Segmented Worlds and Self

Group Life and
Individual Consciousness

Segmented
Worlds
and Self

Group Life and
Individual Consciousness

Yi-Fu Tuan

UNIVERSITY OF MINNESOTA PRESS

MINNEAPOLIS

Published by the University of Minnesota Press,
2037 University Avenue Southeast, Minneapolis, MN 55414
Printed in the United States of America.
Second printing, 1984

Library of Congress Cataloging in Publication Data

Tuan, Yi-Fu, 1930–
   Segmented worlds and self.

   Includes bibliographical references and index.
   1. Self-perception. 2. Social relations. I. Title.
BF697.T74   302.5   81-23094
ISBN 0-8166-1108-4   AACR2
ISBN 0-8166-1109-2 (pbk.)

To

J. B. Jackson

Acknowledgments

I happily acknowledge my gratitude to Ivor Winton for his help with the chapter on "Food and Manners," to Tom Engelhardt for his detailed criticism of an early draft of the book, to Su-chang Wang for the handsome diagrams, to Robert Winthrop for the enlightening discussions on community and tradition, to the University of Minnesota for the quarter leave with pay (a felicitous arrangement that has done so much to stimulate faculty productivity), and to the editors of the University Press whose advice and encouragement over the years are deeply appreciated.

Contents

WHOLE

1

Segmentation, Consciousness, and Self

In any serious reflection on human beings and society, we tend to come up against the bipolar categories of a whole and its parts, a group and its individual members, public and private, a given or a publicly acknowledged reality and its subjective perception. These categories and their paired juxtapositions are particularly prominent in the history of Western thought. More than people in other cultures, Western thinkers have pondered the basic question of how self and group are related, for they have come to realize that to this question is tied a host of other basic ideas concerning the nature of reality and of value. Although a vast literature addresses the topic of self and group, what is missing is a cultural and historical survey touching on how groups and cohesive wholes break down as their members grow in self-awareness and withdraw into fragmented spaces; and also how individuals might then try to regroup, recreate cohesive wholes, regain a sense of unity, or regenerate objective (i.e., public) values, all at the conscious level. Spatial segmentation in relation to developing consciousness and to the idea of self is the theme of the following essay. The approach is concrete, not abstract. What is offered is an interpretative description, not a social-scientific treatise.

Yet we have begun with a number of abstract terms. What do they mean? Rather than provide formal definitions, consider the usage of these terms and the meanings that derive from such usage in a familiar context—the modern middle-class family. It is a small group of human beings. When the children are young, the family is a close-knit unit of authority and dependence. It seems a necessary order of nature. Membership in it is taken for granted. In a young family, the arrangement of space lacks differentiation. A mother puts a small child on her lap and feeds him from her own plate. A bigger child, however, has his own chair at the dining table and eats from his plate with his own utensils. Space in the house becomes more segmented and specialized as the family grows older: children not only have their own places at the table but their own rooms in the house. A further consequence of the children's greater maturity is that they are aware of themselves as centers of consciousness. They no longer simply belong to the family; they can also *see* that fact. An adolescent in the house feels the need to withdraw, periodically, from his or her kin. The need develops from a growing awareness that parents and siblings are not just "family"— a familiar background of warmth and support—but also bafflingly different individuals. Recognition of the concrete particularity of other persons intensifies the sense of one's own individuality and isolation. A family can still maintain its cohesiveness when its members have turned into self-conscious individuals, but it must do so more often through acts of will. From being a fact of nature, something that need not be examined because it is there—real and objective—the family can seem a mere social convention (perhaps a comforting one) in the critical eyes of an adolescent.

What we can so clearly perceive at the scale of the family exists also at larger scales—those of a clan, a village, a small town, or a city-state. A city-state, for example, loses its cohesiveness and its standing as a permanent and natural unit when its citizens begin to question its institutions and values, not necessarily because these are oppressive but rather because the citizens have come to recognize their own separate identities, and to see the public ceremonies and laws as generated by people like themselves, not eternal verities ordained by nature or God. The mystique of a polis dissolves in the clear and critical vision of its citizens. This, of course, need not happen. Unlike members of a biological family, the citizens of a state do not, in successive generations, necessarily become more individuated and self-conscious.

Although we know that changes in society toward complexity and individuation are not inevitable, we also know that directional changes have repeatedly occurred, and that they result in the rise of civilizations. What kinds of awareness, social and individual, are typically associated with complex societies? We shall attempt a detailed (though partial) answer in the body of the book. Here a few general remarks are appropriate.

Consider, first, the individuation of the world as guided by the powers of the mind. One such power is analysis. The mind strives to differentiate the parts from each other and from the whole; it articulates and creates distinctions. A necessary step toward the making of new objects is this ability to attend, to notice and separate the constituent elements. Whether we think of material substances or streams of sensory impressions, they must be divided up in order that new entities, more vividly present than the primitive whole, can emerge. Thus we remove undifferentiated clay from the earth and make it into a free-standing jar that attracts notice; and from a whirl of inchoate and fleeting impressions, only those few to which we attend and may have given names stand out. Interestingly enough, the story of creation as told in Genesis consists of a series of such acts of separation and individuation. God first separated light from darkness. He divided the waters above the heavenly vault from those below it, and then gathered the waters on earth into one place so that dry land might appear. God continued to diversify his creation by introducing new entities, including Adam whom he made in his own image. God's might was manifest in utterance; he called things into being. Adam, endowed with a godlike power of speech, named the animals, and in the process gave them visibility before his eyes; in that sense he too called creatures into being.

Such powers of articulation and discrimination are able to engender a world that is luminously particular, meticulously defined, and richly fragmented. However, it would appear that such powers cannot be confined to the external world. When turned inward, the self loses its unreflexive integrity, becomes fragmented and self-conscious. Adam and Eve, having eaten fruit from the Tree of Knowledge of good and evil, turned their gaze inward and discovered a new fact—their own nakedness. Innocence was lost in the split between "I" as subject and "I" as object. Recognizing their own nakedness, they knew shame and

Segmentation, Consciousness, and Self

felt vulnerable. But what they lost in innocence they gained in the ability to think critically. They were able to raise questions concerning the nature of good and evil. Could "evil"—as in the feeling of shame and vulnerability—also be good, and "good" evil? The womb-like world of Eden was no place for awakened Adam and Eve. They were expelled. Outside Eden their consciousness of themselves was sustained by the memory of what they had been compared with what they had become, and by the pain of labor. Their sense of the world around them was sharpened by the need to exercise judgment, to choose between alternatives in the making of their own world. Only in death could they find ultimate release from the burden of consciousness and of individuality. God guaranteed death by dispatching archangels to guard the Tree of Life so that Adam and Eve and their descendants might not be tempted to eat its fruit and thus be condemned to live forever.

The enduring relevance of the creation myth in Genesis is that it encapsulates the experience of complex societies and of individuals. In early times, people lived in small cohesive worlds in which rules, customs, and ceremonies were elaborated to maintain stability. Where successful, a communal group changes little through time. It remains "primitive." It avoids situations in which conflict among its members might arise. Its culture lays overwhelming stress on the harmony of the whole as against the rights and uniqueness of the parts. Cooperation is routinely encouraged, individual assertiveness and boasting debarred. In such a group, knowledge need not be disruptive. Everyone, given time and a willingness to learn, can potentially know everything that the group as a whole knows. Knowledge is neither an endless pursuit, nor does its possession necessarily isolate the self from others. Moreover, in simple economies, knowledge is rarely self-critical; religion, art, and taxonomic science exist, but not compartmentalized as in a civilization, nor burdened by a reflexive layer of theology, aesthetics, and the philosophy of science. Knowledge in a folk culture is closely meshed with the immediate experiences of life. It is characteristically implicit rather than explicit. To make sense of reality, a nonliterate people must segment nature and society and recombine the segments into a meaningful whole. Myths and legends suggest the existence of such wholes, labeled sometimes as world-views in the social scientific literature. However, except when an anthropologist is inopportune with questions, nonliterate folks have no occasion or reason to articulate verbally and explicitly their understanding of how the universe coheres. By themselves, their understanding is typically expressed with gestures, as in a ritual dance, or by means of the indirect language of myths, rather than with explicit, descriptive prose and diagrams. Nonliterate folks can therefore be said to have a "world sense," or in Walter Ong's words a "world presence," rather than a world-view or philosophy.[1] They are able to save the appearance of their small, harmonious world by not pushing their comprehension of it too far beyond what is sensed and intuitively appropriate.

A civilized society is large and complex. It has had a long and eventful history of change and growth. Group cohesion and shared myths are tenuous, especially in times when external threats do not exist. A modern society's cohesion is almost constantly under the stress of questioning by its component parts—institutions, local communities, and individuals. The material landscape itself provides suggestive cues. A primitive village gives the impression of being a single and rather simple entity if only because few manmade barriers such as curbs and walls are visible, and few places are reserved for exclusive functions. By contrast, in a large city the innumerable physical boundaries that keep people and activities in discrete areas forcefully remind us of the city's delimited and segmented character, its complex hierarchies of space.

The human mind is disposed to segment reality. Words as well as gestures do so. These methods of segmentation are, however, time-bound. Stories draw our attention to a particular place and time, but without dedicated reiteration their messages quickly lose detail and soon fade from memory. A ritual dance, while it lasts, converts a meadow into sacred space, but as soon as the dance ends the space reverts to a meadow. As distinguished from story-telling and ritual, writing and architecture are typical achievements of high civilization. They make it possible for human beings to greatly multiply, elaborate, and refine separate worlds out of inchoate experience, and to make these worlds a permanent part of the human environment. Pericles' funeral oration faded into thin air, but the written version remains effective to this day in lending glamor to Athens. Ancient Greek activities and ceremonies, which partitioned space, have long since disappeared, but the segmented spaces themselves remain in the landscape as ruined temples and agoras. Behavior is evanescent, but its architectural shell may endure. In the modern world, almost every human activity and state of being has its special architectural frame. Clearly defined and marked places exist for eating, defecating, and sleeping, for playing volleyball and badminton, for rich and poor, for drivers and pedestrians. These places have a high degree of integrity. They are reserved for special functions, and departure from the accepted practice is strongly discouraged. Incommensurables no more mix in physical space than they do in the structures of logical thought.[2]

In the Genesis story, God first created an inchoate entity called "heaven and earth," and then proceeded to divide and reconstitute it into more and more parts. Despite this proliferation of parts, God's capacious mind can no doubt comprehend how they are related to one another and form a coherent whole. Human beings have an almost unlimited capacity for analysis but, unlike God, they are less skilled at integration. In small nonliterate societies, both the breaking down and the putting together of the world occur at a modest scale. Moreover, the two processes usually appear at the same place and follow each other so quickly that they seem almost one enterprise. A shaman does not analyze a problem beyond what is necessary for its practical resolution. Primitive builders break the stems of bushes only to reconstitute them quickly as shelters. What they do to maintain their world seems almost a natural function that can be carried out without much conscious effort.[3] With modern people the story is often different: they have the ability to take things in nature and reduce them to their finest constituent parts. They lack, however, the ability and at times even the intention of recombining the parts into new and complex wholes. At the scale of city construction, modern engineers and architects can design and produce endless components such as parks, streets, and factories without really knowing how they cohere and work as a system. Modern humanity, like God, has commanded its creatures to multiply, and they have multiplied until they have reached an aggregate complexity that is beyond our comprehension and control.

More than other human beings, Western men and women have explored and manipulated the world. But they have been almost equally energetic in exploring their own nature, in self-reflection and analysis, in promoting privacy and the idea of a human individual's uniqueness. From the Middle Ages onward, evidences accumulate that suggest a progressive awareness of self. They include: the increasing importance of autobiographical components in literature; the proliferation of family and self-portraits; the growing popularity of mirrors; the concern with child as a stage in the blossoming of human personality; the use of chairs rather than benches; the multiplication of private and specialized rooms in the house; the inward turn in drama and literature; and psychoanalysis.

What is the self? Who am I? To raise this type of question presupposes an ability to stand apart from the group. Individuals must be capable of physical and psychological withdrawal. One withdraws to answer biological needs, to think and be oneself. In nearly all human societies, defecation and especially copulation call for privacy. In many societies, people also move apart from the larger group when they wish to eat or sleep.[4] These are times when men and women feel vulnerable. The sense of vulnerability implies an awareness of self, the kind of awareness that human beings share with other animals. However, human beings also withdraw out of feelings of shame. Biological functions demand privacy because they do not conform to an exalted image that people have of themselves. Biological being is here contrasted with social being, the one animal and private, the other human and public. Transcending the social is a person's sense of the self as a unique channel of experiences that need to be reflected upon in seclusion. Thus at both extremities of being, biological and transcendental, people wish to be alone.

The self is an entity. As with the world it can be decomposed into parts, a process that has no end. An individual is his organic and, ultimately, chemical constituents. He is his upbringing, socioeconomic background, and the concurrence of fortuitous events. As a person reflects on who he is in this reductive way, he may well improve his self-understanding and achieve a firmer hold on certain facets of his personality. On the other hand, he may be distressed to discover that he has no center—that he is a multitude.

In the public sphere, a person may lose a sense of who she is, torn by the many fleeting roles demanded of her. Alone in the privacy of her home, she may find that self-analysis can have a similar discombobulating effect. Parts of herself she understands better, but her sense of her unsundered being is more elusive than ever, for no amount of analysis can reconstitute a self.

Modern consciousness is often felt as a burden. The home or suburb relieves the burden by offering the fractured ego a nurturing and seemingly harmonious world, a pleasing image of self. But it is too limiting. The thinker creates a lucid and coherent world on paper, but such a world is a home fit only for the mind. Any person who seeks identity and justification in mental constructs alone will come to feel insubstantial. By contrast, the ideal city of the potentate and master planner is real, being made of concrete, glass, and steel, and stocked with human beings. Although the ideal city can be austerely beautiful, it does not function well because it is inadequate to the complexity of life. When we look at past and present performances, we must conclude that the human mind is better at taking things apart and at making small intricate entities or large but simple systems than at creating large and complex wholes. A characteristic of consciously designed wholes is their simplicity—their limited number of components and linkages—compared with the organisms and organizations that exist in nature. This simplicity becomes a grievous fault when the created object is a city in which people are expected to live. The ideal city is a supreme testimony to the master builder's inflated sense of self; yet the monument postulates a lack of ego and of individuality on the part of its inhabitants.

Modern man's longing for community or nature is a longing to lose consciousness and self in a greater whole. It is the often-noted desire to return to the womb or Eden. Segmentation, which began well in the early stages of man's creative endeavor has gone too far. Particularization has gone too far. Consciousness and with it an intensifying awareness of self has become excessively isolating and painful. We wish at times that we had not eaten the fruit from the Tree of Knowledge, that we could be back in Eden, sufficiently aware to name objects in the world but not so aware as to be able to name also ourselves. Yet, at other times, we feel proud of our individuality, of our unrelenting consciousness, and of our status as prisoners within our own ineluctable subjectivity.

This dilemma, though often stated, retains its power to baffle. The purpose of this book is to explicate the dilemma with the help of parallel cultural themes that generally do not, but should, appear in tandem within the compass of a single study. We begin with examples of integrated human groups (cohesive wholes) from different areas of the world and from different times of the past. In such groups, the idea of the unique and isolated self is minimally present; and in every case, group cohesiveness arises out of need and is maintained, as we shall see, by the physical presence and ready availability of members to each other.

We will then focus on Western civilization as it developed from the late Middle Ages onward, because it was in the West that individualism —that tension between group and self—found its fullest expression both in literature and in reality. Other cultures will be introduced, not so much to yield a basis for systematic comparison as to provide a context in which to depict the unique tale of the West. For the West, we will trace the progressive segmentation of three kinds of sociocultural phenomena: food and table manners, house and household, and theater. Their histories supply the parallel themes.

With food preparation and table manners we shall see that progressive refinement has meant the serving of carved meats rather than of whole animals and joints; it has also called for the elaboration of specialized utensils and of an etiquette that makes diners increasingly self-conscious. The story of the house from the European Middle Ages onward details a progressive partitioning of space that clearly reflects the people's growing sense of self, their need for greater individual and and group privacy. The theater is the world dramatized, made more visible and self-conscious. In the West, the theater began as religious and communal activity, but by the late nineteenth century it was almost a private experience that spectators have as they sit in the dark

Segmentation, Consciousness, and Self

in their separate chairs, gazing through the proscenium arch at dramas of family disintegration.

Of this period of European history we shall ask whether emphasis on the modes of perception has changed. The concrete surveys of table manners, household, and theater will prepare us to answer this more psychological and elusive question. We wish to know: Is there evidence of an increasing stress on the eye as compared with the other senses? Sight presents us with a vivid and sharply differentiated world "out there." By contrast, smell, taste, touch, and hearing tend to wrap us in a variegated but unfocused ambience. We shall note that folk communities are oral communities, knit by the intimacy of speech, and ask: How does literacy affect a people's sense of their world? Writing and reading, when they are a habit, tend to enforce our perception of the world as causal, linear, and segmented. It is clear that literacy encourages withdrawal. Although story-telling and oratory require a public arena and an audience, reading is best done in the privacy of one's own room.

Community is compatible with individualism if by individualism we mean the freedom of individuals to pursue careers suited to their unique talents, and if we mean behaviors that do not conform to any set of formal rules. Dynamic communities or societies, after all, exist. By definition, they are those that successfully accommodate a wide range of talents freely and even cantankerously expressing themselves. Individualism is, of course, *in*compatible with community or with any kind of social life if it means the total withdrawal of self, or total alienation. Modern society is believed to contain many such individuals who are commonly viewed as failures. However, a paradox of society is that its successes—its most thoughtful and reflective members—are also a threat to its integrity. Thought corrodes value simply by putting it to question. Laws and customs lose their power to bind when they are seen as conventional. Society, to a thoughtful person, is an artifact, lacking the legitimacy of what is natural and objective. Indeed nature itself, under questioning, dissolves into subjective experience.

Subjectivism is the ultimate loneliness. Symptoms of it have appeared in the past, but they seem far more prevalent in modern times. With people of preliterate and traditional societies, reality is given.

Segmentation, Consciousness, and Self

Nature as well as society's rules and customs are simply and objectively there: they are not subjective values and constructs dependent on the mood, perception, and specialized knowledge of individuals. People not radically transformed by modern culture therefore live in a reassuringly objective, shared, and taken-for-granted world. With modern men and women, a sense of insubstantiality and of isolation that derives from subjectivism moves increasingly to the forefront of consciousness. As evidence, we need think only of the rise to popularity in recent centuries of such terms and concepts as scenery, prospect, perspective, point of view, interpretation, and, in our time, construct and paradigm. "The way the world looks depends on where you stand." This is a common belief and attitude in our age, and it suggests how illusory and subjective reality has become for thinking people.

Are there still common worlds that we can take for granted? Efforts to recreate common worlds range from the building of unpartitioned houses and of thrust-stage theaters that encourage warm human exchange to the establishment of integrated neighborhoods and social utopias on a national scale. Success in even the more modest of these efforts is only partial for a variety of reasons, among them being the paradox of consciousness: the need, on the one hand, to be aware so as to sustain a whole that owes its existence to forethought, and on the other to lose oneself in it as though it had always been there—objective and independent—able to subsist and function on its own.

2

Cohesive Wholes

Modern man and woman, believing that they live in a fragmented and impersonal society, have periodically yearned for the greater social cohesiveness of people living in distant times and places. What common characteristics do these vanished and vanishing cultures have? By the more obvious measures, they would seem to have little in common. Nonliterate and traditional communites may be small, the size of a band, or relatively large, with thousands of members. They may be egalitarian or hierarchical. Many discourage self-assertion, a few encourage it. Modesty and privacy are valued in some communities but not in others. Social organization along kinship lines may be strict, or loose. Such divergences notwithstanding, it remains true that all premodern communities differ from modern society in one important trait—cohesiveness. This trait is manifest in the need for the physical proximity of kinsfolk and friends; in the view of the world as given and objectively real; and in the lack of self-awareness and, hence, the lack of a critical stance toward the group and the world.

At the most elemental level, social bonds are maintained by bodily contact. Consider the Kaingáng tribe, hunters and gatherers who live in the forbidding highland forests of Santa Catarina province in Brazil. The anthropologist Jules Henry writes:

Kaingáng young men love to sleep together. At night they call to one another, "Come and lie down here with me, with *me*! . . . In camp one sees young men caressing. Married and unmarried young men lie cheek by jowl, arms around one another, legs slung across bodies, for all the world like lovers in our society. Sometimes they lie caressing that way in little knots of three or four.[1]

But Henry could detect no evidence of homosexuality. The frequent touchings and fondlings served to establish mutual trust and group cohesion rather than provide sexual excitation. Bonds thus established might even transcend those of blood. "Men who have hunted together day after day, raided the (European) Brazilians together, slept together beside the same fire, under the same blanket, wrapped in each other's arms, hold this relationship above their kinship with their brothers."[2]

Social ties in a Kaingáng band are exceptionally fluid. Elaborate rules governing permissible and nonpermissible contacts, so often to be found among primitive peoples, appear to be absent. Parents must not have sex with their children, nor can blood siblings marry, but otherwise sexual relations are conspicuously permissive. Almost every kind of marriage known to anthropology is practiced. Although predominantly monogamous, they are also polygynous and polyandrous; in addition they establish "joint marriages" in which "several men lived with several women in mutual cohabitation."[3] Children are greatly appreciated by adults, not so much for their unique personalities as for their cuddliness—the warmth and softness of their little bodies. Children are at the beck and call of every adult. They sleep all over the place. They waddle up to grown-ups and there, like puppies, absorb the delicious stroking they can always count on receiving.

It is difficult to avoid the impression that the Kaingáng wish at times to deny their individuality altogether. When the men sleep with their arms and legs slung across each other's body, they turn into writhing human lumps. The sexual modesty that keeps people apart is almost nonexistent. "It is not an uncommon sight," Henry writes, "to see a little girl of five or six hovering over a supine man picking the ticks off his genitals." Sexual foreplay between adults is open and boisterous. There is no attempt to hide it from children. Indeed, adults may jocularly tell little children to copulate with one another or with people many times their age. Personal attachments based on frequent bodily contact are so important to the cohesion of Kaingáng society that its people are perplexed when they see an individual without such bonds. No one is spoken of more sadly than a mature person who is alone.

Cohesive Wholes

The Kaingáng have a strong sense of the group self. Awareness of "us" or "one's own people" is maintained by physical proximity, warm personal ties, a keen interest in genealogy, and an antagonism toward other Kaingáng descent groups or bands. Within a band, individual aggressiveness is suppressed. It emerges, however, in sexual play and teasing; it also appears under the influence of alcohol. The Kaingáng are not given to introspective self-analysis. They are little aware of their own feelings, which outwardly are so warm. "When drunkenness uncovers the Kaingáng personality, it does not bubble over in rivulets of tenderness, but pours out in torrents of violence."[4]

Consider another preliterate group, the !Kung San (Bushmen) of the Kalahari Desert. Resembling the Kaingáng in some ways, they differ sharply from them in others. Like the Kaingáng, the !Kung are migratory hunters and gatherers. Their society is egalitarian and its members like to stay close to one another; children are constantly fondled and kissed. Lorna Marshall notes that when "women and girls sit together they tend to huddle, touching one another shoulder to shoulder, knee to knee, ankles overlapping." Boys and young men do likewise.[5] Of course there is no shortage of space in the Kalahari Desert; nonetheless, the camps are compact and densely settled, their average density being 188 square feet per person, much less than the 350 square feet per person considered the desirable standard by the American Public Health Association. Typically in a camp, Patricia Draper observes, the family hearths are located so close that people gathered around them can hand items back and forth without getting up. "Often people sitting around various fires will carry on long discussions without raising their voices above normal conversational levels." In the daytime, about 35 percent of the residents disperse to hunt and gather food, but the rest—children under age fourteen, sick and old people—stay behind in tight little clusters.[6]

Unlike the Kaingáng, the !Kung are modest about their bodily functions. Modesty, however, is difficult to maintain in an exposed environment of bright skies and broad horizons. Other than low scrubs, a few widely scattered trees, and huts, they lack places in which to hide from eyes trained to interpret animal behavior and mood on the faintest evidence. The !Kung, it is true, want to live close together. On the other hand, they recognize the incest taboo and fear the possibility of revealing improper sexual response in the presence of close kin. Self-consciousness and a desire for privacy are the result. When a !Kung wants to urinate or defecate, he or she moves far away from camp and squats behind bushes. Rules of sitting avoidance exist. When a mother-in-law and a son-in-law sit by the hearth they must keep a distance of at least three feet between them; the same rule applies to a father-in-law and a daughter-in-law. The !Kung's attitude toward their huts further illustrates their need for circumspection. Huts are not always built at an encampment. The campfires around which everyone congregates at night are, for them, a more important symbol of home. Where shelters are put up, they may be used only when rain falls or the sun becomes too hot. The !Kung do not normally sleep or live in them. A hut is on the average only five feet long and three feet deep. Its interior space is open to view and can hardly provide any real privacy. Yet a son's wife or a daughter's husband would strictly avoid entering the shelter of his or her parents-in-law. A brother and a sister, once they are married and have built their own huts, must be equally strict in this observance. Not entering each other's hut is a mark of respect. The !Kung's sense of self demands a measure of distance between certain categories of people. The idea of segmented and demarcated space is clearly present among them, as is that of privacy for subgroups and perhaps also for individuals.[7]

Most peasants are villagers, members of cohesive communities. What is the nature of this cohesion and how is it maintained? A large and varied literature on peasants exists—historical studies of villages in medieval Europe and ethnographic surveys of peasant economy and livelihood in the poorer parts of the world at the turn of the century.[8] Though differing from each other in significant details, peasant worlds nonetheless share certain broad traits that distinguish them from urban and modern societies. First, peasants establish intimate bonds with the land: that one must labor hard to survive is an accepted truth that is transformed into a propitiary and pious sentiment toward Mother Earth. Deities of the soil and ancestral spirits become fused. Peasants see themselves as belonging to the land, "children of the earth," a link between past and future, ancestors and progeny. Biological realities and metaphors, so common in the peasant's world, tend to suppress the idea of the self as a unique end or as a person capable of breaking loose from the repetitive and cyclical processes of nature to initiate something radically new. Although peasants may own the land they work on, they work more often in teams than individually. Many agricultural activities require cooperation; for example, when fields need to be irrigated and drained, or when a heavy and expensive piece of equipment (such as the mill, winepress, or oven belonging to the landlord) is to be used. Scope for individual initiative is limited except in small garden plots next to the house, and even there customary practices prevail. Individualism and individual success are suspect in peasant communities. Prosperity is so rare that it immediately suggests witchcraft.

In the peasant's world the fundamental socioeconomic unit is the extended family, members of which—all except the youngest children—are engaged in some type of productive work. They may not, however, see much of each other during the day. Dinnertime may provide the only opportunity for family togetherness, when the webs of affection and lines of authority become evident to all. More distant relatives are drawn into the family net on special occasions, such as weddings and funerals. Besides kinsfolk, villagers can count on the assistance of neighbors when minor needs arise, whether for extra hands during harvest, for tools, or even for money. In southeast China, a neighborhood is clearly defined as the five residences to each side of one's own.[9] Belonging to a neighborhood gives one a sense of security that kinsfolk alone cannot provide. Villagers are able to maintain good neighborly relations with each other because they have the time to socialize. In Europe the men may go to a tavern, where after a few beers they feel relaxed enough to sing together—that most comradely of human activities. In China the men, and sometimes the women as well, may go to a teahouse in a market town, where they can exchange gossip among themselves and with visitors from other villages. More informally, neighbors meet to chat and relax in the village square in the cool of the evening. Peasants desire contentment rather than success, and contentment means essentially the absence of want.[10] When a man achieves a certain level of comfort he is satisfied. He feels no compulsion to use his resource and energy for higher economic rewards.

He has the time and sense of leisure to hobnob with his fellows and bathe in their undemanding good will. Besides these casual associations, peasants come together for planned festivals that might involve the entire village. The New Year and the period after harvest are such occasions in many parts of the world. The number of festivals and the days on which they occur vary from place to place, but without exception festivals come to pass when people are relatively free, that is, during the lax phases of the calendar year.

Festivals, of course, strengthen the idea of group self. These are the times when the people as a whole express their joy in the success of a harvest, or the growing strength of the sun. Simultaneously, they reaffirm their piety toward the protective deities of the earth and sky, their sense of oneness with nature. Group cohesiveness is a product of need, a fact that is manifest in the traditional world of villagers at different scales, ranging from that of family and kinsfolk, through those of neighbors and work team, to the entire community as it celebrates the end of a period of toil or the passing of a crisis of nature, or as it is girded in self-defense against natural calamity or human predators. Necessity is not a condition that human beings can contemplate for long without transforming it into an ideal. Thus, the cooperation necessary to survival becomes a good in itself, a desirable way of life. Units of mutual help achieve strong identities that can persist long after the urgencies that called them into existence have passed. In such groups, forged initially out of need but sustained thereafter by a sense of collective superiority, wayward and questioning individuals have no place.

A common image of America is that it is a land of individualists. Even in the colonial period, when towns were small and isolated, intimately knit communal groups like those of Europe did not exist. The people who lived in them, particularly in the Middle Colonies, shared too few common traditions and habits. Moreover, they were continually moving in and out. In New England, where settlers made periodic attempts to establish communities artificially by means of consciously constructed models, the results were mixed in relation to satisfaction and permanence.[11] In the countryside, the Jeffersonian ideal of the yeoman farmer seems to have held sway. Nevertheless, not

Cohesive Wholes

only individualists but families and clusters of families migrated to the frontier, and in the course of time some of them became deeply rooted agglutinate communities, in which such characteristic American ideals as upward social mobility, individual initiative, and success were alien.

Traditional farming communities, relics from the past, persist in rural America at mid-twentieth century. Consider the sixty-odd families whose roots in the hollows of Tennessee, a few miles south of Nashville, go back to 1756. Over a course of two hundred years, intermarriage has produced the closest bonds. Natural warmth between kinsfolk and neighbors is reinforced by a deep suspicion of outsiders. The community is strongly egalitarian. Work roles differ by age and sex, but social stratification as it exists in most parts of the country is unknown. "In work terms," writes John Mogey, "no one is clearly leader: collective responsibility for work assignment is the rule to an extent that to speak of individual or family farming enterprises would be to violate the facts."[12] In her study of this community, Elmora Matthews notes how warm feelings between farmers can emerge from a combination of blood ties, laboring at common tasks, and informal socializing. One woman described the relation between her four brothers, who have adjoining farms, thus: "They work all day long together, eat their meals together, and then always sit around and visit with each other before they go home." Ambition and even efficiency, when it is obtrusive, are bad. On the other hand, "no one ever condemns a husband who evades his work. If anything, a man who sits around home a lot blesses a family group." One of the most respectable activities for man is to loaf and loiter with other men. The greatest satisfaction lies in the warm exchange of feeling among relatives and close friends at home, church, or store.

People in this Tennessee community almost never organize formally for special ends. There are no communal projects. The community is not a provisional state that might be altered and improved upon, or used for some larger, ulterior purpose. It is the supreme value and sole reality: whatever threatens to disrupt it is bad. Critical self-awareness seems minimal. Thus, although this Tennessee people fervently believe in freedom, anyone who exercises it to develop his talent and becomes

a success is harshly judged. Thorough conformists in thinking and behavior, they nevertheless resent the government for its tendency to
impose rules and regulations, and they regard communism as unimag-
inably horrible.[13]

Close-knit communities of this kind can be found in the more isolated countrysides of western Europe and North America even in the
middle of the twentieth century. By contrast, a great modern city is
a "world of strangers."[14] In its busy downtown district are multi-
tudes of people who notice and address each other only to conduct
specific matters of business; in its suburbs are houses on green pedestals
—private retreats of the middle class and of affluent workers. Of
course, we now know that this picture of social fragmentation is a
caricature. In any large metropolis, pockets of social cohesion—"urban villages"—do exist: studies such as those of Gerald Suttles and
Herbert Gans remind us of their presence.

Gregariousness, a desire to see and be seen in a public place, is an
outstanding trait of the urban villager. Suttles, in his study of Chicago's Addams area, notes: "On warm nights there is hardly a stoop,
corner, alley, or doorway that has not been staked out by some of its
regular habitués. The adults get the door stoops. The young girls stay
close, just out of earshot. The small children are given the run of the
sidewalks in front of their mothers. The unmarried males are relegated
to whatever little nooks or crannies are left." People bring out an old
couch or take discarded automobile seats and install them on the sidewalks as permanent places for socializing. These fixtures may be supplemented by cushions and chairs removed temporarily from the
house. On occasion Suttles has seen "older women come out of their
door stoops and sit in the rain with their umbrellas." Attachment to
the streets—to the public arena where friends and relatives gather—is
strong, especially among teenagers. "After being arrested and released
they do not speak of going home but of going 'back to the streets.'"
The residents of Addams area, who are mostly American Italians,
Mexicans, and blacks, do not necessarily seek the streets because their
homes are too crowded and unpleasant. On the contrary, the streets
are dirty, whereas most homes (particularly those of the Italians) are
clean and well kept. Homes are, however, the women's domain—their

showplace, which comes fully alive only on ritual family occasions. Otherwise, homes are perceived to be merely shelters from inclement weather, places in which to eat and sleep. They are not places set aside for solitude and the intimate exchange of views between friends.[15]

The West End of Boston, before it was judged a slum and demolished between 1958 and 1960, resembled the Addams area of Chicago in several respects. Like the Addams area, West End had a mixed population, mostly of Italian stock but with important subgroups of Jewish and Irish descent. Street life could be animated at times. Its sounds penetrated tenement homes with no objection on the part of the residents. As one West Ender put it, "I like the noise people make. In summer, people have their windows open, and everyone can hear everyone else, but nobody cares what anybody is saying." What is said has far less importance than the warm bubble of sound that chattering generates. Being with one particular individual, outside the context of courtship, has no great value, but being in the midst of one's own group has. West Enders, according to Gans, know about middle-class Boston suburbs but feel no envy for them. "They describe these [newer suburbs] as too quiet for their tastes, lonely — that is, without street life."[16]

West Enders have an insatiable appetite for group experience. The teenagers and even adults are listless and passive when alone, but burst into activity when surrounded by their peers. For men, women, and teenagers, the group is the most satisfactory arena in which to display their individuality. Young males compete vigorously with each other in card games, verbal duels, and physical scuffles. Older people also compete, though more quietly. Self-assertion establishes temporary superiority. Each member of a peer group takes his or her turn before the footlights of approbation and then withdraws. Thus no one becomes a permanent and formally acknowledged leader, and the ideal of equality is maintained. The group is seldom, if ever, convened for a common goal beyond itself. It has no political function and is almost exclusively a social device for individuals to gain a sense of self-importance in the midst of critical, but basically supportive, peers. Although West Enders yearn to display self and can often be assertive in their manners, Gans believes that they lack detachment and self-consciousness. "While they do give of themselves as freely as do other people, they cannot conceive of themselves doing so." Adults are ill at ease with people who try to take their point of view. They suspect that they may not actually have a point of view that others can empathize with and evaluate. The absence of a clear self-image also makes it perplexing for a West Ender to confront himself—hence the fear of being alone.[17]

Thus far, we have looked at social cohesion as it is manifest in egalitarian groups. Conspicuous gregariousness that makes for social solidarity exists also in hierarchical communities. In these communities the fundamental unit is the household. Illustrative examples of large and tightly knit households can be picked from widely different parts of the world. We shall confine our attention to premodern China and Europe. In Sung China during the third quarter of the thirteenth century, wealthy families became magnets that attracted to themselves numerous poor people, who found employment as servants and suppliers in highly specialized capacities. The social structure of the household was pyramidal: at its top stood the prince, the high scholar-official, or (in the flourishing commercial economy of Sung China) the rich merchant; next to his immediate family hovered bevies of relatives, and serving them all at close quarters was a small army of men and women. Their world, highly diversified, was yet united. The French sinologist Jacques Gernet notes that the staff of a great family was divided among various service departments that in Hang-chou were known as "the four services and the six offices."

The four services consisted of servants in charge of furnishings; alcoholic liquors and teas; ceremonies at banquets, marriages and funerals; the kitchen and the kitchen staff. The six offices had functions that were more precise and more limited: the decoration of dishes ready for serving, the purchase of fruits, the purchase of snacks for accompanying drinks, lighting, the purchase of incense and perfumes and of medicines, the heating, cleaning and decorating of the rooms.[18]

This list comprised merely the domestic servants. In addition, many more people, not strictly servants, found employment by virtue of their special gifts. The civilized and sometimes esoteric tastes of a great family called for "tutors, tellers of tales ancient and modern, chanters of poetry, zither players, chess players, horsemen, painters of orchids, literary men, copyists, bibliophiles." Of lower social standing were entertainers who could give exhibitions of cock- or pigeon-fighting, imitate animal noises, train performing insects, or pose amusing riddles. In this complex and richly human microcosm the masters showed paternalistic concern for the welfare of their employees and servants, who in turn demonstrated loyalty and respect. Employees were regarded as members of the family. A job passed from father to son through successive generations in the same house. Whereas revolts periodically erupted among peasants in the countryside and among workers in the big city factories (both public and private), they were unknown in the great urban households.[19]

We obtain glimpses of what it was really like to live in a great family of premodern China from literature, particularly from novels, and uniquely from that great Chinese novel of manners written around the middle of the eighteenth century, *The Story of the Stone*. In this work, the Jia household has more than three hundred members, living in a compound so large that to go from one courtyard to another might call for the service of a palanquin borne on the shoulders of handsome pages or a carriage drawn by mules. The compound swarms with male and female servants of all ages and grades. The more powerful among the female servants have underlings of their own and are so beautifully decked out that they can easily be mistaken for daughters of the house. Bao-yu, a thirteen-year-old boy who is the hero of the novel, and his young female cousins are each attended by a wet nurse, four other nurses to act as chaperons, two maids as body-servants to help with their washing and dressing, and four or five other maids to dust, clean, run errands, serve tea, and be generally useful. Punishment can be swift and harsh. A maid is given twenty strokes of the bamboo for oversleeping and reporting late for work. On the other hand, the great and their servants are so mutually dependent and live in such proximity that much contact is necessarily informal, even familiar, and deep affection often develops, especially when master and page, mistress and maid, have grown up together. We find in the novel a maid asking her young master Bao-yu to peel some chestnuts for her while she makes up his bed. The two of them might even lie cozily on the bed to chat. Bao-yu's pages play practical jokes on him in their own quarters, but fight for him against bullies in the family school-house. When a young lady died, one of her loyal maids took her own life by dashing her head against a pillar, and another performed the duties of the chief mourner since the lady had no issue.[20]

An egalitarian community does not have social barriers that keep its members apart; a hierarchically structured community does. Forces for division exist. To overcome them at the ideological level, Confucians appeal to the family model. Two facts central to the family model are biological inequality and the need for cooperation. A family, despite its inequality, can be cohesive and harmonious because it is a natural association in which the strong help and patronize the weak, and the weak for their part offer service and respect.[21] It is in the order of things in this kind of community for parents to rule their children, a husband his wife, and an elder brother his younger siblings. These relations of power and necessity do not seem excessively harsh because they are tempered by the flow of natural affection. Ideally, the larger society exhibits the same kinds of bond. A term for emperor in Chinese is "Son of Heaven," the local magistrate is addressed by his charges as "parent-official," and good friends become sworn brothers.[22]

At the heart of Confucianist thought is the belief that society thus ordered does not stem merely from arbitrary human will and custom. It is a fact of nature; therefore, an offense against society is an offense against the order of nature—an attempt to disrupt a foreordained harmony. For this reason, Chinese social thought has always emphasized an individual's obligation to society rather than one's rights and privileges. It is the duty of every person from the emperor down to the humblest subject to uphold the proprieties as exemplified by the ancient sage kings. A perfect world order, Confucians seem to believe, runs spontaneously (*wu wei*). All its recurrent patterns, routines, and rhythms—like the primordial harmony of the Tao—can subsist without the stress and strain of conscious striving. Human action, even talk, is redundant. In the *Analects* we find the Master saying, "I would prefer not to speak. . . . Does heaven speak? The four seasons pursue their course; all things are produced by it, but does heaven speak?"[23]

The Taoist's view of society differs radically from that of the Confucian. Whereas Taoists believe that the suprahuman cosmos abides in

Cohesive Wholes

the ineffable Tao and proceeds without striving and calculation, they deny that this can also be true of the sociopolitical order, which is an arbitrary human construct.[24] Taoism is able to promote individualism in ways that Confucianism cannot. It can encourage a person to with-draw from society and commune with nature, and thus advance ro-mantic, nonconformist values. We think of the unconventional be-havior of the great T'ang poets, Tu Fu and Li Po, the one a lonely and rootless wanderer, the other a debauchee and drunkard. Moreover, because Taoism views the sociopolitical order as a willful human crea-tion, it exonerates people from unreflective obedience even in king-doms ruled by virtuous princes.

In premodern times, literacy, if it existed, was limited to a few elite members of society. Touch and speech in face-to-face contact were the only effective means of communication. Social cohesion required that people move almost constantly in each other's presence. Gregar-iousness was a necessity whether the group was egalitarian or hierar-chical, with the difference, however, that in a hierarchical group physical proximity and familiarity must coexist with sharply drawn social distinctions. Both the familiarity and the distinctions were manifest. "All things in life were a proud and cruel publicity," was how Johan Huizinga characterized the European Middle Ages. All must be seen. "Even intimate relations . . . are rather paraded than kept secret. Not only love, but friendship too, has its finely made up forms. Two friends dress in the same way, share the same room, and call one another by the name of 'mignon.' "[25]

Although social distinctions vividly displayed in dress and ceremony tended to keep people apart, stronger was the force for cohesion. In Europe during the early Middle Ages, safety and the ability to act de-pended on the readiness with which kinsmen and servitors could co-agulate into small, intense groups. Even much later, in Italian cities of the thirteenth and fourteenth centuries, essentially the same reason for living in concentrated clusters obtained. Rome, Florence, and Genoa were then each made up of hundreds of fortified family com-pounds that dominated their neighborhoods.[26] A typical compound in Genoa could be recognized from a distance by its tower. Within the compound were the adjacent houses of the several branches of the family, the loggias, shops, market, bath, and church surrounding a small square. Because the houses were small, people spent much time in public places. The bath became a center for family gossip, the loggia a place for family meetings and festivities, and the church a building for family worship. Like the loggia, which was often decorated with house emblems, the church provided a means of family identification through plaques inscribed to the ancestral dead, through splendid tombs and monuments, and through the masses sung to commemorate the deaths of kinsfolk.[27] Swelling the population of the compound and of the precinct beyond were artisans and traders who supplied the multifarious needs of a large noble household. In such manner, a colorful heterogeneity of people and activities developed in medieval and Renaissance cities. The traits of gregariousness and heterogeneity emerged in response to threat and to the political and socioeconomic necessities of the period. People had little choice. To survive in a fractious and violent world, they had to hang together, display themselves, and regularly exchange tokens of power, dependency, and affection.

From the fifteenth to the seventeenth century, in the more prosperous parts of western Europe, the need for self-protection declined in importance as a cause for group living and social cohesiveness in noble households. By the end of the period, security was no longer a significant motivation. Nonetheless, the tendency for the town houses of the rich and powerful to shelter a large and variegated population persisted. In a Parisian town house, for example, one might expect to meet, besides the family proper, variously related kinsfolk, servants, clerics, clerks, shopkeepers, and apprentices as well as an assortment of hangers-on. Friends, clients, and protégés moved in and out of the big residence freely and seemingly at all hours to conduct business and socialize as though it were a public place.

We have briefly told the story of the town house; that of the country house is much the same. In medieval times country houses were castles and seats of power in which kinsfolk and dependents congregated for mutual protection. Their contacts with outside groups varied from caution, through suspicion, to hatred. It was important for a great lord to impress his rivals by projecting an image of might and glory. He could best do this by encouraging crowds of people to come continuously to his house, where he offered drinks in abundance and served gargantuan meals, the leftovers of which could then be brought out to the gate and fed to the poor. In the castles, the servants were mostly men. Chores such as cooking, cleaning, and waiting on tables were all done by men. Since the visiting nobility and gentry often came without their wives, most of the strangers entertained were men. The heavily male constitution of the medieval household could be traced to its origin as a war band.[28] Once more we see necessity as a social bond, powerful enough to overcome the divisiveness of rank.

During late Tudor, and still more, by Stuart times, the great lords no longer needed to maintain large retinues for defense or the waging of war. Power and glory shifted to the politics of the city and of the court. Where hospitality and the social rites were kept up at the country manor, they were exercised in deference to tradition and out of a sense of duty to dependents and tenants, whose only access to the greater world lay in social intercourse with their lord. There was, however, another bond—the economics of farm work on the estate, which required the lord or his deputy to reside in the manor house, maintain a household full of servants, and keep up a table for day-laborers. Peter Laslett notes: "Raising crops and tending stock go on in the night as well as the day, and this gave the household servant system a permanent advantage." Before the coming of the bicycle and the paved highway, laborers could not live beyond a fixed distance from the farm and still do a full day's work. Conditions in the seventeenth century made it difficult if not impossible, "for the landowner to act as entrepreneur in the modern fashion, to run their land as our farmers do, using daytime labour alone, hired from outside the house, on the model of the business or factory."[29]

We have seen that life must be lived in the open, visible to all members of the group, if human ties within the group were to keep up their strength. Maximum opportunity for contact exists in a war band, a tribe, a family, or a household; these are all small face-to-face communities. In the event of conflict between one tribe and another, or one household and another, how can it be resolved without submitting to the violence of a blood feud or war? One answer to this question is theatricality, that is, the dramatization of power as distinct from its actual use.

Before the twelfth century, some sort of consensus between the feuding families of Europe was achieved through the theatrical device of the ordeal. Contestants appealed to a supernatural order of reality that transcended individual and kinsfolk passions. The ordeal itself must be dramatically vivid and cruel to be convincing. Innocent or guilty? The verdict might depend on the effect of a hot iron on the hand that could hold it for nine paces, of boiling water on the arm that had snatched an object from a cauldron, and of whether a man sank (innocent) or floated (guilty) in a pool of holy water. God intervened directly and his ruling in the form of a miracle seemed final.[30]

In the course of the twelfth century, secular law backed by a powerful prince made the ordeal obsolete. However, the prince was obliged to demonstrate his power by victories in the field. He must also periodically expose his person to his vassals and subjects to retain their loyalty; this meant a necessity for almost constant, exhausting travel through the realm. To enhance personal authority, the medieval ruler, and later the Renaissance prince, sought to concentrate ceremonial grandeur upon himself. A numinous aura of might accrued to the regal figure to compensate for his declining ability to keep direct contact with the people. Legitimacy and authority required the support of grand spectacles. After 1100 the idea of direct supernatural intervention began to wane, but not the idea of God as magistrate and of magistrate as God. A preternatural solemnity persisted in the machinery of justice.

Even in eighteenth-century England, justice was enacted as though it were a combination of cosmic ritual and psychic drama. Douglas Hay notes that in provincial assizes, "there was an acute consciousness that the courts were platforms for addressing 'the multitude.' " The judge played the part of the just but merciful Christian God. An awesome figure of majesty, he could impress the onlookers by word and gesture, "fuse terror and argument into the amalgam of legitimate power in their minds." The smell of brimstone seemed to be more pervasive in the courts than in the churches of that time.[31] Of course, there was also mercy. Judiciously applied, it served to enforce the

Cohesive Wholes

structure of paternalism. An important self-justification of the ruling class was that a gentleman always looked after his own people, even a thief, once he had been sufficiently chastised to protect property. "A Norfolk gentleman asked for mercy on the grounds that 'all his man's family live in the neighborhood near Norwich and are employed occasionally by me.' . . . Men facing imminent death tried to exploit some improbably remote connections."[32]

Certain ideas contribute to social cohesiveness. In traditional China, we have seen how under the influence of Confucianism the biological model of the family was extended to the neighborhood, the village, the province, and ultimately the empire or the civilized world. Society thus conceived encouraged submission and discouraged radical criticism because its hierarchical orders were understood as part of the overall harmony of nature. A similar model of social relations existed in Europe. Thus classical Roman writers, notably Cicero, characterized the ruler as "the common father of all." In medieval times the relation of the king to his subjects was envisaged as similar to that of a father to his family.[33] Two other ideas exerted an influence on the perceived nature of society during the medieval and Renaissance period: the "body politic" and the "great chain of being." Both ideas supported the belief that social institutions and ranks were natural, beyond mere human desire and will. The idea of the body politic played on the images of a biological metaphor. Social distinctions were necessary. It would be as absurd to level them as to create a human body out of a number of the same limbs. In *Courtier's Academy* (English translation 1598), Count Hannibal Romei argued:

Now a city being nothing else but a body of men united together, sufficient of itself to live, it is necessary that like to a human body it be compounded of unlike members, the which, in goodness and dignity among themselves unequal, all notwithstanding concur to the good establishment of a city.[34]

If the state is an organism like the human body, then each part of the body must help the others and be helped by them. The idea of "body politic" stresses not only the necessity of hierarchy but also of mutual dependence. Nicholas Breton (1551?–ca. 1623), a prolific English author, asked: "Can the labourer, the foot, be wounded, but the body of the state will feel it, the head be careful, the eye searchful and the hand be painful in the cure of it? And can the commonwealth, the body, be diseased, but the king, his council and every true subject will put to his hand for the help of it?"[35] In such a conception of society, obviously no room existed for social mobility and the fulfillment of individual ambition: the foot must not usurp the functions and dignity of the hand, much less those of the head.

The other great idea of world order was the vast chain of being.[36] Derived originally from neo-Platonic doctrine, it permeated much of medieval thought, but became far more vivid and elaborate through the enthusiastic exposition of Renaissance Platonists. Basically, the idea combined the notion of hierarchy with that of an unimaginable plenitude. The chain stretched from the meanest of inanimate objects to the angels at the foot of God's throne. Every speck of creation was a link. God in his enormous fecundity and goodness had filled every vacant space in the cosmos. Creation seemed less the result of arbitrary or deliberative commands than the outcome of a natural prolixity. No gap separated the different orders of created things. Thus Ranulf Higden (ca. 1364) noted that oysters, occupying the lowest position of the class of animals, were like plants in the way they clung to the earth and could not move. Moreover, "The upper surface of the earth is in contact with the lower surface of water; the highest part of the waters touches the lowest part of the air, and so by a ladder of ascent to the outermost sphere of the universe." No part of the universe was superfluous; even the humblest creature had its own special dignity and its use in the large whole. As Davies of Hereford put it, "The noblest creatures need the vil'st on ground, the vil'st are served by the honour'd most" (1602).[37] This conception of world order persisted into the eighteenth century. Its catholic compass was one reason for its appeal. It promoted a calm image of order but also an almost overwhelming sense of abundance. It insisted on a hierarchy of being but also on the dignity of all classes of creatures bound to one another by relations of interdependence and accessibility. In this conception of a perfected and finely stratified world, there was little scope for individual initiative and for the kind of withdrawal into self that could lead to the incubation of radical doubt.

Cohesive Wholes

Withdrawal nonetheless had occurred, and has been increasingly common. The freer and more technically developed a society is, the easier it is for its members to isolate themselves from each other and from society as a whole; and the greater the desire to do so in the interest of nurturing an integral sense of self. A heterogeneous sociocultural whole becomes, in the course of time, fragmented. Objects, people, and activities are compartmentalized, taking on individually a distinctiveness they did not formerly possess, but also, in the case of people, acquiring a wistful air of self-conscious isolation. We shall examine this process in the next four chapters, beginning with food and table manners. Our center of concern will be the culinary style and dining-hall etiquette of medieval and modern Europe, but first we shall look briefly into those of ancient China and Rome. By thus broadening the cultural canvas, we should be in a better position to assess the special case of Europe—the emergence there of a heightened fastidiousness and sensitivity as the physical and social environment of the dining hall changed.

PARTS

3

Food
and Manners

With most people, mealtime is a happy social occasion.[1] Kinsfolk and friends forgather in anticipation of food and entertainment. They are able to relax among their own kind and take pleasure in feelings of solidarity. Yet, in societies where some degree of social stratification occurs, mealtimes also contain unavoidable elements of stress. Eating is a biological imperative, but human beings who take pride in their supra-animal status want to transcend this natural act by making it into a ceremony and an art. The techniques of cooking, the formalities of service, the placement of utensils, and the etiquette of consumption all support an exalted image of human dignity. They remind people not only of their distance from animal needs and raw nature but of differences in status among themselves. Moments of tension arise in the midst of all the bonhomie. A guest may feel, for instance, that he is seated too far from the host, that his witticisms have fallen on deaf ears, and that he has probably committed a solecism by scooping up peas with his spoon.

A characteristic of high culture is its tendency to elaborate categories, to separate things, sometimes as a step toward the creation of new patterns. In cooking, for example, chefs recognize that for a meat to retain its unique flavor it must not be mixed with other incompatible meats or smothered in a rich sauce. Etiquette, more arbitrarily, dictates that a fish knife not be used to butter bread. The effect of discriminatory sensitivity on food and table manners is to reduce hearty gregariousness, and substitute for it self-conscious behavior and the view that food preparation is a serious art. Consider this process as it transpired in China and the West.

The Chinese story is well told by K. C. Chang and his colleagues in their book, *Food in Chinese Culture*. Among the wealth of details they provide, we shall focus on those that bear on our theme. Two outstanding facts about food in China are its importance and its precocious development. It may seem superfluous to assert the great importance of food to the Chinese. Surely this is true of all human beings. And of course it is, but for survival and nurture rather than as an art and even as a philosophy of life. The ancient Greeks, for example, made no great fuss over food. It may be that Sir Alfred Zimmern's definition of the Attic dinner as consisting of two courses, "the first a kind of porridge, and the second a kind of porridge" is unjustly spare, yet it does express forcefully and correctly the simplicity of Greek cooking.[2] Even in the middle of the fifth century B.C., the Greek manner of eating their evening meal (the most substantial for the day) was unceremonious. Reay Tannahill observes that the "symposium or banquet so dear to literary tradition was a type of dinner party at which the food was disposed of rapidly before the real business of the evening—talking and drinking—began."[3]

Unlike the Greeks, the Chinese have always shown a tendency to treat food with high seriousness. When Duke Ling of Wei asked Confucius (551–479 B.C.) about military tactics, Confucius replied, "I have indeed heard about matters pertaining to *tsu* (meat stand) and *tou* (meat platter), but I have not learned military matters."[4] In those times, one of the most important qualifications of a gentleman was his knowledge of food and drink and his skill at preparing them. The reason is that food was intimately connected with ritual. *Li Chi*, a Confucian classic with materials dating back to the fifth century B.C. and earlier, is full of references to the right kinds of food for various occasions and the right table manners, and it contains some of the earliest recipes of Chinese dishes. The elaborateness of table setting and manners among the upper-class members of the Late Chou (480–221 B.C.) society is suggested by the following rules from the *Li Chi*:

The cup with which the guest was pledged was placed on the left; those which had been drunk (by the others) on the right. Those of the guest's attendant, of the host himself, and of the host's assistant;—these all were placed on the right. In putting down a boiled fish to be eaten, the tail was laid in front. In winter it was placed with the fat belly on the right; in summer with the back. . . . All condiments were taken up with the right (hand), and were therefore placed on the left. . . . When the head was presented among the viands, the snout was put forward, to be used as the offering. He who sets forth the jugs, considered the left of the cup-bearer to be the place for the topmost one. The jugs and jars were placed with their spouts towards the arranger.[5]

The ritual books also contain simple rules on table manners reminiscent of those that can be found in the *courtoisie* books of Renaissance Europe: for example, "Do not make a noise in eating; do not crunch the bones with the teeth; do not put back fish you have been eating; do not throw bones to the dogs; do not snatch at what you want."[6] However, a modern reader is surprised not so much by such simple directives as by the elaborateness of the prescriptions in these ancient times. Occasionally, refinement seems to have been carried to excess. It was reported of Confucius that "he did not eat meat which was not cut properly, nor what was served without its proper sauce." Utensils, too, were highly particularized. Grain foods required several types of vessels distinctive enough to call for special terms such as *kui*, *hsü*, *fu*, and *tui*. Vessels for holding vegetable and meat dishes belonged to a separate category and they were also subdivided into types known as *tou*, *pien*, and *tsu*. The *Li Chi* tells us that during the Late Chou period the Chinese used their fingers for eating condiments and certain meat dishes. On the other hand, as early as the twelfth century B.C., Shang aristocrats already used chopsticks, spatulas, and ladles to convey foods at the dinner table.[7]

Eating could be a simple affair in cultures that are otherwise sophisticated. But such was not the way of the Chinese. They turned banquets into rituals, which is to say, they segmented and particularized every aspect of the process of serving food and drink. Ritual heightens awareness. Particularization makes one sensitive to differences. Eating ceremonially asserts, at the most basic level, that one is human, not animal; civilized, not barbarian. It also reminds a person of his standing within society. In ancient China, where one sat and the cardinal point toward which one faced boldly marked one's social

Food and Manners

position. At dinner, knowing how guests of different rank should behave toward each other was a part of the savoir-faire of all cultured
persons. Feasting, however, might go beyond good fellowship and
manners and turn into an occasion for ostentatious display. Insecure
officials then suffered from knowing that everything they owned, including vessels for food and drink, somehow revealed not only their
wealth and social standing but also their taste and indeed the quality
of their being. An excess of sensitivity encouraged hypocrisy, a defect
of character that was sufficiently widespread and obtrusive to call for
public censure. Thus the modern scholar Ying-shi Yü notes: "Toward
the end of the Earlier Han dynasty (202 B.C.–A.D. 9), a ranking official, T'ang Tsun, was accused of hypocrisy because he used earthen-
ware vessels [rather than the lacquered ones that enjoyed prestige].
Under the Emperor Kuang-wu's reign, Huan T'an, in a memorial essay
for the monarch, attacked some of the hypocritical court officials of
ministerial position who sought to achieve reputations of frugality by
using plain wooden cups for eating and drinking."[8]
There was surely a time when aristocratic Chinese ate and drank
with gusto, free from the constraints of an overwrought etiquette. We
gain such an impression from the poems of the *Shi Ching*, which contains materials dating back to the early part of the Chou dynasty.
Even much later, in the Western Han period, the feast that followed a
hunting expedition in the great park outside of Ch'ang-an was probably more hearty than ceremonious. Uninhibited drinking and noisy
entertainments by dancers, clowns, and jugglers were likely to have
taken place in these post-hunting revels.[9] On the other hand, both
archaeological and literary evidence supports the antiquity of the
Chinese manner of preparing and consuming food. Utensils, in their
form and function, go back to the prehistoric period, and those traits
of Chinese cooking that distinguish it from other national styles are
already plainly evident by the Chou dynasty.
Chinese culinary art has two basic characteristics. One is the division of food into two balanced parts: *fan*, grains and other starchy
edibles, and *t'sai*, vegetables and meats. The other characteristic is
the chopping up of vegetables and meats, and their mixing to produce
hundreds of dishes of differing texture, aroma, and flavor. Except for

small crustaceans and the fish, whole animals seldom appear on the table of a ritualized feast. Disseverment hides nature. Recombining the severed pieces results in a work of art. Food thus prepared is an ancient Chinese tradition. In Chou texts, culinary art is often referred to as *ko p'eng*, that is, "to cut and cook." Many culinary words mean "to cut" or "to mince." Cooking in Han China carried the art of cooking further.[10] Several writers of the Later Han dynasty (A.D. 25–220) spoke of mincing and slicing fish and meat to the thinnest degree as a discriminative feature of fine food.[11]

The recombined meat-and-vegetable dishes must be tasty as well as pleasing to the eye. However, the Chinese have given food an importance beyond gustatory pleasure and art. Food is also medicine. The kind and amount of food one takes are closely related to one's health. True, other peoples (including Westerners) subscribe to this idea, but the Chinese have tied the quality of food to the fundamental principles of their cosmos, *yin* and *yang*. Good health comes out of harmony between the yin and yang forces of the body; imbalance between them brings sickness. To the Chinese, many foods have qualities of yin and yang; they can therefore be eaten to counteract the body's yin-yang disequilibrium. This belief appears in documents of the Chou period, and it remains a viable concept in Chinese culture today.[12] The success of Chinese culinary art, and indeed of Chinese civilization, lies in an ability to segment and particularize on the one hand, and on the other, to recombine and reintegrate the particular—without destroying their individuality—into large wholes: that is, while the components retain their individual virtues, new creations of subtle and complex flavors can emerge.

Compared with Chinese banqueting, which acquired genteel tones by its early association with ritual, banqueting in the Western world had been a much more open and boisterous affair. Of course, a great feast boasted moments of high ceremony, but until modern times these tended to be mingled with crude behavior and also with activities that now seem incompatible with the conduct of eating. When we read about a Roman banquet or a great feast in medieval England, we have the impression that it was a sort of public event, exuding an atmosphere compounded of religious seriousness, orgiastic reveling, and

Food and Manners

the merrymaking of villagers. A feast was a tumult of movement (the crowd of servitors and entertainers whirling about the diners), of color, noise, music, laughter, and the yelping of dogs fighting over a bone. To modern fastidious eyes, there was a grossness not only in the manner of eating but also in the amount of food, in the way whole animals appeared at the table, and in the bewildering number of barely differentiated dishes served en masse.

Thus, in miniature, dining revealed the rich humanity of an older world, unselfconscious and fully engaged in the externals of living. From the Renaissance period onward, the story of dining was largely one of simplification and of discernment, in the course of which incompatible flavors in the food were kept apart and behaviors discordant with the idea of a dignified table were excluded. Table manners evolved gradually toward an ideal of discrimination. The vulgarity of food piled high on a plate and smothered in gravy came to be recognized. The unique flavor of individual meats and vegetables were increasingly appreciated. Segregation proceeded along all fronts: musicians were retained but not clowns and jugglers; guests no longer sat on a common bench but in separate chairs; the variety of dishes diminished along with the quantity, but the number and kind of instruments used to cut and separate foods vastly increased. Table manners promoted self-consciousness. They drew more and more boundaries around people and things, and made diners feel shame when these boundaries were unwittingly crossed.

A Roman feast still evokes an image of orgiastic abandon, thanks to the vivid prose of Petronius and the extravagant re-creations of Hollywood. It is an unfair image because ancient Romans were normally sober diners, the sound of their eating interrupted by nothing more raucous than a slave's recitation of uplifting prose or a musician playing on the lyre. On the other hand, Petronius's description of Trimalchio's dinner party, though a wild satire, nonetheless captured an air of dissoluteness and of excess that was not too far from what could very well have happened at feasts given by the newly rich of Rome during the first century A.D.[13]

Several customs contributed to a picture of moral lassitude in Imperial Rome. The use of couches suggested languor. Diners slouched over them, propped up by their left forearms, and using their right hands to procure food and drink. Knives and spoons were available but not the fork. Romans preferred in any case to use their fingers, and this could be messy when the meat was covered with sauce. Napkins were spread along the edge of the couch to catch the drippings. Whole animals or large chunks of meat carved to look like animals appeared at the table. The obscenely rich landowner Trimalchio offered his guests a hare decorated with wings to look like Pegasus and a wild sow with its belly full of live thrushes, among other more or less fanciful meat sculptures. To modern taste, the dishes offered at the table pell-mell were nauseatingly rich. The acme of extravagance was the food that the emperor Vitellius dedicated to the goddess Minerva, which Tannahill describes as "a very cloying mixture of pike liver, pheasant brains, peacock brains, flamingo tongues and lamprey roe."[14] The Chinese idea of balance between "cold" and "hot" foods with their yin and yang properties did not exist. Again, in contrast to the Chinese rule of eating until one felt only "seven-tenths full," the Romans seem to have sought relief from bloating by using the emetic.

A confusion of movements and activities marked the Roman feast. Numerous servitors, those of the host as well as those who accompanied the guests, danced to the needs of their masters, bringing to them food, wine, and water to wash their greasy fingers with. Guests customarily discarded the food they could not consume, spattering the ground with snail shells, egg shells, lobsters' legs, cherry stones, and apple cores,[15] which were fought over by dogs. In a cultured household, literary readings entertained the guests. The Roman scholar Pliny (A.D. 23–79) habitually took notes as his slave read out aloud to his guests. Pliny was ever conscious of the shortness of the human life span and hated to miss any opportunity for acquiring knowledge.[16] His behavior was not, however, all that eccentric for his time. Between servings at a party, guests might well write or dictate letters at the table or play with the dice. In a less cultured household, a rich host might entertain his guests with performances by buffoons, effeminate men, dancing girls, and even with the spectacle of a gladiatorial contest.[17]

Medieval feasting resembled Roman feasting in several respects. It too was a tumult of noise, color, and movement, a giddy mixture of

Food and Manners

ceremony and farce—the utmost refinement in art and manners side by side with animal appetites and crudities. As at a Roman banquet, a grand dinner in late medieval times was full of bustle. Guests often arrived with their own retainers, who hovered about behind their masters, ready to supply them with any drink and food that was out of reach. The host's servants, supervised by household dignitaries, rushed back and forth between the sideboards and the table. Grace was said before and after meals; pages served their lords on bended knees: such was the pomp and high seriousness.[18] On the other hand, entertainment by troubadours, acrobats, and jugglers was noisy and frivolous. Beautiful tapestries decorated the walls, whereas only humble rushes were strewn on the floor, barely hiding what Erasmus described as an "ancient collection of beer, grease, fragments, bones, spittle, excrements of dogs and cats, and every thing that is nasty."[19] Rich cloth covered the table. Noble lords drank out of bejeweled goblets and displayed tableware made of silver, gold, crystal, coral, and ophite. But few utensils were available to the less privileged guests who, until the fifteenth century, ate from trenchers. A trencher was originally a thick slice of stale bread rather than a wooden plate. By the end of a meal the bread-as-plate was soaked with juice, and the diner could eat it himself, give it to the poor, or throw it to the dogs.[20]

Food appeared at the table in confusing variety, without discernible order. How restrained modern gourmets are compared with their ancestors! Plantagenet kings of the fourteenth and fifteenth centuries ate everything that had wings, from a bustard to a sparrow, and everything that swam, from a minnow to a porpoise. The game list was prodigious and included many birds, such as herons, egrets, and bitterns, that have long since passed out of favor. As to vegetables and herbs, medieval cooks used them in abundance and indiscriminately. Many dishes were created by combining every scrap of greenstuff that came to hand. In a hare stew one might find cabbage, beets, borage, violets, mallows, parsley, betony, the white part of leeks, and the tops of young nettles. The inclusion of violets on this list reminds us that flowers were used not only for decoration but also for cooking. Besides violets, other flowers that might find their way into a dish included roses, hawthorn, and primroses.[21]

A dinner was made up of two or three courses. This sounds modest, but each course could easily contain more than a dozen different kinds of food heaped high on large platters. Guests were confronted with such rich fare as shields of boiled and pickled boar, hulled wheat boiled in milk and vension, rich stews, salted hart, pheasant, swan, capons, lampreys, perch, rabbit, mutton, baked custard, and tart fruit. If a diner felt surfeited and longed for a salad or a vegetable dish in the next round, he was doomed to disappointment. The second course was again made up of a large array of rich meat and fish offerings hardly distinguishable from the first.[22]

The ideal of an orderly sequence—soup, fish, meat, and dessert— did not exist until the end of the seventeenth century. Copiousness, rather than discrimination, was the key concept in premodern culinary art. Cooks were singularly indifferent to the unique textures and flavors of the materials that went into a cauldron. Their clients showed little awareness that the flavors of the different meats piled on a platter would conflict. The French critic and poet Boileau (1636–1711) mentioned an enormous mixed grill consisting of a hare, six chickens, three rabbits, and six pigeons, all served on the same plate. Messiness was aggravated by a tendency to overcook everything, especially the boiled meats and *ragoûts* that Louis XIV and his subjects were so fond of. The recipe for ragoût called for putting a number of different kinds of flesh and fowl in a cauldron, adding a large quantity of spice, and stewing the mixture for twelve hours. This heavy broth does not sound at all appetizing to a modern gourmet, and one hardly imagines (says W. H. Lewis) that it "would be saved at the twelfth hour by a lavish top dressing of musk, amber, and assorted perfumes."[23]

Before the seventeenth century, most dishes did not require thoughtful preparation, not even the pâtés, meats and side dishes of the most ostentatious feasts. Thereafter, gourmet meals for discerning people began to appear. During the seventeenth and eighteenth centuries the French terms *gourmand* and *gourmet* won general acceptance in urbane Europe; they were used to express approval, without a later age's hint of derogation. Another sign of refinement in taste lay in the serving of foods on a large number of small dishes rather than on a few large platters.[24] Incompatible flavors were thus kept apart. After 1700, more and more cultivated people recognized that the distinctive quality of a dish rather than the quantity and expense of the ingredients that went into it was the only acceptable criterion of excellence. The care that went into cooking by the middle of the eighteenth century is suggested by the menu for a reception in honor of the Archbishop of Besançon. Among the dishes listed were: "Bisque d'écrivisse, potage à la reine, grenouilles à la poulette, truites grillées, anguilles en serpentin, filets de brochet, carpes du Doubs avec coulis d'écrivisse, tourte de laitances de carpes."[25]

To modern taste, the amount and richness of the food of earlier times are rather vulgar. Gross too is the idea of cooking and serving whole animals and large joints. In the medieval period, entire pigs and quarters of oxen were roasted on spits at the center of the hall. Upper-class members of late medieval society dined not only on the whole fish and on whole birds (sometimes with their feathers stuck back to look as though they were alive), but on whole rabbits and lambs, and on quarters of veal. In seventeenth-century England, beef, mutton, and pork occupied a large place in the diet of the yeoman. At big dinners and on local feast days in the village, it was a common practice to roast a whole animal or even several of them. Indeed, if there existed no special occasion, the roasting itself might serve as one. On a Sunday, while a whole sheep with "a puddinge in the Bellye" was being cooked over the fire, the guests went to prayers and then returned to the feasting; at which, inspirited by plenty of ale, they danced and made merry with fife music.[26]

From the Middle Ages to the beginning of the eighteenth century, carving meat at the table was a skill that every well-bred man was expected to have. By the seventeenth century, upper-class Frenchmen began to lose interest in this bellicose art, together with their passion for hunting and fencing. It was also from this period onward that the urban society of France and Germany showed an increasing aversion to the display of animal forms at the dining table. English society was more laggard or tolerant in this regard. Great lumps of meat survive to our day as the "joint." Still, a joint is not a whole animal, and in the middle of the nineteenth century, some English arbiters of good taste objected to even the joint. One book on proper behavior, published in 1859, asserted:

The truth is, that unless our appetites are very keen, the sight of much meat reeking in its gravy is sufficient to destroy them entirely, and a huge joint especially is calculated to disgust the epicure. If joints are eaten at all, they should be placed on the side-table, where they will be out of sight.[27]

The evolution of table manners and utensils was indicative of a growing sensitivity to what it meant to be civilized. A civilized person was someone who consciously sought to put a distance between self and all that hinted at animality, natural functions, violence, messiness, and indiscriminate mixing, whether of different kinds of food or of people. By these criteria, medieval people still had far to go. Manners even among the great lords could be crude, especially when hunger removed restraint and a favorite dish appeared on the table. As the Scottish clergyman and poet Alexander Barclay (1475?–1552) put it, no doubt with a touch of sardonic exaggeration,

> If the dish be pleasant, eyther fleshe or fishe,
> Ten handes at once swarme in the dishe;
> And if it be fleshe, ten knives shalt thou see
> Mangling the flesh and in the platter flee;
> To put there thy handes is perill without fayle,
> Without a gauntlet or els a glove of mayle.[28]

In the Middle Ages, peasants as well as the high-born ate with their hands. By the sixteenth century, an elegant diner dipped into the communal plate with only three fingers. This was still sticky business when we remember that most of the dishes were either big chunks of meat covered with gravy, or hashes and stews. Forks came into use first in Italy, then in Germany and England. Elizabeth I provided forks on her table; Thomas Coryat's claim that he introduced the tool to England in 1601 must therefore be disallowed. It is a fact, however, that the fork did not find easy acceptance. Coryat was laughed at for his affectation and rebuked from the pulpit for assuming that God's gifts were unfit to be touched by human hands. Throughout the medieval period, guests normally brought their own knives to the table. These were sharp, pointed implements, suitable for cutting and impaling meat. When did table knives first become rounded at the tip? The credit for the change probably should go to Cardinal Richelieu,

Food and Manners

who in 1669 promulgated an edict that forbade the manufacture, sale, and use of pointed knives. He was disgusted when Chancellor Séguier, a guest at his table, made such an implement serve as a toothpick[29] (Fig. 1).

In the Middle Ages, sharing was much admired as an ideal and colored all behavior at the table and beyond. A generous host provided victuals not only to his honored guests, but also to the poor at the door and to the dogs beside the table. It was good manners to share food between equals too. A gracious diner was one who offered his companion delicacies from his own trencher. The few utensils on the table were often shared. A knight sat next to his squire, and close relatives were sometimes seated together so that they could use the same tools. For the same reason, a gentleman sat next to his lady love. Knives, ladles, spoons, wooden trenchers, and cups might all be shared. The custom began to irritate fastidious people in the sixteenth century. Montaigne, commenting on table manners, considered it worth noting that an old soldier had grown so refined in his drinking that he would use only his own private cup. Montaigne himself confessed that he did not like to drink from a common glass or be served by a common hand.[30]

The growing delicacy of table manners can be traced through the various acceptable ways of consuming soup. At first, soup was simply drunk from the communal bowl, or from a ladle passed from hand to hand. A more delicate diner might, however, use his own spoon, perhaps the silver one he had received as a christening present, which he had remembered to bring along with his knife. When Samuel Pepys dined at the Lord Mayor's table he ate with his own utensils. The next stage in refinement, recorded in the *courtoisie* literature of the later half of the seventeenth century, was to refrain from taking the soup directly from the common bowl to one's mouth; rather one poured some first into one's own plate. And it came to be regarded as offensive to dip a used spoon into the common dish; one should first wipe it clean with a serviette. Finally, only a clean spoon could be used.[31]

In the nineteenth century, the number of utensils and their specialized functions increased to a peak that was never to be surpassed. After 1800, for example, a well-laid table displayed fruit knives and forks as well as fish knives and forks. These implements were made of

Fig. 1. Sixteenth-century woodcut of King Arthur and the Knights of the Round Table at a banquet. Note that there is only one goblet on the table, for general use, and no forks or spoons. From *History of the House*, Ettore Camesasca, ed. (New York: G. P. Putnam's Sons, 1971), p. 384.

silver or plated with silver because fastidious diners believed that the delicate flavor of fruits and fish would be spoiled by contact with steel. In the late seventeenth century, each guest was allowed one wine glass even though several wines might be served. In the course of the nineteenth century, the number of wine glasses, as also the number and variety of wines drunk, increased greatly. By the 1890s, a guest "might enter the dining room and find on the table before each place, individual wine glasses for sherry, red or white Bordeaux, red or white Burgundy, Moselle or Hock, Champagne, perhaps one glass for wines drunk with the sweet course such as Tokay, and one glass for the dessert wines of Port and Madeira."[32]

Food and Manners

What was distinctive about an upper-class Victorian banquet (especially after the 1850s) lay not in the sheer quantity of food, which could not match that served on a grand occasion in antiquity and in medieval times, but rather in the elaborate delicacy with which foods and drinks were conveyed in their separate containers and consumed with specialized tools. A glittering array of crystal and silverware surrounded the plate of every guest. Even before the first dishes were put on the table it already looked overburdened: it groaned not so much with food that catered to the needs of the body as with the segmenting tools and containers of high culture[33] (Fig. 2).

As evidence of a growing self-consciousness in the Western world, we may also turn to books on etiquette, which began to appear in the late Middle Ages. Late medieval society was large and flexible enough to allow a degree of geographical and social mobility among its more ambitious members. Aspiring courtiers moving up to serve in princely courts soon recognized the need to acquire acceptable manners. Thus, guidebooks were in demand. One popular guide, Tannhäuser's *Hofzucht* (Courtly Manners), dates back to the thirteenth century. Tannhäuser provided rules such as these: "Do not pick your nose while eating" because you have to use your hand to take food from the communal dish. "A number of people gnaw a bone and then put it back in the dish—this is a serious offense." And "a man who blows his nose on the tablecloth is ill-bred, I assure you."[34] In the *Contenances de Table* of the fifteenth century, written in metrical French, the aspirant to good manners is told that he must not spit on the table at dinner time; the proper thing to do is to spit on the floor. And when he washes his mouth at table, he must not reject the water into the basin, which other guests will want to use, but again he should spit the water on the floor.[35]

It was, however, early in the modern period, during the sixteenth and seventeenth centuries, that books on manners began to multiply and gain wide influence. Demand for them rose because social stratification during this time had become notably less rigid and moving up the social ladder was a possibility for a larger segment of the population. By far the most influential of these guides was a short work by Erasmus, *De civilitate morum puerilium* (On Civility in Children).

A.

Fig. 2. The elaboration of utensils in the nineteenth century. (A) Table glass, 1851. (B) Formal dinner in Victorian England. Note the cluttered table even before food is served. Fig. 2A from *Early Victorian England*, G. M. Young, ed. (London: Oxford University Press, 1934), opposite p. 114. Fig. 2B from W. J. Reader, *Life in Victorian England* (New York: Capricorn Books, 1964), p. 153.

B.

Food and Manners

First published in 1526, it quickly achieved the broadest circulation among the upwardly mobile families of Europe.[36] What distinguishes Erasmus's treatise from its medieval predecessors is not in the rules themselves, which closely parallel those of earlier times, but (as Norbert Elias points out) in its psychological perspective. It is a work that reflects the mind of a far more self-conscious people. Erasmus's rules, unlike those of the medieval period, impress us as coming out of his own experience and reflective observation. He did not simply assert, "Do not gorge yourself with food." He would have said that some people devoured their food as though they were about to be carried off to prison, or were thieves wolfing down their booty. Erasmus noted that outward manner, including clothing, revealed the man—indeed his soul. He gave examples of what kind of dress corresponded to this or that spiritual condition. Civility, as he understood the term and fostered it on the European consciousness, was closely bound with a psychological manner of seeing. To be really courteous, one was obliged (as Elias interprets Erasmus) "to observe, to look about oneself and pay attention to people and their motives."[37]

There can be little doubt that table manners both reflected and nurtured an increasing tendency in European life to eschew hearty gregariousness in favor of differentiation, order, understated elegance, and an extraordinarily inflated sense of human dignity, which implies not only the necessity to distance oneself from nature but from other human beings as well—even from other guests around the table. The Chinese, by contrast, have not moved so far. Early in their history the Chinese, unlike the Europeans, have introduced elements of high formality into their feasts. They did this because food and eating were seen to be closely tied to the yin and yang principles of the cosmos. Eating properly and with the appropriate gestures were ways of enforcing the harmony of nature, to which human beings and human society belonged. Rules of etiquette were intended to enjoin, not separate. The Chinese had an early start on table manners, but chose not to elaborate them to the point of making diners excessively self-conscious. With Europeans it was otherwise. In the nineteenth century, a Chinese dinner is a relaxed affair in comparison not only with a formal European banquet—awesome in its display of tableware—but even with an ordinary meal in an affluent bourgeois household presided over by master and mistress, sitting stiffly at the two extremities of a long table.

Preparing food and eating it is one activity within the house. We may now turn to the larger stage of the house itself, and note how architectural history as well as the history of what constitutes membership in a household throw additional light on the relationship between progressive spatial segmentation and heightened self-awareness—even self-preoccupation.

4

House
and Household

Space, to become a world and a home for self, must be defined. All human beings make some conscious effort to define space, though not necessarily by constructing a material house. What a material house does supremely well is to make the character of the human world vividly present to the senses and to the mind. An enclosed space contains, concentrates, and focuses the human psyche. Sitting by a fire alone or with friends inside a shelter, a person is likely to acquire a more intense awareness of self and of human reality than can occur in the midst of open and undifferentiated space. Within protecting walls, our capacity to attend, feel, or think is spared the distractive buffeting of events beyond our comprehension and control. Enclosed space sheathes the kernel of our being; from the focused center of self, house, and intimate world, we venture forth to engage the wider world.[1]

In addition to these personal and psychological relationships between enclosed space and human reality, the house is an architectural embodiment of social structure and values. A house of many rooms distinguished from each other by size and furnishing, suggests that the people living there differ in social status, that they know what is and is not appropriate in the different rooms, that their awareness of self intensifies as they play their varied roles in a complex arena, and that periodically they may feel the need to withdraw so as to recapture a sense of their unique nature in solitude.

In all civilizations the story of the house is one of enlargement and of progressive partitioning. The earliest Neolithic dwellings were single rooms, round or oval in shape, and partly underground. Separation from Mother Earth was not yet complete. In the course of time, the round semi-pit dwellings gave way to larger houses built above ground, internally partitioned, and of rectangular shape. In China during the Shang dynasty (ca. 1500 B.C.), houses of high prestige stood on terraces; the terrace and the gabled roof hint at aspirations toward the sky (Fig. 3). As the round Neolithic dwellings might be arranged to form a circular encampment, so the rectangular buildings characteristic of a higher stage of civilization were often arranged to form a courtyard. Where courtyard and semi-pit houses existed side by side, the former possessed ceremonial functions and belonged to people of power, the latter were the habitations and workshops of the humble. Archaeologists have discovered courtyard complexes in the ancient Near East, the Indus Valley, north China, and Mesoamerica. Interior courts became a standard feature of upper- and middle-class domiciles in widely different parts of the world.[2]

The higher the status of a family the greater the number of interior courts such a family would have in its residence. Typical of the courtyard residence is the separation of ceremonial space from private space. The house's physical layout reveals its occupant's acute awareness of the public and private roles of the self. China's courtyard house antedates the Western Han dynasty (207 B.C.–9 A.D.). By then, there existed already an elaborate code governing the proper reception of an honored guest who was also a personal friend. In a large residence of traditional north-south alignment, the privacy of the quarters increased as one moved north. The host received his guest ceremonially in the central guest hall, which faced south toward a courtyard that still had the character of a semipublic space. If the guest were also a friend, he might be asked to step into the family compound behind the ceremonial hall. This signified a special kind of honor—that of being accepted as a member of the intimate world of the family. The guest, as he moved along the principal axis of the house, progressed from a formal to a more personal welcome. Yet, in a typical Chinese house, individual privacy was not easy to obtain even in the family quarters. All rooms opened to the common courtyard. The thin walls and screens could not keep out household noises. If the head of the

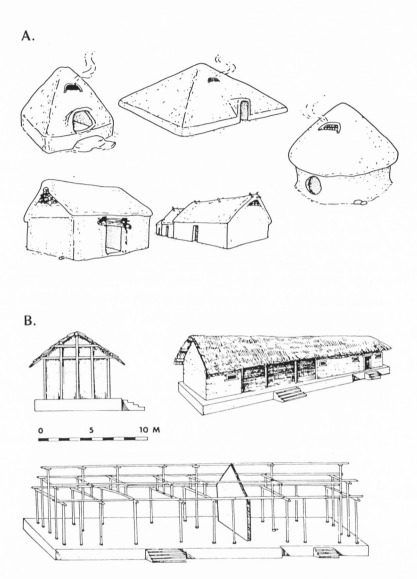

Fig. 3. Evolution of the house from (A) Neolithic Yang-shao culture (6000–3000 B.C.) to (B) Shang culture (1300 B.C.) in China. The Shang house is at Hsiao-t'un, An-yang. The changes are toward the enlargement and progressive partitioning of space. From *K'ao-ku Hsueh Pao*, 1975, no. 1; Shih Chang-ju, *Annals of Academia Sinica* I (1954): 276, and K. C. Chang, *The Archaeology of Ancient China* (New Haven: Yale University Press, 1977), pp. 107, 249.

house really wanted solitude, he might have to retreat beyond his bedroom or study into a small high-walled garden, where he could contemplate undisturbed.[3]

The courtyard house was a common feature of ancient Athens and Rome. Its blank walls facing the streets suggest a desire for privacy, but in fact little personal privacy could be found in the city domiciles. Athenians of the fifth century poured their energies into the construction of public rather than private buildings. Residences, with few exceptions, were small and modestly appointed, the rooms arranged around one or more courtyards. Inside the room, which had no window to the street, an Athenian enjoyed a measure of privacy free from the intrusions of the outside world, but not from members of his own household, because the interior of his room, like that of other rooms, could be seen from the common courtyard. Although the city domicile was too small to allow individual privacy, after dark solitude for contemplation or study became possible. Most Athenians retired early, but a few stayed up late to take advantage of the quiet hours. It is well known that Demosthenes prepared nearly all his speeches at night. For longer periods of peace and seculsion the wealthy Athenian withdrew to his country estate.[4]

Ancient Rome had two principal types of residence, the *insula* and the *domus*. Most people lived in the insula, which offered little or no privacy because the windows and doors of this multistoried structure opened out to the street. By contrast, wealthy Romans lived in the horizontal courtyard house, the domus, which turned a blind, unbroken wall to the street; all its windows and doors opened to the interior court. Architecturally, private and public spaces seem well defined. The cacophony and bustle of the streets were kept out as much as possible.[5] However, many activities occurred inside the domicile that we would not now regard as private. A tradition of the Republican period was the morning call, during which unofficial businesses were transacted in the households of the great. The occasion allowed clients to solicit the advice and assistance of their patrons, politicians to engage in political maneuvers in support of their candidates at forthcoming elections, and foreigners charged with diplomatic affairs in Rome to gain the sympathy of influential senators for their cause.

House and Household

By the time of the Empire, the morning call had lost its work character and sunk to the level of either a tedious social chore, or the routine dispensing of charity to hangers-on.[6] But whether the business conducted was political and serious, or merely social, the great Roman clearly enjoyed little privacy in the confines of his own domus. Solitude was to be found not in the city but in the peaceful surroundings of his country estate. At his Laurentine villa the younger Pliny could relax: "I hear nothing said, I say nothing myself. . . . I never have to listen while somebody is being criticized or abused. I criticize nobody —except, occasionally, myself when I am writing badly." And at his estate in Tuscany he had the leisure to think: "I wake as I please. . . . I keep the shutters closed. In the quiet and the dark, with no distractions, free and left to myself, instead of thinking about what I see, I direct my gaze towards whatever I am thinking about, which eyes can do when they have nothing else to look at."[7]

Western man, more than people in other societies, has raised the idea of the human individual together with that of privacy to a supreme value. How has such an exalted view of the self developed in relation to the story of the house? We shall try to answer this question by focusing on changes in the house—its internal arrangements and furnishings, its social functions and significance—from the Middle Ages to modern times.

In the early Middle Ages, the house, whether that of a lord or a peasant, was basically a barnlike structure with a central hearth and a roof open to the ceiling. In the course of time, more and more rooms were added to this central feature known as the hall (Fig. 4). Needless to say, at first only the powerful and the rich could afford these additions. Privacy and the exploration of self were luxuries confined to the elite of society.

Through most of the medieval period, the large, uncluttered and unpartitioned hall served as an open and almost public arena, in which all manner of people might meet, conduct business, and find temporary hospitality. Contributing to the atmosphere of bustle and noise were animals. On a festive occasion, as a guest entered the hall he would find in the midst of a boisterous crowd game-loving barons with their favorite bird on their wrist. Some of these birds were placed on

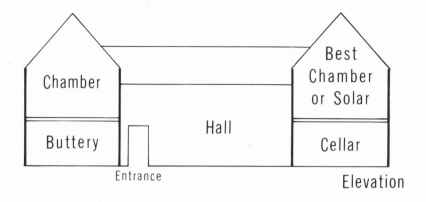

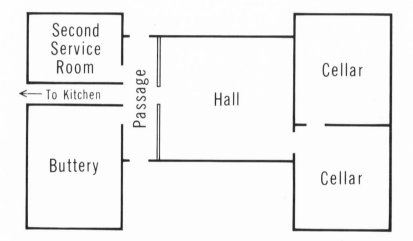

Fig. 4. Elements of the later medieval house, shown in section and plan. The essential feature is the hall, open to the roof and flanked by storeyed ranges. By the end of the Middle Ages, the ground-floor room (or rooms) at one end of the hall was sometimes used as a parlor. From M. W. Barley, *The House and Home* (Greenwich, CT: New York Graphic Society Ltd., 1971), p. 23.

a T-shaped perch that stood on the floor. There they flapped their wings and periodically swooped across the hall, disrupting the conversation of their masters. Besides hunting birds, popinjays or parrots from the Middle East and an occasional raven swelled the avian population. Dogs, not all of them house-trained, trotted at their masters' heels or gamboled on the rush-strewn floor. A few monkeys would almost certainly be present, as also a tame badger or weasel. A menagerie of animals thus mingled with human beings, who were colorful and strange in their own way.[8]

House and Household

While dinner was being served, there might be ceremony at the high table on the dais, but in the main body of the hall the atmosphere was far from calm as from time to time hungry diners reached out for food and argued loudly with their rude servitors. The job of gentleman usher was no sinecure. Charged to maintain peace, ushers paced up and down the aisles shouting, "Speak softly, my masters!" The mixed guest list made a degree of rowdiness inevitable. Almost any traveler could make a claim on the hospitality of a manor; indeed, some barons took pride in the openness of their house to all conditions of men. An extreme example from the thirteenth century is furnished by the old Shropshire chronicle of the Fitz-Warines of Whittington. The story is told that Fulke Fitz-Warine turned the king's highway so that it ran through the middle of the hall of his manor at Alleston. He did this to forestall any excuse a traveler might have to pass by without partaking of his liberality.[9]

Not all men of power even in Saxon times welcomed the promiscuity of the hall. Some wished to withdraw from it after dinner and seek quieter amusements elsewhere, but such retreat (the temptation of King Edwy of Wessex, for example) was frowned upon as effeminate. In the thirteenth century, the person who shut the hall door (*huis*) and retreated to the privacy of an upper chamber or solar was taken to be a rude and avaricious miser. A contemporary poem noted,

> Encor escommeni-je plus
> Riche homme qui ferme son huis,
> Et val mengier en solier sus.[10]

Bishop Grosseteste of Lincoln (ca. 1175–1253) reminded the Countess of Leicester, sister of Henry III, of the importance of dining in hall with her people, an injunction that she scrupulously obeyed. On the other hand, the need to issue such an injunction suggests that by this time it was already a fairly common practice for the lord and lady to dine apart. William Langland noted in *Piers Plowman* (1362):

> Wretched is the hall . . . each day in the week
> There the lord and lady liketh not to sit.
> Now have the rich a rule to eat by themselves
> In a privy parlour . . . for poor man's sake,

House and Household

> Or in a chamber with a chimney, and leave the chief hall
> That was made for meals, for men to eat in.[11]

Royal personages, like their humblest subjects, suffered from a lack of privacy. Henry VIII in the end was compelled to issue an order in which he explained why he had to retreat periodically to his "Priueye Chamber and inward lodgeings."

In so muche as in the pure and cleane keepinge of the kinges Priueye Chamber, which the good order thereof consisteth a greate parte of the Kinges quyett, reste, comforte, and preservation of his healthe; the same above all other thinge is principally and most heighlie to bee regarded. And consideringe that righte meane persones, as well for their more commodity, doe retyre and withdrawe themselves aparte, as for the wholesomenesse of theire Chambers, do forbeare to have any greate or frequent resorte into the same.[12]

To retreat implies the existence of private quarters. A large domicile is so partitioned that its residents can forgather for sociability and withdraw for intimacy or solitude. Obviously the poor in all times lacked this choice. Crowding was so much the daily experience and a necessity of life that even the desire for solitude seems to have disappeared. In the Auvergnat villages of eighteenth-century France, one-room cottages were forced to accommodate twenty or more individuals. Ten to a cottage was a common occurrence. Brothers, sisters, cousins huddled together in a tiny space of twenty square yards, and three generations might sleep in the same bed. In Brittany, livestock actually shared the family's room; elsewhere they were separated by a slight partition that allowed some animal warmth to penetrate.[13] Extreme rural crowding persisted for at least another century in France, Germany, and Switzerland. The cities, too, packed the poor in tiny quarters. In the 1880s, 49 percent of Berlin's population lived in one-room households, 55 percent of Dresden's, 62 percent of Breslau's, and 70 percent of Chemnitz's.[14]

The reconstruction of rural dwellings began in France only during the nineteenth century. It was then that cellars appeared, second stories were built, and roofs reconstructed with fire-proof tiles.[15] In England the rebuilding of rural cottages began much earlier, in the late Tudor period. Between 1560 and 1650, the number of laborers'

House and Household

houses having three or more rooms rose from 56 to 79 percent.[16] A
three-room cottage had, besides the common-purpose living space, a
separate room for sleeping called a chamber in the south of England
and a parlour in the midlands, and a storage room called the buttery.
"Chamber," "parlour," and "buttery" were all upper-class terms that
had diffused to the world of prosperous farm laborers by the seventeenth century.[17]

Much better off than the laborers, the tenant farmers and freeholders—the husbandmen and the yeomen—lived in houses that on
the average had three to six rooms, rising to eight or ten among the
affluent yeomen, whose style of living could barely be distinguished
from that of the lesser gentry. In Elizabeth's time, a yeoman's house
might include the hall, two or three bedrooms, parlor, buttery, and a
servants' chamber. The hall was the main living room, styled sometimes "the bodie of the house," or simply "the house," eloquent
testimony of its prominence in earlier days. When construction was
limited to renovation, a ceiling might be fitted into a medieval hall,
formerly open to the rafters, so as to provide bedrooms above the
ceiling and a living room and parlor on the ground floor. Partitioning
the bigger rooms into smaller ones further enabled privacy, as did the
establishment of a master bedroom that could be entered through
only one door, and the setting aside of space for servants.[18]

Unlike the gentry, people of the yeoman class worked in the fields
and at home. A yeoman and his wife might enjoy the help of several
servants, both men and women, who lived with them. In addition,
they might accept the responsibility of sheltering a few of the parish's
charity children, who would serve as apprentices in husbandry.[19] Even
a house with six rooms could seem cramped, given the number of
people and of activities both economic and social that it had to accommodate. There was a clear desire on the yeoman's part for bigger
and more specialized space, for a room or two in which a measure of
privacy was possible. During Elizabethan and Stuart times the better-
off tenants and freeholders had the means to realize, at least partially,
their desire. In turn, the experience of living in a house where limited
withdrawal was possible no doubt whetted a person's desire for even
greater privacy.

House and Household

Houses that belonged to artisans, tradesmen, and merchants varied greatly in size and shape, depending on the wealth of the owner and on the importance of the city. Compare, for example, Leicester with Exeter. Leicester in the reign of Elizabeth I was a small provincial town. Many of its houses had only two rooms: a hall and a parlor or bedroom. If a third room existed, it would be the buttery. The hall very likely served a variety of social and economic functions. An artisan could have worked there and a shopkeeper could have used it to display his wares. A few houses had a second and even a third story: these narrow, tall structures might have six to a dozen rooms. Leicester's prime example of conspicuous wealth, in the 1530s, was a merchant's house. Its seventeen rooms, courtyard, chapel, barn and barnyard sprawled over valuable space off one of the town's principal streets.[20]

In the late Tudor period, Exeter's wealth and political importance far exceeded that of Leicester. Merchants' houses in Exeter commonly had a dozen or more rooms distributed through three to four floors. A typical house presented a narrow front, perhaps only twenty feet wide, to the street; its total depth, including large and small courtyards, might be six times greater (Fig. 5). Rooms, many of which served specialized needs, included hall, parlor, master chambers, separate quarters for male and female servants, shop, kitchen, buttery, warehouse, counting house, and stable. Prestigious rooms faced the street, if we can judge by Prestwood house as it stood in 1576. On the ground floor, the shop fronted the street; on the first floor it was the hall; on the second floor a principal bedroom called the forechamber overlooked the street by means of a handsome mullioned window. Behind the forechamber was the broad chamber, which faced an inner court.

Was there much privacy in such a house? That at least some rooms were set aside for specialized use indicated discrimination and the availability of privacy. On the other hand, many houses were only a single room wide. The absence of a separate passageway to which all the rooms opened meant that a person would have to cross an occupied chamber to traverse the length of the house. Even in a large building of more than a dozen rooms, only the one or two principal

House and Household

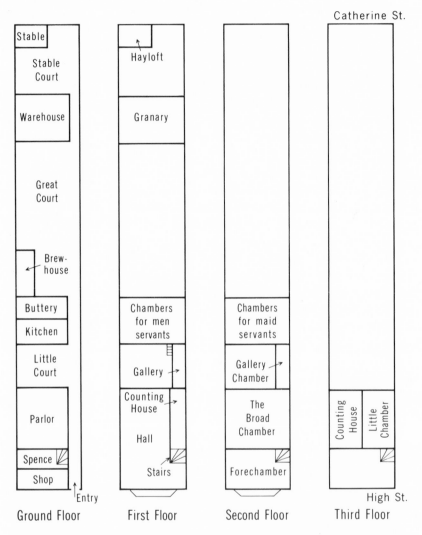

Fig. 5. Conjectural plan of the Prestwood house — the house of an Elizabethan merchant in 1576 (not drawn to scale). After W. G. Hoskins, "The Elizabethan merchants of Exeter," in *Elizabethan Government and Society* (London: The Athlone Press, 1961), p. 181.

bedchambers enjoyed real privacy. The other rooms were either common spaces such as the hall and the parlor, or specialized work and storage areas such as the kitchen, the counting house, the granary, and the stable. Opportunity to be alone must have been rare. This conclusion seems reasonable when we consider the size of a household, which could easily include a dozen members: parents, five or six children, two apprentices, and two or more maidservants.

Did the Exeter merchants lead a public life? In other words, to what extent were the affairs of the city and of people in the streets allowed to penetrate the domestic premise? The position of the shop and of prestigious rooms next to the street suggests that the merchant family was not averse to the noise and bustle of street life. Moreover, the major offices of the city were drawn from members of the merchant class, which indicates that the opulent interiors of the larger houses justified themselves as places for civic entertainment. On the other hand, Exeter's high civic offices were few compared with the number of qualified merchants, most of whom, apart from their business contacts, must perforce have led private lives.[21]

What was the situation in urban France? Between 1590 and 1637 the population of Paris increased rapidly from about 220,000 to 415,000. Much construction took place during this period. In the crowded medieval quarters, where allotments were narrow, people who could not afford to buy up adjoining properties built and lived in small houses, one room wide and two or three stories tall. Pressure of population might cause some dwellings to rise to six or seven stories. Bourgeois houses with two or three bays fronted the streets in the wealthier parts of Paris, such as the interior of Île Saint Louis.

During the reigns of Henri IV and Louis XIII, Parisian houses that served the needs of prosperous traders and artisans resembled the English merchant houses in several structural features. They were elongated in shape, stretching backward from their narrow street fronts; they rose to three to four stories; they had shops on the ground floor and one or two courts. However, the interior arrangements differed. In the Parisian house the two most important rooms on the ground floor (besides the shop) were the *salle* (hall) and the kitchen. The salle either faced the street or an interior court. It was a multipurpose room in which people assembled, dined, and played. At night a bed might be put there for a guest. Above the ground level, each floor contained a principal room known as the *chambre* and one or two subsidiary rooms (Fig. 6). Such interior arrangements suggest that the house was built to accommodate a single family; indeed, a house of this type in a prosperous English or Dutch city would have served the needs of only one bourgeois household.[22] But in Paris it was more common for several families to occupy the same building. The proprietor or main tenant took over the full complement of more or less specialized rooms in the first two stories. Other tenants filled the rest of the house. A family might occupy a room or two on one floor, and as it grew in size it would rent a room on another floor so that its living space spread over more than one level to interlock with the disconnected living space of another familial group.

Under the circumstances a family enjoyed little privacy. Individual privacy was even harder to achieve because too many people crowded into the few rooms. From seventeenth-century documents we read about a master tailor who lived with his wife and five young children in two rooms, and about a major of the Gournay regiment, a man of substantial position, who with his wife and two children had only two rooms to themselves on Rue de Richelieu.[23] The multiple use of space discouraged privacy. For example, the chamber that held the principal bed was also used for cooking. People cooked over the chamber's chimney fire because most apartments did not have a separate kitchen; only the proprietor had a real kitchen in his complex of rooms on the ground floor. The chamber served other purposes as well: family members and their guests ate, sat, and socialized in it. Above the ground floor, each story had a chamber of the kind described and one or two smaller rooms; if two, one of them was the *garde-robe* and the other the *cabinet*. A garde-robe contained cupboards and chests, but it might also have a fireplace and serve as the bedroom for servants and small children. The cabinet was a tiny cell used for storage. Even though it did not have access to daylight, a bed might be put there to accommodate an extra guest.[24]

We have sketched the bourgeois house in English towns and in Paris. We must now turn to Florence, because it was there that the private

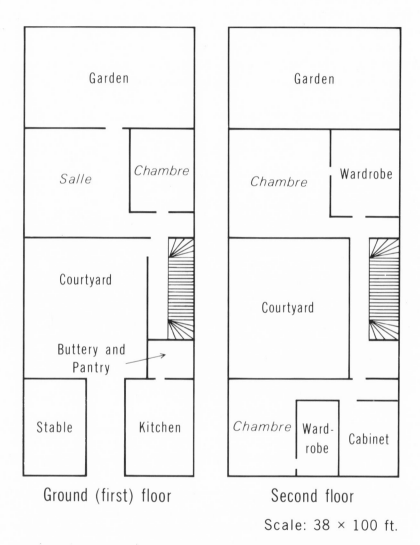

Ground (first) floor　　Second floor

Scale: 38 × 100 ft.

Fig. 6. A two-story Parisian townhouse according to the plan of Le Muet (1623). Such townhouses were built for a single owner, but in fact it often happened that the proprietor occupied the first floor and the second floor was rented to lesser occupants who had to manage without a kitchen. The wardrobe could also be used as a bedroom for children or servants. Modified from Jean-Pierre Babelon, *Demeures Parisiennes sous Henri IV et Louis XIII* (Paris: Le Temps, 1965), p. 104.

House and Household

residence early effloresced to become, by 1400, a conspicuous feature of the urban scene. It was also there that private familial life developed precociously, only to wane some two hundred years later, at a time when familial life started to acquire importance in other parts of western Europe. This story, as told by Richard Goldthwaite, neatly illustrates relationships of interest to us: those between segmented space and place identity, privacy and a sense of self.[25]

In the late medieval period, leading Florentine families still lived gregariously in protected compounds of common-wall houses and fortified towers that overlooked interior courts around which artisans and traders set up stalls (Fig. 7). Outside of these compounds were other privately owned buildings (*palazzi*), which, like those within the compounds, lacked functional specialization and architectural identity. Public and private worlds freely penetrated each other. Shops at street level led by stairways directly into residential apartments, as in a modern *palazzo*. The private residence of even a patrician might not take up a whole building. "When the very wealthy Messer Paglio di Bacuccio Vettori (1331–1377) wrote out in his diary a description of his house, he found that it was structurally all jumbled up with his neighbor's, with common walls, shared loggias, and division by floors."[26]

By the second half of the fourteenth century, patricians began to abandon the architectural hodgepodge and strove for monumental identity and definition in their residences. As a first step, they sought to create a distinctive facade that aesthetically separated one house from its neighbors. Multiple openings to the street gave way to one principal entrance. Shops were progressively eliminated. A rich Florentine merchant of the fifteenth century needed warehouses and shops in the manufacture of silk and wool, but he preferred to pay rent for space elsewhere rather than make room for such activities in his residence. His attitude thus contrasted strongly with that of a rich merchant of early Tudor England, who could build a palace grand enough for acquisition by royalty and yet see fit to rent its street frontages for shops and tenements.

A Florentine patrician of the Renaissance period yearned to display wealth, power, and individuality to the world and achieved this end by the style and monumentality of a palace. On the other hand,

Fig. 7. The tower houses of Florence, A.D. 1200–1300. The houses all belong to one family and are grouped together so as to form a single tower or block with an internal courtyard. The external galleries were used to fend off attacks by enemies. From Leonardo Benevolo, *The History of the City* (London: Scolar Press, 1980), p. 438.

the palace was also designed to keep the world out. Familial apartments faced inward to a landscaped court. To see the street or public square from the interior called for special effort because the windows were located so high up the wall that one must climb steps to peer over the sills.

The palace of a banker or merchant in Renaissance Florence, though impressively big and tall when viewed from the street, normally contains only three floors and no more than a dozen or so inhabited rooms. A large palace, compared with a smaller one, has bigger rooms but not necessarily more of them. The design of a palace suggests that it was meant to accommodate a small family in extraordinarily spacious quarters. Members of such a family included the owner, his wife, his children, and perhaps an unattached relative. The family was not, at least originally, a tentacular clan. Even when a father built a palace for his sons, the building was partitioned into an appropriate number of distinctive parts. As Goldthwaite puts it, "The privacy of a man's home meant not only withdrawal from public life but also detachment from most relatives who were not members of his immediate family." Servants did not intrude either, because it would seem that even a

House and Household

wealthy family living in a large house employed no more than two or three of them.[27]

Unfortunately, very little is known about life in such a household. We can infer, however, a trend toward increasing privacy and intimacy. Rooms, by the fifteenth century, were beginning to have specialized domestic functions and to be recognized as spaces reserved for individual members of the family. Women and children received attention in Renaissance culture. The status of women improved. Parents showed an increasing concern for the proper way to raise and formally educate children. The art works of the time revealed a tendency to idealize home life, childhood, and womanhood. On the scale of values, the private sphere matched the public sphere in importance. Individuality was recognized as an attribute not only of men, but of women and even of children.

However, this precocious development of a bourgeois mode of life did not last: it began to fade in Florence toward the later part of the sixteenth century. Renaissance houses were altered to suit the needs of more aristocratic households in the baroque period. Residential rooms and public chambers were added to meet the demands of the sumptuous life of this later age.

Having surveyed the possibilities for privacy and isolation among the lower and middle classes of premodern European society, we may now return to the ruling class with which we began. A chieftain or lord traditionally moved and lived among his people in relations of mutual dependence. Power and prestige required exposure. A lord, to maintain his privilege and effectiveness, must be seen. Unlike a merchant, he could not freely withdraw from the company of people with whom he might, personally, have little in common. Yet, as we have noted, the desire to withdraw was present even in Saxon times. Houses grew in size and rooms multiplied to make retreat possible, though it never seemed easy. The first room to be abandoned was the hall: in England, from the second half of the fourteenth century onward, a great man no longer dined there except on special occasions. By 1500, in both royal palaces and private houses the hall had become the dining room of the lower servants; princes and nobles

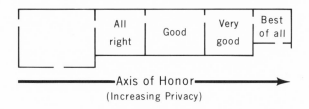

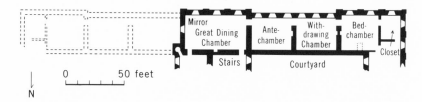

Fig. 8. The axis of honor in a formal house. The lower figure shows the state apartment on the second floor of the south front, Chatsworth house in Derbyshire (1687–1688). From Mark Girouard, *Life in the English Country House* (New Haven: Yale University Press, 1978), pp. 144, 155.

themselves moved upstairs to feast in the great chamber, not in privacy, but ceremonially, surrounded by people closer to their own status.

The great chamber, however, was no more specialized in its functions than the hall in its heyday. As late as 1500 a bed might occupy a prominent place in it. Dining in the great chamber became so common that late in the sixteenth century it was sometimes called the dining chamber. On the other hand, it could also be used for music, dancing, games of cards, family prayers, and the performance of plays and masques. The great chamber was obviously not the sort of place in which Henry VIII and other potentates of his time could find peace of mind. For privacy they must withdraw in their respective palace along the axis of a suite of rooms, each more exclusive and offering the possibility of greater intimacy than the one preceding it (Fig. 8). In Elizabethan and Jacobean England, a withdrawing chamber lay beyond the great chamber. It was the private eating, sitting, and reception room of the family. Personal servants might sleep there at night. Beyond the withdrawing room was the bedchamber. Here at last the occupant was free from intrusion, though valets and personal maids still had access by virtue of the essential services they rendered. Finally, there was the closet, the one truly private room in the house. By 1500 it served principally as the place for private devotions and for private study and business. Shakespeare showed that Ophelia had reason to feel alarm when Hamlet unceremoniously intruded into her

House and Household

closet; and when Queen Gertrude wished to speak with Hamlet in her closet she intended to convey the idea that they would be utterly alone. The privacy of the closet was a luxury to the Elizabethans, being the one place in which a man's or a woman's personality could find expression. Perfume was burnt in a censer to clear a closet of its mustiness but also to reveal a person's individuality in the choice of a special fragrance.[28]

Domestic architecture in both England and France began its career with the basic system of hall (salle) and chamber (chambre). However, subsequent evolution showed significant differences in the two countries. Changes in the French house suggest a lesser degree of concern for privacy. The family did not abandon the salle to the servants as had occurred in England by the end of the medieval period. Instead, the servants withdrew; that is, they (at least the retainers of lower status) lost the right to eat and sleep there. On the other hand, until well into the seventeenth century the salle was still a busy place open to all conditions of men. As Philippe Ariès has observed, before 1600 European society lacked true public houses and shelters in which members of the middle and upper class could forgather to socialize informally and transact business. Cafés and pubs did not then exist. Taverns were crowded, noisome, and filled with laborers and disreputable transients. Perforce the halls of the larger residences, though more so in France than in England, catered to this need for points of assembly.

Crowding and perviousness to the outside world were a common state of the big house. In the period from 1500 to 1700, a minor Parisian nobleman might have some twenty-five people living with him: his own family, protégés, clerics, clerks, servants, shopkeepers, and apprentices. It was recorded of a bachelor *seigneur* in the reign of Louis XIV that he surrounded himself with thirty-seven servants, including a chaplain. Besides this resident population, the big house catered to an almost constant flow of visitors. People came at all hours, disrupting the routine of the household, but they were rarely shown the door.[29] French kings likewise led more public lives than did their English counterparts. Foreigners often commented on the ease with which the lower classes were able to enter the palaces of

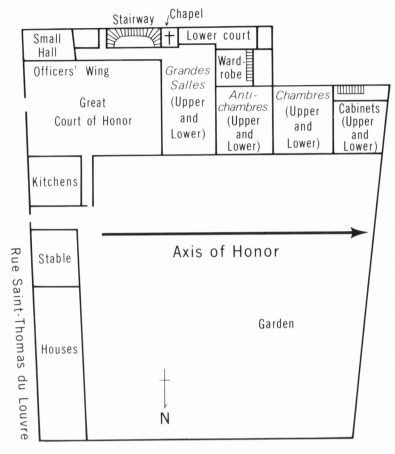

Hôtel de Rambouillet (ca. 1640)

Fig. 9. The axis of honor at the Hôtel de Rambouillet from the great court of honor, through the *grande salle*, *antichambre*, and *chambre*, to the cabinet. In palaces such as Rambouillet and Lambert, the lower suite of rooms belongs to the master and the upper suite of rooms belongs to the mistress. Modified from Jean-Pierre Babelon, *Demeures Parisiennes sous Henri IV et Louis XIII* (Paris: Le Temps, 1965), p. 185.

France. Sightseers swarmed into the king's chambers almost the moment he left them. Even so reserved and ceremonious a king as Henry III (1551–1589) was spoken to by anyone who wished to do so when he dined in public. Louis XIV continued this tradition of maximum exposure: when he dined in public at Versailles, sightseers from as far as Paris came in streams to gawk at the spectacle of a royal repast.[30]

In a French mansion, behind the salle stretched two rooms, called the *antichambre* and the *chambre* (Fig. 9). Departing from the English tendency to specialize, the French chamber remained basically a bed-sitting room even in the middle of the seventeenth century. It was used to sleep in, for private meals, and as a reception room for a more select group of visitors. The antechamber served as a waiting room for clients hoping to get into the chamber, and so it lacked the private character of the English withdrawing room. In the same way that the English had their closets behind their bedchambers, so the French had their cabinets. The cabinet, as the only private room in a French mansion or house, played an important role in French aristocratic life that was not characteristic of closets among the English. A richly furnished cabinet was indicative of the truly great and powerful. Admittance into it was considered a high honor, an opportunity for the privileged person to savor life in the innermost ring of power. Cabinet and closet thus offered different meanings of privacy. The former signified the exclusivity of privilege, the latter the hiddenness of self.[31]

To bring a sharper focus to questions of privacy and self, we need to look at the furnishings and internal arrangements of living space. Where did people sleep and what did they sleep in? However public a person's life may be in day hours, some time in the course of night one must withdraw from the world to be alone with one's detached consciousness before it is dimmed by slumber. Sleep is clearly an asocial need of the body, and it seems natural to regard the place we sleep in as private. In a modern home, the bedroom is very much a private place, second only to the bathroom, even exceeding in a sense the privacy of the bathroom, which, after all, is used by the whole family and occasional guests. The bedroom belongs to the married couple or to one person. The bed may well be the single most personal piece of furniture in the house.

Sharing a bedroom with strangers offends modern sensibility. Yet in earlier times people, both proud and humble, did not feel that sleeping required a room apart. The farther we go back into the Middle Ages the less we find that people segregated sleeping (Fig. 10). In a twelfth-century manor house, retainers and servants slept in the hall, kitchen, or storeroom—anywhere, in fact, that was fairly dry, warm, and comfortable. The lord, his family, and perhaps also high-

Fig. 10. The exterior and interior of a public hostel of the fifteenth century. The bed-chambers illustrate not only the practice of lodging a number of persons in the same bedroom, but also that of sleeping in a state of perfect nudity. From Thomas Wright, *The Homes of Other Days* (London: Trübner and Co., 1871), p. 345.

status guests occupied the upper-floor chambers. However, little per-sonal privacy could be found there, both because the rooms were used for purposes other than sleeping and because it was a custom for sev-eral people to sleep in the same room and even in the same bed.[32]

A French tale of the thirteenth century depicts a bedroom scene in which a duke's younger female relatives and their attendants all sleep in the same room. One of the young women is shy and indicates a reluctance to remove her chemise until the light is extinguished. Her bedmate, a daughter of the duke, thereupon blows out the candle, and "Roseite tantost la soufla, qu'a s'esponde estoit atachie."[33] It was not uncommon for members of the same sex to share a bed in the sixteenth and seventeenth centuries. Michelangelo (1475–1564) slept with his workmen, four to a bed. In colonial New England, the Reverend John

House and Household

Cotton of Plymouth wrote his cousin Cotton Mather "to thanke you for your late courteous entertainment in your bed."[34] Personal servants slept in the same room as their master or mistress. A cot, foldable or capable of being rolled under the master bed, served this purpose. Louis XIV, even as a young man of twenty-two, shared his bedroom with his nurse. In the full dignity of middle age, the Sun King shared his bedchamber with his First Valet, who had the duty to wake him every morning at a quarter to eight.[35]

Until the end of the seventeenth century, interconnecting rooms made privacy difficult if not impossible to secure. Imagine, wrote Ariès, the promiscuity that "reigned in these rooms where nobody could be alone, which one had to cross to reach any of the communicating rooms, where several couples and several groups of boys or girls slept together (not to speak of servants, of whom at least some must have slept beside their masters), in which people forgathered to have their meals, to receive their friends or clients, and sometimes to give alms to beggars."[36] This rather chaotic scene must be toned down somewhat to fit the reality of aristocratic life in England. The Englishman's desire for greater privacy was manifest by having more rooms and by limiting their functions. And yet in the later part of the seventeenth century, English manners approached those of France. Charles II, upon his return from exile, set the example of adopting certain continental customs, including a more public and promiscuous use of residential space.

Across the Atlantic, early colonists in New England lacked the resources to build large houses. They did, however, inherit a tradition of living in multiroomed dwellings. Many immigrants to the New World came from East Anglia and the southeastern counties where, by 1640, even laborers lived in cottages with at least three rooms. An average house in early colonial New England had perhaps four rooms. Families tended to be large, and a significant minority of these had domestics, farm laborers, or apprentices living with them. The Puritans valued family cohesion; home life was communal in nature. Nonetheless, partitioning of the larger rooms became increasingly popular. Dividers might be permanent walls, or such temporary devices as blankets that could be hung from the beams. Colonial houses lacked visual and sound privacy. Wooden partitions, both the floors and walls, were often only a single board thick. Sound penetrated easily through the numerous knotholes and cracks, which also served as peepholes for the curious. David Flaherty notes the haphazard scattering of beds throughout the house, from the parlor and upstairs chambers that were primarily for sleeping, to the garret that could serve as a dormitory. "While parents were in the best bed in the parlor, servants and children sometimes bundled on straw pallets and animal skins before the fire."[37] Until the introduction of a corridor in the larger eighteenth-century homes, people could not move from one part of the house to another without passing through intervening rooms. For this reason, "three servant girls in their early twenties had the following experience in the Salem home of Nicholas Manning in 1680, while his wife was away. They went downstairs early one morning and, while going through their master's bedroom to reach the kitchen, found him in bed with his sister."[38]

The bed itself changed over the centuries, gradually allowing greater privacy. In Saxon times it was merely a sack filled with straw that could be thrown over a bench or board. People of rank, however, had a special frame or place for their bed, which is what the word "bedstead" means. By the twelfth century, the tester bed made its appearance. The tester was a canopy hanging from the roof or extending from the wall, under which the head of the bed could be lodged. By the first part of the fifteenth century, the roof of the canopy had reached over the full length of the bed. When the curtains along the sides of the canopy were drawn, the bed nestled in a private enclosure. Large four-post bedsteads appeared in the sixteenth century and developed into lavish mini-chambers in the course of the next hundred years.[39] The four-poster was the single most important piece of furniture in those times, a valuable possession that received special notice in wills and deeds. Unlike the tester bed, the four-poster was an independent unit. It could be placed anywhere in a chamber, and there with curtains drawn, it turned into a private world of its own (Fig. 11). In seventeenth-century France, the chamber was almost a public place through which residents passed more or less freely and in which various activities were pursued. Within it stood these four-poster beds

Fig. 11. (A) Fifteenth-century suspended canopy or tester bed. Note how the canopy is hung from the ceiling. From Elizabeth Burton, *The Early Tudors at Home* (London: Allen Lane, 1976), p. 124. (B) A four-poster bed in the grand manner, ca. 1680. From Elizabeth Burton, *The Pageant of Stuart England* (New York: Charles Scribner's, 1962), p. 119. Illustration by Felix Kelly.

that constituted separate, private realms. While people ate or chatted in the chamber, a husband and wife might be asleep or making love inside the curtained enclosure.[40]

The evolution of seats and sitting arrangements provides another line of evidence for a growing sense of self and for an increasing appreciation of privacy and comfort. Medieval halls were very sparsely furnished. As in a public square, people did not sit but stood about or moved around to chat, socialize, and conduct business. At dinner time, tables were put up, benches and stools brought in. These were dismantled and set aside at the end of the meal. The bench was the most common type of seat. People shared a bench at the dinner table and in the bed-sitting room where it was normally placed at the foot of the bed. "In the French Carlovingian romances," wrote Thomas Wright, "the earlier of which may be considered as representing society in the twelfth century, even princes and great barons sit ordinarily upon benches. Thus, in the romance of Huon de Bordeaux, Charlemagne invites the young chieftain, Huon, who had come to visit him in his palace, to sit on the bench and drink his wine."[41]

Benches equipped with a high back and armrests are known by the Anglo-Saxon word "settle." Ancient prints show that a settle might accommodate a family consisting of father, mother, and child, or a group of monks engaged in earnest discussion (Fig. 12). The chair was a "chair of state" in Norman times and belonged only to great people. Draped in rich cloth, it had the aura of a throne. Even in the Elizabethan house, chairs were still seats of honor reserved for the master, the mistress, and other personages of distinction. A popular place to sit was by the bay window, which began to be a feature of stylish houses toward the end of the fourteenth century. The bench by the bay window was an alcove of peace in the noisy and bustling great chamber; there people could rest or carry on intimate conversation.[42] Chests, receptacles for clothes and household goods, also served as seats throughout the house. During the reign of Elizabeth I, cushions were everywhere—on chests, window benches, and the floor, so that one could sit, squat, or recline on hard surfaces in some comfort. Occasionally the Queen herself sat on a cushion on the floor of the antechamber, to converse with various individuals whom she

House and Household

summoned, and who were obliged to kneel before her all the time.[43] When the Queen sat on a chair her courtiers were permitted to sit on unpadded stools. Even in the reign of James I, chairs were not plentiful.[44] Upholstered chairs, however, made an appearance in the middle of the sixteenth century; a few decades later, even window seats were padded. Although the adoption of individual, soft, and comfortable seats was rather slow, once started the process seemed irreversible.

Changes in the physical character of the house mirrored new trends in society and in sociocultural values. The family, an institutional pillar of society, underwent rapid transformation. Throughout the fourteenth and fifteenth centuries, family and household were overlapping concepts, all-embracing in their meaning. A nobleman's household included everyone from master and mistress, their children, down to the lowliest servitors. Together they formed an unbroken hierarchical chain, their bond symbolized by communal feasts in the hall. In the late Middle Ages, when the institution of monarchy was relatively weak, the barons sought to maintain a large retinue, because its size meant effective power. By the late Tudor period, however, power for a great lord meant favor in court rather than the maintenance of many servitors; thus, the size of a nobleman's household began to decline. Its character also changed: The ancient sense of bond up and down the social scale was weakened by the loss of its upper-class servitors and by alterations in the composition of the lower ranks. In the seventeenth century, gentleman-servants were more likely to be recruited from among the sons of merchants, clergymen, and army officers—youths of the middle class—than from the old county families. Women of working-class background came into service as domestics increasingly from the Tudor period onward. Thus the ancient warrior bond between a chief and his men was eventually broken. Servants, except for valets and personal maids, were pushed further and further away from the sight and consciousness of the family, a term that now assumed the meaning of blood relations only.

The spatial organization of the house adapted to these changes of society. Late in the sixteenth century, first in France then in England, architects introduced back stairs and basement rooms for the service

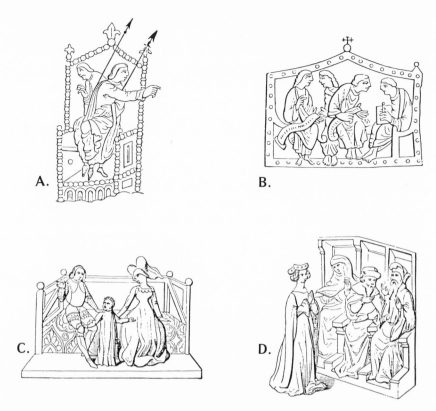

Fig. 12. (A) A chair of the twelfth century with two figures on it. (B) A conversational group on an Anglo-Norman settle. (C) A family group on a settle of the fourteenth century. (D) A partitioned seat of the fourteenth century. From Thomas Wright, *The Homes of Other Days* (London: Trübner and Co., 1871), pp. 108, 109, 380, 381.

functions of the house. Servants, after toiling in the dark basement during the day, must climb several flights of the dark back stairs to reach their cots in a gloomy garret.[45] Separate arrangements of this kind suited the family well. In the period between 1500 and 1700, when the portable stool (*chaise percée*) was widely used, a gentleman or lady walking up the front stairs no longer risked encountering last night's feces coming down. Toward the end of the eighteenth century, a new fashion dictated that the main rooms of the house be flush with the ground and open to nature, that is, to the garden. As the main rooms were lowered to the ground level, Mark Girouard writes, "the servants' rooms underneath them were pushed further and further underground. By the end of the eighteenth century they were sunk so far down that light had to be got to them by digging a pit or dry moat round the house. The moat in turn isolated the main rooms from the landscape."[46]

House and Household

Another innovation of the eighteenth century had a more pleasing consequence for the servants, but it tended to isolate them even further from their employers: this was a system of bell pulls that made it possible for members of the family in any part of the house to summon their valets and maids from a distance. Under such a system, the servants could move out of the basement into a separate wing of their own above ground. By the nineteenth century, two types of the big house were widely distributed through western Europe. One type showed a vertical structure, with the family domain sandwiched between the servants' quarters above and below. The other, more commonly to be found in the countryside, stretched horizontally in the form of two wings. Social exchange between the occupants of these two wings was minimal. Whereas in the seventeenth century servants might banter with their master or mistress and Louis XIV gallantly took off his hat to any charwoman he encountered in the corridors of Versailles, in the nineteenth century servants who entered the family wing to clean up must try to be invisible to their employers, a trick made possible by an intricate system of back stairs and corridors.[47]

Withdrawal from the communal hall and limiting the range of social contact at the end of the medieval period did not at first mean individual or even familial privacy. Much of life was still lived in the midst of company in the great chamber, parlor, or long gallery. The long gallery, an architectural innovation of the 1550s, had taken over some of the earlier functions of the hall.[48] Basically a covered walk linking different parts of the house, it served as a spacious general purpose room for entertaining the neighborhood, dancing, making music, and walking when the weather was bad. At any time a number of activities might be in progress. Here children played at skittles and blindman's buff. The young flirted with each other. Older people walked for exercise while listening to a chaplain or attendant read to them from the Scriptures or from a more amusing type of literature. And here men engaged their important visitors in light or serious talk. The master of the house, strolling with his guests, might point to those details visible through the windows that revealed the magnificence of his home (Fig. 13).[49]

Fig. 13. Multiple use of the long gallery, Haddon Hall, Derbyshire, ca. 1600. From a lithograph by Joseph Nash and reproduced in Christina Hole, *English Home-Life 1500–1800* (London: B. T. Batsford, 1947), opposite p. 10.

This scene differs significantly from the mixture of ceremony and rowdiness characteristic of festivities in the medieval hall. Much sociability transpired in the long gallery, but it transpired among people of the same class. To aristocrats, family bond and intimacy among close relations were gaining importance, at the expense of the ideal of feudal allegiance in a large and heterogeneous household. We have commented earlier on the emergence of familial privacy in Renaissance Florence, a precocious development among the upper-middle class that did not spread beyond Florence or endure beyond 1600. By contrast, the tendency to withdraw into family circles, evident in western Europe by the late sixteenth century even among aristocrats, was the start of a social trend that did spread geographically and through time.

As evidence of this trend, we may note a striking new feature of Elizabethan and early Stuart houses—the family portrait.[50] For the first time, in England as well as on the Continent, the halls and dining parlors began to be filled with paintings of the family and its individual members. These portraits showed pride not only in lineage but also in individual distinction and achievement. Engravings and paintings of family life, rare before the year 1500, were commonplace in the seventeenth century. As a part of this new concern for domestic and

House and Household

interior life, children attracted greater attention from moralists, educators, and parents. Adults grew more sensitive to the fact that young people, rather than being mere diminutive adults, had their own ways of feeling, seeing, and thinking, and their own special needs. This new awareness, it is true, did not immediately result in the curtailment of contact between children and promiscuous adults. In aristocratic households, young children continued to mix indiscriminately with nurses and servants, and were thus exposed to their bawdiness, sexual teasing, and abuse. During the eighteenth century, however, attitude toward children was increasingly colored by moralism. Educators and parents began to emphasize the innocence of young children and the special purity of the relationship between parent and child. These tender qualities were thought to require protection from society at large.[51] Responsible people believed that a new type of moral and physical environment must be created for the young. Before 1800, children were usually put up on the top floor, in the same kind of rooms as those occupied by the maids. In the course of the nineteenth century, rooms furnished especially for children and located near those of parents gained favor in the big house.[52]

A process of interiorization began some three hundred years ago, marked by withdrawal into the intimacy of the family, to interior scenes and the comfort of padded chairs, but also by a withdrawal into self and an intensification of self-awareness. Wall mirrors became popular as the seventeenth century moved to a close. Early in the eighteenth century, the library, a quiet place for study and reflection, was a feature of more and more gentry and aristocratic homes, although for a long time the books themselves (too intimate, perhaps, for the public eye) were hidden behind glazed panels or curtains. During this period, literate people used "I" in their writing with greater frequency. Words such as "self-love," "self-knowledge," "self-pity," "ego," "character," "conscience," "melancholy," and "embarrassment" were finding their way into English and French literature and were used in the modern sense.

Before 1700, although middle-class homes in a metropolis might be crowded with furniture for lack of space, palaces and great houses tended to be sparsely furnished; thereafter great houses too gathered

Fig. 14. Cluttering was common even in the houses of the great. White Lodge, Richmond Park, Surrey. The Duchess of Teck's boudoir in 1892. From Mark Girouard, *Life in the English Country House* (New Haven: Yale University Press, 1978), p. 228.

more furniture and knicknacks (Fig. 14).[53] The presence of clutter, not from necessity but apparently out of desire, reached a peak in the bourgeois home of the late nineteenth century. Oscar Wilde threw up his hands in horror at the "wax flowers, atrocities perpetrated in woollen cross-stitch, and the antimacassars without end." Edmond de Goncourt counted on one wall, "every kind of showy, striking object, gilt pots, Japanese embroideries, shining branches, and even stranger objects astounding the beholder with their originality and exoticism."[54] The desire for comfort and clutter in the home emerged at a time when not only medical specialists but educated laymen as well showed a keen interest in the workings of the mind. Psychoanalysis, almost predictably, was born. "The interior furniture of houses appeared together with the interior furniture of the mind," John Lukacs observed.[55] Both phenomena signified an inward turn, a greater awareness of the complexity of an individual's emotional life combined with a readiness to explore it.

An inclination to identify the house and its contents with the human body and soul might have deep roots in the human psyche. As an articulated idea it can be found in the dream interpretations of

House and Household

Artemidorus Dalianus, who lived in the second century A.D. Our own consciousness of this bond, whatever its distant origins, owes more to the well publicized writings of modern thinkers such as Freud and Jung.[56] Freud's conception of the human personality seems grounded in the structure of the bourgeois house. Thus the cellar is the id, the dark ground of being, the place of the furnace that fuels the passions. The living room is the ego, the public and social self. The attic is the superego, dream place for the poet and the introspective child. In a somewhat similar fashion, Jung took the vertical section of a typical middle-class house, which appeared to him in a dream, as a representation of his psyche, the levels of the house being the levels of his consciousness. Freud, in a more calculated manner, turned the consulting room of his house into a womb. Withdrawal into self and mastery of self could both be attained in a cluttered, womblike room. Carpets lay upon carpets in Freud's office. "Carpets covered tables, a carpet hung on the wall adjacent to the couch, which rested beneath another carpet, blankets and cushions. At one end of the couch, where the patient's feet would lie, stood a tile stove equipped with water pipes to supply humidity. At the head, hidden behind a mountain of pillows and in the corner of the room, was the large, graceless easy chair where Freud sat to listen."[57]

The late medieval house was a microcosm of society. The nineteenth-century bourgeois house, by contrast, was a family haven and a symbolic embodiment of the psychic dimensions of the self. From one point of view, horizons had shrunk; from another, they had greatly expanded. What was lost was a feeling of mutual help and obligation across different social classes, a feeling undergirded by a coherent, vertically structured conception of the universe. The gain was in the appreciation of nature. From 1600 onward, partitioning the house, and a concern with privacy and the nature of the self represented one direction of change. The other direction led to the opening up of the geographical horizon and to a heightened educated interest in the natural things of this world. Paintings of household interiors rose in popularity at the same time as paintings of landscape. Seventeenth-century halls and parlors were decorated not only with family portraits but also with landscapes and even county maps. Nature study was a fashionable pastime for the gentry in the Age of Enlightenment; a walk by the seaside would have seemed incomplete without some attempt at identifying and classifying the natural fauna and flora.[58] In the same period that Victorians were withdrawing into their familial havens, they flocked to lectures on science given by such luminaries as Alfred Russel Wallace and Thomas Huxley. Less distinguished speakers could still attract an appreciative audience in cities and provincial towns. The exploration of the self proceeded side by side with the exploration of external nature. A Victorian who appreciated the "inscapes" of Gerard Manley Hopkins might also read Darwin and enjoy a peek into the telescope. Curiosity, once aroused, is not easily confined. Although people do specialize—some showing more interest in the nature of the self, others more in the nature of external reality —it would seem that a society that strongly encourages one form of inquiry is also likely to nurture the other.[59]

5

Theater
and Society

"All the world's a stage." And the stage represents a world; it is a model of the world; it holds a mirror to the world. Unlike literary or architectural achievements, the theater mirrors the world in two important ways: first, there is the play's message; then there is the physical arrangement of the stage and of the theater as a whole. Our question, how spatial segmentation is related to a deepening sense of self, is exemplified and clarified in the history of the theater. In its history, we see in essential outline the change from cosmos to landscape; from public square to drawing room; from participation to spectatorship; from communal rites that cope with matters of sin and salvation, through the tragedy and farce of social intercourse, to the inability to connect, the loneliness of the self, and private despair. Of course, a theatrical tradition may petrify and never move beyond cosmic themes, never evolve from a high degree of participation to pure spectatorship. The reverse process, however, has not been known to occur, except as the result of deliberate experimentation in modern times; and only in the history of the West do we see the entire sequence from communal celebration to the projection on stage of the segmented world within.

The word drama is derived from a Greek term meaning "do" or "make," not just any kind of doing but *effective* doing—a powerful act that is distinguished from ordinary acts. The purpose of the dramatic act is to make ordinary living possible. Drama, as many scholars have noted, has its roots in communal rites performed to rejuvenate nature and society. In archaic and primitive societies, the ritual act (which usually involves dancing and singing) is not necessarily confined to able-bodied males: the old and the young, and sometimes women, may also participate. Key figures in the dance probably wear masks, which by their size and design command awe and create the illusion of union with the spiritual world. Masked figures do not represent the gods; even less are they trying to portray them. The idea of acting in the sense of artfully portraying superhuman personalities is alien to the purpose of the ritual dance. Masked figures at the dance are spiritual powers incarnate. On that sacred occasion, community embraces both gods and mortals. Ordinary human differences that irritate and isolate, or cause frustration and conflict, disappear in the drama — in effective doing, in the unified singing and vertigo-producing motions of the group. Figures in a ritualized enactment are not all equally important; some wear more imposing masks than others and some may not wear masks. Supporting actors become from time to time spectators. In this differentiation of roles and perhaps also of space in the performance area, we see how drama can emerge from communal cult. Furthermore, faith in the effectiveness of a ritual may wane. When this happens, more and more members of the community are inclined to stand aside and watch rather than participate. *Dromenon* (thing done) is performed for them rather than by them and becomes *drama*.

According to Gilbert Murray, the material of Greek tragedy arises from mythology but its form goes back to the rites for the new-year daemon, a tribal god whose own resurrection ensures the renewal of life.[1] Some scholars believe that Attic comedy originated in the ritual combat between on the one side Winter and his henchmen, and on the other New Life and his followers. Again, the underlying themes are struggle, suffering, death, and resurrection. Greek drama thus has its roots in the needs of survival. Human problems are played on a cosmic stage that amply provides for the machinations of the gods. Aeschylus's characters are superhuman and embody cosmic conflicts. His plays are often magnificent spectacles, with lavish costumes, large choruses, horse-drawn chariots, and sometimes frightening mythological figures. By comparison, Aeschylus's younger contemporary Sophocles had

Theater and Society

put greater emphasis on individual characters and reduced the role of the chorus, which in Greek drama normally served as a public and objective commentator, an intermediary between actors and audience.

It is in the history of the comedy, however, that the narrowing of the arena from the cosmic to the social and the domestic is most evident. Tragedy, even in a domestic setting, implies a larger fate. But this need not be so with comedy. The comic impulse finds expression first in the boisterous choruses and dialogues of the fertility rites of the Dionysian feast; here we see comedy's early link to religion.[2] Later, in what theater historians call the Old Comedy, situations such as a major political event or an incident in the Peloponnesian War are exploited through farce and satire in a series of loosely connected scenes that end in a celebration of unity. Invective began to lose its pungency with the death of Aristophanes; moreover, drama tended to shift away from the larger political and social issues to those of personal love, financial mismanagement, and family conflicts. The New Comedy, which gained popularity after 336 B.C., was primarily concerned with the domestic affairs of the Athenian middle-class citizenry.[3]

Classical theater was public and communal (Fig. 15). Its public character is symbolized by the open and outdoor auditorium and acting areas. The overarching sky from which the gods descend is a part of the scene. In general, scenes are out of doors: they are the open spaces in front of temples and palaces, the public squares and streets, and, more rarely, the army camps and tree groves. The communal character of the theater goes back to its roots as a festival. A festival involves all conditions of men and women, it occurs at a particular time of the year, and normally takes up a whole day; its activities are a mixture of solemnity and fun. These traits aptly describe the theater in antiquity. The stone auditorium of fifth-century Athens could accommodate a large and mixed audience of some 15,000 men, women, boys, and slaves. Because several dramas might be presented in sequence the entire show could last from morning to dusk. People attending it must have felt free to come and go, eat and drink. There was not much formality: although we can envisage interludes of rapt attention, members of the audience were known to have loudly voiced their opinions and even to have hissed actors off the stage.[4]

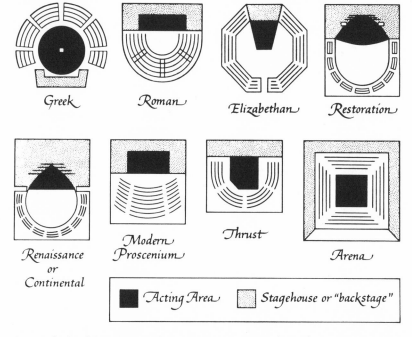

Greek   Roman   Elizabethan   Restoration

Renaissance   Modern   Thrust   Arena
or   Proscenium
Continental

◼ Acting Area   ▢ Stagehouse or "backstage"

Fig. 15. Cycle of change in the theater from encirclement (whole), through separation (parts), to encirclement (the ideal of the whole). From Vera Mowry Roberts, *The Nature of Theatre* (New York: Harper & Row, 1971), p. 332.

In Rome, admission to state-supported performances was free. All classes of people attended. Plautus the comic poet (ca. 254–184 B.C.) refers to children and their nurses, magistrates' attendants, women, slaves, and prostitutes. Although officials were present to maintain order, much jostling for places occurred and people did not hesitate to go in and out during a performance. Under the empire, serious drama yielded to variety entertainment: the theater became increasingly diversionary, with novelties of all kinds demanded and offered— spectacle, sex, violence, and bloodshed. We are familiar with this picture of the Roman theater. It fits with our perception of the tumultuous and promiscuous Roman world—its orgiastic feasts, its public baths and latrines. Nonetheless, we need to recall that at least the state-sponsored performances had never wholly lost their connection with religious festivals, or *ludi*, that honored the various gods. Plays and entertainments, insofar as they were a part of a religious celebration, occurred on official festival days: if any irregularity or flaw were discerned in the enactment of the rituals, then the entire festival might have to be repeated, including the *ludi scaenici* or plays. A deep seriousness lay buried under a towering excrescence of spectacle and farce.[5]

Theater and Society

The genealogy of the modern play reaches back directly to the rituals of the medieval Church. From communal worship in an edifice that was a clear symbol of the Christian cosmos, there emerged in the course of time that intimate little theater of our age, in which spectators in the privacy of a darkened hall can watch the incommunicable agonies of sundered selves. How did such a transformation come about? What were the intermediate steps? First, we should note that the Christian ritual had a natural affinity for song and dance, that its own central drama encouraged the histrionic talent. As early as the fourth century, Athanasius accused Arius of enlivening divine service with ungodly mime. Repeated conciliar denunciations, culminating in those of the Trullan Synod of 692, showed how difficult it was to eradicate these signs of pagan and human exuberance.

Nevertheless, drama did not grow directly out of such extraneous display. It emerged rather from an integral part of the Christian ritual. During the tenth century, the sung dialogue in the scene of the *Visitatio Sepulchre* of the Easter Introit was lengthened and supplemented by dramatic gestures. St. Ethelwold of Winchester (ca. 970) explained that a certain part of the altar could be made to look like the sepulcher, and that two deacons might lay a cross wrapped in cloth as though they were burying the body.[6] Later in the service, St. Ethelwold noted, three monks (representing the three Maries) might approach the altar as if they were looking for something in the tomb. Despite these theatrical additions, in the tenth century the Easter Introit was deemed *officium* (office), and not *ludus* (play or game). The monks were dressed as monks and did not pretend to be women. In the course of the eleventh century, however, the narratives became longer and the imitative aspects of the ceremony seemed to possess a value more aesthetic than religious. In the thirteenth century in France, characters in the *Representatio* (no longer Officium) began to dress for their parts. By this time it is clear that the drama of the Church approached what the Romans had known as ludus and what we describe as a play.[7]

An effect of this change in divine service was to divide an original unified body of worshipers (celebrants and congregation) into performers and spectators. This division must occur before drama can develop into a separate art. When in the twelfth century religious plays started to move out of the church, the separation of actors and audience became still clearer. The audience could see that the actors were independent of any office within the church. The performance, despite its religious message, offered a different kind of experience from that which transpired within the church and which could still be seen as constituting a part of the church's service. The chasteness of ritual yielded to dramaturgic exigencies, to an embellishment of the message beyond that necessary for the arousal of devotion. By the close of the twelfth century, sacred drama had joined a wide range of secular entertainments offered out-of-doors in the summer months. Clerics might still compose the scripts for the sacred drama and even occasionally act in it, but clearly the staging of the performance passed increasingly into the hands of municipal authorities and citizens. Inside the church, liturgical plays continued to be presented in Latin; outside it, the vernacular was used in a variety of performances and ceremonials that from the thirteenth century onward began to attract large crowds.

A major impetus toward the development of a vernacular drama, epic in scale and cosmic in the scope of its setting, was the popularity of the Festival of Corpus Christi in the period roughly between 1300 and 1600. This new drama, centered on the Eucharist, emphasized the humanity of Christ's ministry, his suffering and passion rather than his burial and resurrection.[8] Death and rebirth, the central idea of the Easter liturgy, was a belief common to all fertility cults. Nothing specifically Christian adhered to celebrating either winter solstice or the renewal of life in spring. Everyone yearned for abundance and if possible some assurance of immortality. The Eucharist, however, focused on a unique sacrifice by a unique individual for the salvation of the world. Unlike Christmas and Easter, the time for celebrating the Feast of Corpus Christi did not have to fall in line with nature's seasons; the Feast came around in summer because it happened to be a time when people could comfortably gather out-of-doors to watch a play. The cosmos of the play was not that of nature, defined by the stars and their motions; rather, it was framed by the theological space of Heaven and Hell, and by a concept of linear universal time that began with the Fall and would end with the Last Judgment.

Theater and Society

From the outset the new drama of the Corpus Christi festival was didactic rather than ritualistic in intention. No one conceived it as an officium. From the start it was scripted in the vernacular languages of Christendom and thought of as a ludus, a game or a play. Although its dominant message was moral and deeply serious, it also strove to entertain. Games figured within the game: soldiers played dice for Christ's clothes; there were word games, dances that could be licentious, such as the *Zarabanda* performed in the Corpus Christi *autos* in Seville, and mechanical marvels such as flying angels and fire belching out of the mouth of hell.

Stage equipment and mechanical marvels, being merely the props of a game, were not intended to create an illusion of reality. As children used sticks for horses, so adult players might use a bench for Noah's Ark or a painted canvas for the Red Sea. To spectators, such devices were fun in themselves and at the same time they vividly conveyed the play's serious message. In the medieval theater, suspension of disbelief was absolutely essential for both actors and spectators. Human beings dressed in robes and paper wings were obviously not angels: and if illusion were the aim, who would dare to play God? "Those who played God," notes V. A. Kolve, "would not have sought . . . to *be* God, not to get inside His personality; such a notion would have seemed to them blasphemous and absurd. They presented not the character of God but certain of his actions." The role of Christ might have invited closer identification. However, since more than a dozen actors might be used to play him in the same cycle it is clear that no effort was made to present Christ as a single personality.[9] This lack of compulsion to penetrate the core of another's being—this stress on emblematic figures and their clearly observable actions—further encouraged the actors to treat their roles as solemn make-believe and a game.

To put on a Corpus Christi cycle in England or a Passion play on the Continent called for full cooperation between the clergy, city authorities, and townsmen. A typical site was the town square. Spectators, leaning out of the windows of buildings and piling on top of temporary scaffolds, enveloped the play area; to a medieval crowd the idea of viewing a performance from the front only would have seemed unduly restrictive. Months of work preceded a performance. Time and labor were required to prepare the play area and establish on the grounds such stage props as sacrificial altars, wells, gardens, tables and benches where meals could be eaten, an area where Lazarus was to be buried and from which six souls were to arise at the crucifixion. On the second day of the performance, workmen might erect three crosses at the site that on the first day was allocated to the earthly Paradise with its apple-laden Tree of Knowledge (Fig. 16).[10]

A performance, then, could last several days: three full days in Chester, a week in London, and as many as twenty-five days in Valenciennes in 1547. The townspeople were unavoidably caught up in the affair. Before the play itself began, the festival opened with a procession and a High Mass. Representatives from religious fraternities, crafts, and trade guilds took part in the procession, accompanied by apprentices and novices carrying banners and pictorial accessories. The festival ended with a service of general thanksgiving and a banquet. During the actual performance we can assume much moving about among the spectators. People laughed and jeered at the farcical by-plays and were no doubt rowdy at times because we know that the Church, to encourage good behavior, offered remissions of time in Purgatory.

Is it possible to say when the festival bustle began, or who watched whom? These questions are not easy to answer. A festive mood could well emerge even before the procession, with the workmen's arrival at the principal site of the performance. As they put up the scenic props in the town square, onlookers gathered around and some of them might have offered help. The procession was certainly a part of the festival. Representative townsmen walked in it, observed by other citizens. Processioners in their turn sat to watch when the play proper commenced. Actors, who might number a hundred or more, were also spectators. As the actions moved from one locale to another in the performing area, the actors who had roles in an earlier scene either remained at their stage prop or climbed up a scaffold to watch.[11]

Easter and Christmas plays retained elements of an immemorial ritual for the worship of the sun and the renewal of life. In the period when the Corpus Christi festival flourished, dramaturgic attention shifted

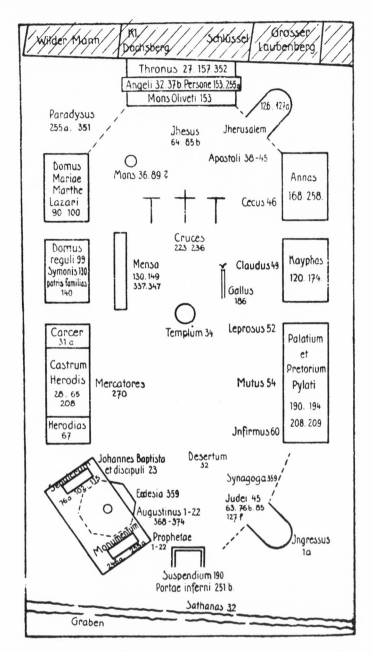

Fig. 16. The Frankfurt Passion Play (ca. 1450) on the Samstagberg, Frankfurt. Julius Petersen's reconstruction in "Aufführungen und Bühnenplan des älteren Frankfurter Passionsspiels," *Zeitschrift für deutsche Altertum* 59 (1921–22): 122.

from the sun to the incarnate God, to his sufferings on earth for human salvation. In outdoor religious plays known as the *miracula*,
which were performed as early as the twelfth century, not Christ but
rather the Virgin Mary and the saints and martyrs were offered to in-
spire people. Following the miracle plays were the morality plays and
the shorter moral interludes, which began to appear in the late fourteenth and the early fifteenth century in the Low Countries, France,
and England. "The Morality Play," writes Glynne Wickham, "owed
its ritual pattern to the drama of Christ the King or Christ Crucified."
But "within the ritual there was a sharp shift of emphasis away from
narrative and towards argument with a corresponding stress placed
upon the personal responsibility of every individual in the matter of his
own salvation or damnation. If misfortune overtook a man, the prob-
ability was that the root cause lay within his own nature: there was
however time to recognize the fault, to repent and pray for grace."[12]

Compared with the Corpus Christi drama, morality plays were rich
in allegorical figures such as Good Deed, Virtue, Fame, and Mercy. Of
equal prominence were the Seven Deadly Sins, which battened on the
frailties of Everyman. Whereas the role of Virtue called for dignity,
other roles—those, for example, of Riotous Living, Insatiability, and
the Devil himself—invited humor and indeed ribaldry. Morality plays,
with their religious themes, were necessarily didactic. However, by
the early part of the sixteenth century, they had also become secular
entertainments performed by troupes of quasi-professional actors.
What the actors did on stage must be light and engrossing enough to
be acceptable to the paying audiences of the banquet hall or fair-
ground where alcohol flowed.

The public theater built to accommodate morality plays captures
many facets of the medieval cosmos and society. Consider a performance in an outdoor staging area called the round, a type of theatrical
setting known to exist not only in Cornwall, where it is best studied,
but also in other parts of Britain and in other countries of medieval
Europe. According to Richard Southern, a round consists of a play
area (the Place) encircled by an embankment, on which spectators
can sit and on which also the scaffolds for staging certain set scenes
stand: beyond the embankment might be a circular ditch filled with

Theater and Society

water (Fig. 17). The performance area does not represent any locality: it is the whole cosmos. For example, in the play "The Castle of Perseverance" (ca. 1425) the four scaffolds located at the cardinal points house God, Devil, World, and Flesh. At the center of the round is the Tower of Mankind. The play itself is epic in scale and depicts Mankind's progress from birth to death and thence to the final judgment on his soul. These were matters of high concern to people in medieval times. Yet, also characteristic of the times was a tendency toward uninhibited bawdiness. Solemnity and levity could appear side by side, as in "The Castle of Perserverance," where the stage for the majesty of God stood next to that for the Seventh Sin, silly Covetyse.

Social space, we know, was not clearly demarcated in the medieval city. Rich and poor lived as neighbors and rubbed shoulders in crowded streets. Likewise, well-to-do and needy clients huddled together during outdoor theatrical performances. The boundary separating actors from spectators also lacked clear definition and wavered as the play progressed. Spectators occupied the embankment but they probably took over part of the central acting space as well. Southern, in his reconstruction of the theater-in-the-round, asks us to imagine the dynamics of motion in a packed theater. As the play opens, World speaks from his scaffold. In response the crowd throughout the round will turn to the West. "World's speech lasts perhaps two minutes, and then the Devil speaks from the North. Now the crowd will turn to the North. And so forth." Actors descend from the scaffolds to play at the center of the round and cross it as the needs arise. We have to envisage "the frequent disappearings behind spectators' heads of the moving players, and all the resultant swayings and risings and movings and redistributions . . . of the Place-crowd. It will recoil and surge back, it will divide like the Red Sea and flood in again like a river in spate."[13]

When contact between players and playgoers reaches this level, we may well wonder how the crowd can be prevented from choking the show. Using functionaries to maintain some sort of order was one solution. Nevertheless, the atmosphere during a performance must have been rather chaotic. People climbed the scaffolds to get a better view; actors waited behind half-drawn curtains for their turn to appear; and to judge from a miniature painting (the Fouquet miniature) done

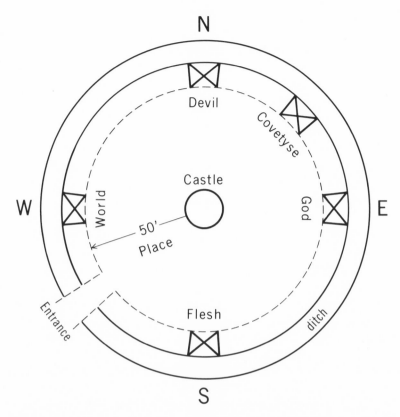

Fig. 17. Conjectural plan of a theater-in-the-round for the performance of the morality play *The Castle of Perseverance* (ca. 1425). Reprinted by permission of Faber and Faber Ltd from Richard Southern, *The Medieval Theatre in the Round* (London: Faber & Faber, 1975), p. 77.

between 1452 and 1460, some of the scaffolds that formed a ring around the Place were occupied by the audience, who might not only listen and watch the central drama but also put on a show of their own, chatting among themselves or embracing each other as the mood struck them.[14]

Medieval theater was informed by the concept of *teatrum mundi* — the Theater of the World. Its acting area still aspired to represent the whole of God's creation, including Heaven and Hell, rather than a particular locality. The same may be said of Elizabethan and Jacobean theater in London. Perhaps for the first time since the Romans, a half dozen or so buildings were put up for the special purpose of giving public theatrical performances. The shape of the building was mostly round or hexagonal, which might reflect the influence of the Renaissance interest in circular and polygonal forms, but which in any case aptly

Theater and Society

symbolized the theater as a macrocosm wherein Man, the microcosm, was to play his parts (Fig. 18). Cosmic symbolism was enhanced by a cover printed with stars to represent the "heavens," extending over the inner part of the stage. Below the stage was Hell and the Devil's realm. Religious themes were prominent. "The popularity of the Elizabethan drama," wrote John Danby, "might be explained by its religious content. In it the Elizabethan could see the every-day and temporal beside the unusual and eternal, 'the time' in a perspective of God and Magistrate."[15] Elizabethan drama retained the essential earnestness of the morality play, as well as its concern with abstract ideas. But to these were added a profound interest in human personality: the major characters in a Shakespearean drama, far from being standard types or allegorical figures, are flesh-and-blood men and women, self-aware, capable of growth and of suffering from the ambiguities of situation and fate.[16]

As with the medieval theater, public theater in Shakespeare's time made no attempt to produce realistic scenes. Shakespeare himself frankly denied the possibility of verisimilitude on the stage. In the prologue to *Henry V* he asked:

> . . . Can this Cock-pit hold
> The vasty fields of France? Or may we cram
> Within this wooden O, the very casques
> That did affright the air at Agincourt?
> O, pardon! since a crooked figure may
> Attest in little place a million,
> And let us, ciphers to the great accompt,
> On your imaginary forces work.

The scale of Elizabethan plays made realistic scenery impossible. The theme might no longer be the Fall and Salvation of Mankind but it still dealt with the affairs of a large and public world. Battlefields, palaces, and seas could not be crammed in a "wooden O."

Whereas scenery might not engage the attention of the theater patrons, voice did. A resonant delivery, as in the theater of classical times, was all important. "From the great stage," Frances Yates tells us, "the voices of the actors reached the ears of the audience in the yard and galleries. 'Lend me your ears,' cries Mark Antony in *Julius Caesar*."[17]

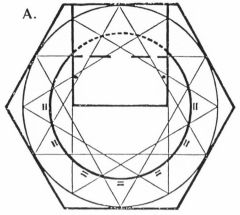

A.

1 Inch = 40 Feet

The Globe Theater

B.

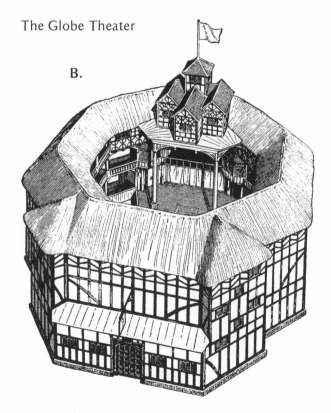

Fig. 18. (A) Hexagon, circles, and triangles as the geometric bases of the microcosm —
the Globe Theater, according to Frances A. Yates, *Theatre of the World* (London:
Routledge & Kegan Paul, 1969), p. 132. (B) The Globe Theater. From the frontispiece
of Irwin Smith, *Shakespeare's Globe Playhouse* (New York: Charles Scribner's, 1956).

Actors addressed the audience and sought to capture its attention in the direct manner of the more flamboyant preaching friars of an earlier age. But spectacle was also provided in abundance. While the ears registered the ringing rhetoric of a poetic drama, the eyes could feast on the resplendent costumes of kings, queens, and warriors. As in the larger world, spectacle was social and personal: people displayed their status and wealth on their persons and felt no compulsion to gain additional glamor from the quality of the public places in which they happened to find themselves.

Public theaters that emerged in London during the last quarter of the sixteenth century were spacious, roofless buildings, each of which could accommodate more than a thousand people. Tiers of seats rose in galleries around the central yard, into which an open stage projected. For a penny, playgoers could enter and stand in the yard; for another penny they commanded seats in the gallery, and for a shilling they might have a gentleman's or a lord's private box. People from different layers of society attended, jostling each other as they entered the narrow doors of the building and as they departed in swarms at the end of a performance. In the theater, merchants sat next to lords as equals on the good front seats of a gallery. Actors and playgoers were not always kept in their separate spheres. A few playgoers of rank exercised their right to enter the theater by the stage door and view the performance from the second level of the actors' dressing rooms (or tiring-house). Even though the privileged clients were thus placed to the rear of the stage, they could see well enough, for the acting was "in the round" rather than addressed forward as in modern theaters. Actors and the humbler members of the audience might find themselves jostling each other in the yard when the action of the play required the actors to perform at the edge of the stage and beyond.[18]

An atmosphere of festive informality was encouraged by the time of the show, which started in broad daylight around two in the afternoon. Vendors of a wide range of goods—wine, beer, ale, nuts, apples, cards, and playbooks—circulated freely in the theater. Noise from the crackling of nuts irritated the more sensitive and serious patrons. Pandemonium could and did break out when the audience felt itself defrauded of its fare, but this seldom occurred. Playgoers hissed at a poor delivery, but when pleased they could applaud heartily and with loud cries of approval. Without inhibition, they wept at the fate of heroes and laughed at the buffoonery of clowns.[19]

Although the Elizabethan public theater was truly public, nonetheless it discriminated against the poor—those who could not afford the small admission fee; and it was not the communal effort that dramatic performances had been in medieval times. The very existence of a building, with its different kinds of demarcated space, suggests a felt need for segmenting peoples and activities, and an awareness that not only the dress but the larger environmental setting defines the self.

In France, the emergence of secular drama from Church sponsorship followed a somewhat different course.[20] France did not have a playwright of genius who, like Shakespeare, could work within the religious tradition of the morality plays but who could also enrich them enormously by substituting dynamic human personalities for their static figures. In France, humor played such a prominent role in dramatic presentations that it was often difficult to distinguish between *moralités, sotties, farces*, and *entremets*. The distinction between street entertainment and semiprofessional theater was also fuzzy. On the streets of Paris, particularly in and around the area of Les Halles, numerous entertainers, with a minimum of equipment, were able to put on an act and attract a following. Often these performers attached themselves to an herb dealer or a medicine man who made extravagant claims to be able to effect cures. The farces of the street players were of the same kind as those that provided comic relief in the long and cumbersome miracle plays and in the pastorals and tragicomedies of the sixteenth and seventeenth centuries. A little more than two blocks from Les Halles stood the first public theater to be built (in 1548) for a semiprofessional company—the Confrèrie de la Passion. Its struggling actors, like the street entertainers, bought their costumes from the old-clothes dealers of Les Halles.

By the late sixteenth century, when miracle and mystery dramas had lost much of their appeal to Parisian audiences, the Confrèrie saw fit to rent out their theater—the Hôtel de Bourgogne—to professional companies, which began to offer pastorals, tragicomedies, and that old standby, the farce. Quick action and risqué dialogue were the essence of farce; scenery was much less important. A tragicomedy or pastoral did, however, require the services of a decorator. Painted canvas scenes were used in the early public theater, along with medieval stage sets or localities known as "mansions." A typical scene was not a unified place but rather a cluster of places that in reality might be miles apart: it was possible to see on the same stage "mansions" for a palace, ships along the seacoast, a city hall, fountains, a tent. Not only the spectators but the actors themselves might be confused by this jumbled setting. Unintended farce could erupt in the midst of the most solemn drama.[21]

A major problem with the indoor play was how to publicize it and how to attract enough patrons into the hall by a set time so that the show could start. In the Middle Ages the amateur actors of miracle plays paraded through the streets in their regalia shouting and proclaiming their programs. Some of these techniques carried over to the professional troupes of the late sixteenth century. By one device or another the offering was announced to the public. In time a motley crowd of artisan patrons gathered inside the theater and milled around the ground floor (the *parterre*), which had no seats.[22] Company officials would try to delay the start of a performance until as many persons as could reasonably be expected had entered the hall. By then early arrivals might have already waited an hour or two. They grew impatient, shouted and fought, or they played games of dice, carried on amorous affairs, ate and drank. A prologuist was sometimes hired to divert them. Once the performance began, the audience did not by any means stay quiet. Much talking and stamping of feet occurred in the parterre. Wealthier patrons seated in the galleries and loges were only relatively less rowdy. At times an actor would have to come out of character to beg the audience to make a little less noise. "Yet," wrote W. L. Wiley, "it was to satisfy this sort of audience that the sophisticated products of Corneille, Molière, and Racine appeared.[23]

The public theaters of France, both inside and outside of Paris, were elongated in shape. The reason is that most of them also served as racquet courts until about 1600. The elongated shape, as distinct from the round public theaters of Britain, tended to discourage audience empathy with the actors on stage; spectators all had to look in the same direction and those who stood at the back of the hall could hardly see over the heads of the people before them. Those who sat in the back galleries were high enough to command a good view, but what they saw was essentially a distant picture.[24]

Even the roof had an indirect effect on the separation of the auditorium from the stage. On cloudy days, the interior of a roofed hall was gloomy. Candles, because of their cost, were lit only at the last possible moment before the play began; and in the years when business was poor, only the stage was lit, thus accentuating the contrast between the two parts of the long hall.

Another factor that contributed to the distancing between actors and audience was the change in the character of the plays. From the Middle Ages to about 1600, religious drama presented questions and issues that meshed with the daily experiences of men and women; it invited audience participation. During this period street entertainment, the humblest form of theatrical life, also called for active involvement: actors sought to engage their listeners—to cast a spell over them so that they would not resist the purchase of panaceas. After the 1630s, however, the appearance of sophisticated plays of an increasingly secular nature invited spectators, themselves more sophisticated, to assume a somewhat detached stance. Playgoers came to view drama as animated pictures, removed from the urgent needs of life that religion and medicine answered. Events on stage were "out there," not a continuation of the world in which the audience sat or stood. When the proscenium arch and the curtain were installed in the public theaters, the separation of actors from spectators would seem to be complete. But in Paris this final step was not yet to transpire. An incident forestalled it. In 1638, the performance of Corneille's *Le Cid* at the Théâtre du Marais aroused so much enthusiasm that important people crowded into the sides of the stage to hear better the speeches of Corneille's young hero and heroine.[25] This event established a precedent that gave privileged patrons a right to penetrate the actors' world, a right that was to endure for another hundred years.

Shakespeare's characters are vivid presences. One reason for their liveliness and substantiality is that they often are identified with particular places. By verbal means alone Shakespeare can evoke a sense of

Theater and Society

place. Unlike his contemporaries, Shakespeare seems to have felt a need to provide his major figures with specific physical settings.[26] His sensitivity to place was ahead of his time. However, as consciousness of the self grew in Western society, more people came to share Shakespeare's view that a place or landscape—no less than speech, gesture, and clothing—revealed the character of an individual. Scenery's move toward realism was concurrent with a deepening idea of the self in the real world and in the theater. When the stage was the entire cosmos, the characters portrayed were of necessity allegorical figures, stereotypes, even Everyman. But by the time the stage showed specific as distinct from generalized scenes, the dramatic personages themselves assumed greater individuality.

An even closer relationship exists between individual and scenery, namely, that between the perceiver and the perceived. Unlike the round theaters of medieval and Elizabethan times, which offered no single privileged viewpoint, perspective stage scenery in an elongated hall could be seen ideally from only one privileged position in the auditorium. Scenery came to mean the view of a particular person at a particular point. This emphasis on perspectival illusion signified a growing personal and subjective conception of reality.

The impetus for the development of stage scenes emanated from the court theaters of Italy, beginning around 1500. A major source of inspiration for design came out of the Roman architect Vitruvius's work, *De Architectura*, which was discovered in manuscript form in 1414. According to Vitruvius, there are three kinds of scenes:

One is called the tragic, second, the comic, third, the satyric. Their decorations are different and unlike each other in scheme. Tragic scenes are delineated with columns, pediments, statues, and other objects suited to Kings; comic scenes exhibit private dwellings, with balconies and views representing rows of windows, after the manner of ordinary dwellings; satyric scenes are decorated with trees, caverns, mountains, and other rustic objects delineated in landscape style.[27]

Vitruvius's ideas, with changes and additions, reappeared in the highly influential works of Leone Battista Alberti (1404–1472) and of Sebastiano Serlio (1475–1554). Renaissance architects designed for their princely patrons unified tableaus as distinct from the fragmented props of the medieval stage. However, these tableaus were standard sets that remained unaltered as the action of the play moved on. Character and setting resonated only within the three general categories of tragic, comic, and satyric. Vitruvius himself assigned only a minor role to changing scenery in the Roman theater. To him, the musical quality of the player's voice mattered much more. Throughout the Renaissance period and later, sound was able to maintain its primacy over sight on both the public and the private stage: actors and actresses demonstrated their power by the artfulness of their declamations. Nevertheless, the new thrust and appeal of Renaissance theater lay in the direction of sight. Grand spectacles behind the proscenium arch quietly gained favor with the public at the expense of mental worlds evoked through the verbal medium.

A pictorial and illusionist stage called for artistry in design. Although the idea of stage scenery as a perspective painting already existed when Aeschylus lived, it was much later, during the Renaissance, that this type of design turned almost into an obsession. A magic art dependent on perspective at last found support in the rapidly expanding knowledge of geometry and optics. Pictorial illusion was able to engage the best minds of the age. Leonardo da Vinci (d. 1519), for example, discussed "aerial perspective" in a posthumous work. He opined that to create a sense of distance, it is necessary to imagine the air thick; and that if one building is to appear five times as far off as another, it should be painted with color to which has been added five times the amount of azure used in the color for the other.[28]

Ideas applicable to the two-dimensional canvas must then be adapted to suit the character of the three-dimensional stage. One early technique of staging (already in use by the 1480s) was to divide a scene into its architectural units and then rearrange them so that from a point in the auditorium they appeared as elements of a single picture. The illusion of pictorial depth was greatly enhanced by putting a frame around the scene. During the early part of the seventeenth century, this frame (the proscenium arch) became a permanent and standard feature of court theaters. Elongating the performance area was another device for augmenting a sense of depth. The length of the Hôtel de Bourgogne was 108 feet, of which only 18 feet were taken up by the shallow stage. In striking contrast is the huge Salle de Machines, built

Theater and Society

by the Italian scenic designer Vigarani (1586–1663) in a wing of the Tuileries Palace. Though only 52 feet wide, it was 232 feet long; and of this length only 92 feet were occupied by the auditorium, leaving 140 feet of depth for the stage.[29]

Fascination with perspective in the theater was part of a wider cultural engrossment. In the seventeenth century, as John Evelyn's *Diary* reveals, people added perspectives to garden walks and painted them outside the windows of rooms to feign views that were not there. What did this cultural taste signify? It signified humanity's increasing confidence in itself and in its power to manipulate the world. Standing by a picture window, one commands a view. One does not belong to the world so much as one organizes and orders it from a pivotal and circumferential point. Any person who has learned to see the world as perspective scenery enjoys at least an illusion of power, for all the elements of the landscape before him cohere into one unified picture only because he is where he is. Reality loses a little of its massive givenness and stability when the way it appears is recognized to depend on the position and sightlines of the spectator. Move a few steps and the world subtly changes. An individual experimenting with perspectives can hardly escape an increasing awareness of the self as a unique source of knowledge—a knowledge not exactly shared by another person standing only a few feet apart.

Court and power being synonymous in the Renaissance period, it is not surprising that the court theater promoted extravagant perspective scenery. A scene based on perspectival illusion can be appreciated, ideally, from only one place in the auditorium, and that is where the ruler sits. In reality the court theater has two separate audiences: monarchs from their unique position enjoy what they have commanded to appear, and the courtiers for whom the monarchs on their elevated seats are themselves a part of the show.[30] As for public theaters, they made little use of illusionary scenes until the second half of the seventeenth century. The major reason was that they lacked the financial and technical resources to put on spectacles. Changing perspective scenery called for complicated and expensive machines. After the Industrial Revolution, people have tended to associate machines with the control of nature. In the early decades of the seventeenth century, however, this power of machines was exercised primarily over the illusory world of the theater. Before and during each production, armies of technicians must be on hand. In those years when people talked of "machines," they meant the lifts, cranks, and wheels of the stage.[31]

Spectacular scenes appeared, for the most part, during the intermissions between the acts. They were a dramatic entertainment in their own right. But what must seem curious to us is that even when the spectacles materialized in the course of the drama they need not be related to the actions performed on the forestage. Stephen Orgel notes that in the play *Florimène* (1635), while the shepherds and shepherdesses suffered the agonies of passion and confusion, "a distant landscape parted to reveal four elegant tableaux of the seasons, the cycle of the pastoral year." What was the message intended for the spectators? It could be the notion that whereas turmoil might reign on earth, the harmony of the spheres remained unaffected.[32] A court drama often required a cosmic setting, as was true of the religious play in medieval times. However, instead of feeling humble before the grandeur of God's universe, the monarch and courtiers, as they beheld the spectacles they commanded to appear, were likely to be inflated by a sense of pride and of power.

The idea of cosmos began to weaken in the seventeenth century. In its place the idea of landscape, a particular segment of nature, emerged. As view, landscape implies the existence of a single, ideal point of observation and a single observer. As environment, it frames and exhibits a single person or a particular group of persons, a single event or a set of related events. Landscape paintings reveal the different kinds of tie that artists conceive to be possible between human beings and their environment. In portraits the scenic background displays the personality and status of a man or a woman; nature here is subordinate to the human figure. Where ordinary working people and their activities are depicted (e.g., fishermen by the strand), the scenes and the human figures appear to merge into each other. We behold in such artifacts images of a placid or serene world—a deeply humanized world. In landscapes that show nature on the rampage, favored by certain romantic artists of the nineteenth century, what we see ostensibly is a dwarfing of the human ego, but what we apprehend at a deeper level is the temperament and mood of the artist.[33]

How have such shifts in sensibility affected the theater? If pictorial art showed an increasing preferment for landscapes, this trend was not immediately apparent on the stage. In England, it is true, scenery did become more important in public as well as in private theaters after the Restoration, but it was stock scenery, and this situation remained little changed for another one hundred years. Stock scenery served the theater's purpose in part because of the neoclassical belief that time and place were irrelevant to drama, and that attempts to particularize only diminished universality. Designers aimed to capture a generalized type of place rather than to re-create a particular place. Types of scenery increased beyond the standard sets of "tragic," "comic," and "pastoral" of Renaissance theater, but they were still sufficiently generalized to be serviceable in different plays.

Major changes in stage design occurred in the eighteenth century. It was a period during which Europeans showed a growing fascination for nature and place, for human beings and their customs, at home and abroad. At home, nature study became a popular recreation. Cultivated men and women pretended an interest in geological features, in plants and animals, and might keep an eye out for fossils as they took their country walks. Scientific reports on distant lands were read by educated laymen. Abroad on grand tours, they kept note of the localities they had visited in their journals and diaries. Such predilections found their way into the theatrical world. In France and England, the landscape artist and designer Philippe Jacques De-Louterbourg (1740–1812) won fame for his realistic stage scenes. Under his influence "local color" became a vogue. For the English stage he produced spectacles such as "The Wonders of Derbyshire" (1779), which depicted real places, and "Omai, a Trip Around the World" (1785), based on Captain Cook's voyages. In the nineteenth century, nature was more than scenery. Its rampages were shown to play an active role in human lives. Rather than count on the gods or angels to resolve an impasse, a flood inundated the stage and carried the heroine to safety on a plank.[34] Not the deities and the stars but nature and places on earth impinged on human fate.

Landscapes and house interiors are both personal worlds. Unlike the cosmos and the public square, they are capable of deeply reflecting personal moods and values. During the period that European artists were drawn to landscapes, they also showed an interest in and a respect for domestic events and for interior spaces (furniture included) of the house. Private life, Philippe Ariès notes, began to invade "iconography in the sixteenth and above all in the seventeenth century: Dutch and Flemish painting and French engraving show the extraordinary strength of this hitherto inconsistent or neglected concept."[35] Playwrights and stage designers responded to the new awareness. While some of them experimented with melodrama and geographical spectacles, others turned to explore the intimate worlds within the house.

Until the beginning of the modern period, it was widely assumed that significant events—those that plays dramatized—normally took place under the open sky in the public realm, such as a courtyard in front of the palace, or a street lined by domiciles and taverns. Human follies would be observed out-of-doors, witnessed by people peering from the windows of houses in the real world, as well as on stage. Tragedies, on the other hand, were thought more likely to occur within the family and inside a building. A problem for the producers, then, was to reveal tragic events on a stage that traditionally represented some type of public space. Greek and Renaissance theater resorted to such devices as the messenger's speech, the cries of characters murdered behind the scene, and the sudden opening of a door in the background to expose a homicidal drama.[36]

Until about 1650 most stage scenes were exteriors. In France, Molière by exerting his influence played a part in transferring comedies from outdoor places of classical inspiration into drawing rooms. He seemed aware than an indoor setting could help to focus the personality and social status of his highly individualized characters.[37] In England, we know that domestic scenes were popular in Restoration plays, but the convention of a broad forestage beyond the proscenium arch persisted. It persisted because the plot of Restoration plays continued to require a common ground or public arena for casual encounters, confrontations, and assignations.

Theater and Society

An intimate and enclosed world on stage was not finally achieved until the second half of the nineteenth century. Restoration plays, even though they were often set in the drawing room or in the bed-chamber, did not explore human vulnerability at the core of private and intimate experiences. Appropriately, Restoration plays came to be known as "comedies of manners." Manners are our public selves: they hide and protect the inner being. An aggressive manner is wit; and Restoration comedies are sparkling exchanges of wit. The "polite" society that patronized the one or two London theaters of the late seventeenth century was not at all emotionally involved with the characters in a play. Spectators sat as Olympians in judgment of the verbal duels on stage, and they would from time to time join the battle themselves with a loud and witty comment. The eighteenth century saw the emergence of sentimental drama, and with its ac-ceptance, comedy took on some of the functions of tragedy. An audience is expected not only to laugh at the characters, but to feel for them—to share their joys and sorrows. A private world is revealed, and vulnerability becomes an explicit theme. But the vulnerability of sentimental drama is in fact spurious because virtue always wins in the end.[38] Virtue is itself manner—manner without wit. In the early part of the nineteenth century, the European stage was dominated by melodrama, for which a major source of inspiration had been the Gothic novel. Skeletons rattled in closets, and there were plenty of dark secrets on the verge of being exposed. Spectators were invited to look at the hiddenness of things. Individuals had secrets, as, in the hidden sufferings of the poor, had society. After the French Revolu-tion, the theater found it profitable to exploit the world's seamy un-derside. Melodrama pretended to dip beneath the bright surfaces of social manners; what it came up with, however, was not a deeper knowledge of self and society, but mere spectacles and thrills. Serious plumbing of the human predicament, of human lives trapped by their social and material environment with no hope at all of dramatic rescues through trap doors or newly discovered wills, did not prevail until after the 1860s; and then such drama was only for a small discrimi-nating audience attending the small intimate playhouses that were being built in the late Victorian period.[39]

The presentation of an intimate world on stage in earlier times was also hindered by certain conventions of acting and of audience behavior, and by the physical character of the playhouse. In the eighteenth century, the division between the reality of the play and the reality of the actors and spectators remained fuzzy. Privileged members of the audience were allowed to sit on the stage, thus destroying any possible illusion of a separate enclosed world of domestic drama. Spectators, moreover, still exercised their right to disrupt a scene to express their approval or displeasure. They might call on an actor to repeat an effectively delivered speech or plague him with boos and hisses when he faltered. The actors themselves encouraged exchange with the audience. They habitually performed at the front of the stage, and at certain high points in a drama, were inclined to address the audience in the hope for applause, rather than each other in the interest of preserving an illusion. They seldom turned their profiles, and almost never their backs, on the spectators.[40] Although furniture began to increase toward the end of the eighteenth century and in the early decades of the next, it served more as background than as something integral to the actions, standing in the back part of the stage while the actors declaimed at the front. Victor Hugo was among the first directors to encourage players to move about freely over the entire expanse of the stage and turn their backs on the audience when necessary.[41]

Intimate dramas of human bonds and conflicts in an ordinary house and using naturalistic language became feasible as the division between players and audience was more sharply drawn. In Paris and London, highborn patrons were finally evicted from the stage in 1759 and 1762, respectively. The apron that thrusted beyond the proscenium arch dwindled in size until by the end of the nineteenth century it was used almost solely for curtain calls.[42] Actors withdrew step by step into the world of the play, until they could act as though the audience did not exist (Fig. 19). Progress in lighting techniques accelerated the division of the theater into two worlds. In the eighteenth century, producers still depended on candles and oil — immemorial means of illumination over which they had little control. For example, they could only with difficulty dim or brighten different parts of the

Fig. 19. Even in the nineteenth century the contact between players and audience can be surprisingly close. This closeness of contact is especially characteristic of the larger theaters where melodramas are presented for the entertainment of the populace. From Richard Southern, *The Victorian Theatre: A Pictorial Survey* (Newton Abbot, Devon: David & Charles, 1970), p. 11.

stage while a drama was in progress. Limelight, invented in 1816, sharply augmented the power of a producer to create mood and atmosphere. Scenery composed in part of light and shadow gained a subtle kind of realism that it did not formerly possess. Scenery became more than a backdrop, or an exotic locale in a distant country that spectators could gawk at. In certain naturalistic plays of the late nineteenth century, it was a pervasive and unifying presence, assuming this role as explanatory and eloquently descriptive speeches went out of fashion.[43]

Gaslight was widely used in the theater by the 1820s. Gaslight helped to accelerate the process of establishing a separate world of illusion and it powerfully affected acting style. As early as the sixteenth century, the Italian architect and designer Leone de Somi championed the darkened auditorium, but his idea could rarely be implemented. During the next two centuries a common method of illumination in western European theaters was to hang a row of chandeliers somewhere in the neighborhood of the proscenium arch. Candles cast light on the auditorium and on the forestage, where the players—in order to be seen—tended to congregate, seldom retreating to the gloomy backside. Players and spectators were thus drawn together by the same pool of light. With the introduction of gas, the illumination of the entire stage no longer presented any difficulty. Players were able to withdraw upstage, move among the furniture placed there, and still be clearly visible from the auditorium. Fully exposed to light, players performing in the small theaters of the late nineteenth century found that they had to subdue their gestures and develop more intimate modes of expression. Darkening the auditorium itself could be executed with ease; after 1880 it was the generally accepted practice.[44]

The spectator, isolated from his fellows in the darkness, turns into a voyeur. Whereas he once stood among the milling crowd alternately listening and chatting, he now sits silently in his own chair gazing as though through a window at the illuminated stage.[45] And what can he see? Not the cosmos or the great world, but a private room, or a private garden that is the "summer room" of a country house. In the realistic dramas of the late nineteenth and early twentieth century, spectators encounter lives similar to their own. They see solid members of the middle class—a perplexed people who yearn to communicate but often speak at cross purposes, who suffer moments of self-doubt, wonder about their own identity, and yet feel the urge to confess. A major theme in the plays of Ibsen and Chekhov is this search for self. In *A Doll's House*, Nora is compelled to leave her husband and children in order to discover who she really is. In *Peer Gynt*, Peer is driven to discover self at whatever cost to others. Near his journey's end he peels an onion and finds to his horror that it has no heart—the self is untenanted at the core. In Chekhov's *The Seagull*, Treplef asks plaintively, "Who am I? What am I—?"

6

Ambience
and Sight

In the last three chapters we have focused on the general tendency in Western society to move from communality toward increasing social and spatial segmentation. Paralleling this trend was the rise in the number of individuals who, as a result of their greater self-awareness and need for privacy, have become proudly but also sadly isolated from their groups. By observing the histories of table manner, household, and theater, we learn that how people perceive external reality and self has undergone striking changes during the last three hundred years. We can now explore these perceptual shifts.

Consider, first, that the modern built environment makes its appeal almost exclusively to our eyes. A lean skyscraper, its glass-sheathed walls reflecting the tinted clouds of twilight, is beautiful to behold from the outside. The interior, too, may display a trim handsomeness of glass, aluminum, and wood. But the senses other than sight tend to be underfed. The place has neither odor nor sound other than the muted noises of office work or of soft canned music; and it discourages touch. The forum of a modern building, whatever its visual appeal, has a limited sensory ambience. The place maintains, as it were, a distance: people in it feel somewhat detached and isolated. By contrast, the interior of a Gothic cathedral is often an enveloping presence. All of one's senses come to life under the impress of soaring stone pillars, of organ music that reverberates across the cavernous space, of odors from moist stone, incense, and melting candle wax, and of the feel of hard ground underfoot.

Comparing the two buildings thus, we are led to ponder on the differences in sensory experience of peoples who lived in different historical periods. Before modern times the sensory world was small and complex, full of competing and conflicting sights, odors, and sounds. In modern times, perceptual experiences tend to be separate and distinct, with visual stimuli and experiences prevailing above all others. A result of this change is that, whereas the size of the perceived world expands, its inchoate richness declines. Another result is the fostering of a heightened sense of a self detached from its milieu. Emphasis on seeing, and particularly on seeing with the mind's eye, has had the effect of isolating the individual and of promoting an awareness of the self as the lone framer of knowledge.

To understand why this is so, we need to assess the character of the senses. Let us begin with hearing. Sounds are an ever present part of our milieu: we are steeped in a world of rustling leaves and whistling winds, of the gentle hum of air conditioners and distant traffic. Such noises are usually taken for granted. Silence, when we are suddenly aware of it, seems uncanny. The sounds of our everyday environment are diffuse and unlocated. This is true of continuous background noises, and even the discrete sounds to which we attend, such as the droning of a small airplane or the barking of a dog, are not precisely located. We have some idea as to where they come from, but that is all. The world of sounds lacks spatial definition. Sound, even when it is perceived to emanate from a specific source, fills space and tends to envelop the listener.

Another attribute of sound is its power to stir human emotion, a power that probably exceeds that of vision even though the human world is predominantly visual. Sound is dynamic. It generates a sense of life. Looking out of a soundproof building to the streets below, we see moving cars and pedestrians and yet the scene appears curiously static until a window is thrown open and noises pour in. Dramatically the street scene comes to life. Furthermore, natural sounds such as the rhythmic beat of waves on the lakeshore and artificial sounds (particularly those of music) are able to reproduce the basic pulses of life—heartbeat and breathing. By replicating the pulses of life, circumambient sounds can arouse feelings of excitement and

Ambience and Sight

fervor, or of peace and happiness. The self is united to the world through sound both because an auditory event tends to fill space and surround the listener and because it can powerfully stir the emotions.[1]

Many animals have an acute sense of smell. A male silkworm moth can follow upwind the come-hither scent of a female moth at a distance of seven miles.[2] A dog's ability to detect distant and faint odor far exceeds that of any human being, as we are well aware. For many animals, the nose opens up the world. For human beings, however, the eyes are the distance sensor. Compared with adults, children live in a more odoriferous environment, both because habit has not yet blunted their sense of smell and because children live closer to the earth—to the flowers and grass, the moist soil and the sun-baked pavement—from which most odors emanate.

Odors do not give us a sense of structured space. Whatever we can smell is already, as the saying goes, "right under our nose." We rarely use our nose to tell direction, to locate the things of importance to us. The image of a hungry man following the scent of roast beef into the kitchen is humorous because people do not normally use their olfactory organ that way. The vapors of fragrance diffuse through space. We live wrapped up in a world of imprecisely located odors, which are important to us because they undoubtedly affect our emotions and our sense of well-being. Such biological necessities as food and sex are stimulated by fragrance. Food that we cannot smell loses all appeal. As to the relation between odor and sexual arousal, Somerset Maugham once said that one can tell whether a woman loves a man from the answer to the question, "Does she like the smell of his raincoat?" Young children are perhaps more dependent on smell for their sense of well-being than are adults. It may be that a child's attachment to an old blanket or teddy bear has much to do with its reassuring odor. With adults, too, there is comfort in certain commonplace odors, such as the clean smell of a freshly laundered shirt.

Odor and what we consider to be natural (real or authentic) are somehow associated in the mind. A reason for this is that nearly all natural substances, including rock, have a distinctive fragrance. Many artifacts, on the other hand, are odorless. A manufactured object does not successfully imitate nature if it cannot exude nature's characteristically complex fragrance. Besides giving us a sense of the authentic, the nose, like other sensory organs, gathers information about the environment. A person with a cultivated sense of smell responds critically to a wide range of odors in nature and in the artifactitious world. However, the sense of smell contributes little to the development of mental life, considered as abstract or symbolic thought. The world that smell yields lacks firmness; it is diffuse, inchoate, transient, and emotional. Odors arouse feelings of pleasure, well-being, nostalgia, affection, and revulsion. They are direct, specific, and ungeneralizable experiences—ends in themselves. As with sound, we can say that the self is united to the world through odor because odor is pervasive and because it stirs the emotions.[3]

The tactile sense is the most fundamental of all senses. Without it no animal can survive. Through the broad surface of the skin, our largest sensory organ, we are in constant contact with the environment. Eyes can be closed and ears plugged, and at times we cannot smell and taste. But the tactile sense is always functioning. Some part of the skin surface is always registering the pressures and the stimuli of an environment—the feel of wind and drizzle, cool bedsheets, and prickly underwear. Exceptionally discerning is the tactile sense of the human hand. In the animal kingdom, human beings are unique in the way that hands are used to explore the texture and form of objects. We like to touch and feel things, and we can tell through touch alone the subtle difference in texture between bond paper and magnolia petal. Touch, moreover, is the ultimate test of reality. Seeing is not necessarily believing because the eyes can deceive, but the tangible is indubitably real: what we are able to touch and hold in our hands is truly there—right before us and immediately accessible. However, we can *handle* only a few objects at a time. A world thus known is limited in size and in the number of things it holds. The tactile sense does not encourage intellectual leaps; perhaps for this reason, it is able to affect strongly our sense of well-being and our emotions, even more so than do hearing and smell. For example, unless a newborn child's body is adequately stimulated by touch and handling, its ability to digest food and eliminate waste will suffer. And we all know that touch is "touching," and that by touching another person we show love and give comfort. Touch literally unites self to the world.[4]

Hearing, smell, and touch are all proximate senses. The worlds known through them tend to be cozy and emotionally rich, but lacking the characteristic of locational specificity. All three senses intimately involve the individual with an environment. Human beings, however, are predominantly visual. Vision opens up a sharply detailed world of objects spatially disposed "out there." At close quarters, all our senses respond to the environment, and what we are aware of is not just a picture but a circumambient world pulsating with life. At the middle distance, odor drops out of our perception and we are confronted by a picture with sound—a sort of movie screen. Emotional involvement with this simplified world is still possible. At an even greater distance, sound also drops out and we are left with a mere picture. The things in the picture may move, but because of the absence of sound, they can seem curiously lifeless.

Vision is our intellectual sense par excellence. It discriminates and defines. "We prefer seeing to everything else," says Aristotle, "because, above all the other senses, sight makes us know and brings to light the many differences between things."[5] Sight provides us with a spatially structured universe. All the objects are visible at the same time, and they are stable long enough for us to apprehend their relationship to each other. Sight is the "coolest" of the senses: it stirs our emotions the least. The visual field does not enwrap; we can see only what is in front. We stand at the margin of the visual field. All objects in it, no matter how close, still seem "out there." We cannot wholly possess what we only see: there remains both a physical and a psychological distance between the onlooker and that which she looks at. A beautiful face or sunset can arouse powerful emotions, but because neither can be touched, an aesthetic distance persists. Since we normally perceive with all our senses and not just with our eyes, we do not ordinarily feel cut off from our setting. That sight alone is ineffective in merging self with the world is suggested by the experience of soldiers who lost their hearing suddenly during the war. At first they found the noiseless world peaceful; in time, it seemed to them static, lifeless, and unreal. They feel isolated as though they lived behind glass screens.[6]

Self-awareness is possible in a human being by virtue of the human brain and eyes. We have already noted the ability of vision to segregate and differentiate impressions into discrete objects, each in its own place. Turned inward, vision discerns that the self is fragmented; or that if it is an entity, it is one such entity among many others, all in some ways different. Again, we have noted the fact that what we see is necessarily "out there," and that we always stand at the margin of our own visual field. How this fact might stimulate self-consciousness is illustrated by the following common experience. You push open the door and see a crowd at a party. You are keenly aware of being the outsider surveying the field ahead, until you plunge into the crowd. In an instant, you belong. Of course, what you *see* is still "out there," but the sense of isolation wanes in the midst of the hubbub and the smell of tobacco, food, and sweat. One more point: seeing promotes a consciousness of self because it is often experienced as a personal act, an initiative that one takes and maintains with one's will. The other senses are relatively passive. Sounds and odors reach us and we respond. Most of the time, we hear rather than listen, smell rather than smell out; and our skin simply registers the agencies—wind in the hair, sand between the toes, the human touch—that move over or press it.

Infants, we know, lack a sense of self. Their world is an undifferentiated whole compared with that of older children and of adults. Immature brains and perceptual systems account for these limitations. However, the perceptual organs are not all equally immature. An infant's ears are very much like those of a grown person. Infants even enjoy an advantage over adults in that they can hear sounds of a higher pitch. Emotionally, sound may have a greater effect on an infant's sense of well-being than sight has. An infant has definite preferences as to sound—the soothing lullaby, the gentle voice of the mother, and her heartbeat which the infant hears from the position he is normally held, in the mother's left arm. Infants are sensitive to odors, liking some and disliking strongly others. They can locate odor sources and, very soon after birth, will turn away from odors they find unpleasant. Infants have a delicate skin, through which much awareness of the environment comes. The first environment that infants actively explore is their mother. They do this by making skin contact at the breast and nipple, by clutching at the mother with their restless hands, and through their sense of smell. The eyes are less important, being often closed. When open, they do not open up much of the world. A new-born can see only about a foot from his face. His peripheral vision is also poor, much poorer than an adult's. Until an infant is four months old, his eyes cannot focus properly. Stereoscopic vision, nearly absent at birth, develops slowly. Attention span is fleeting.

In short, it appears that visual perception—the sense most closely associated with abstract thought, differentiation, and distancing—is the least developed part of a young child's perceptual system. The security that the very young need to feel may depend on the immaturity of vision relative to the other senses. A baby's perceptual world is adaptively small and cozy, caressed by the emotionally reassuring stimuli of sounds, odors, and touch. Significantly, schizophrenic children between the ages of eight and twelve seek security by withdrawing into a small world of reassuring sensations. Compared with normal children, they learn to depend more on the proximate senses of hearing, smell, and touch, and less on the differentiating and isolating sense of sight in coping with people and the physical environment.[7]

Healthy human adults in different parts of the world have similar capacities to hear, smell, touch, and see. How they develop their potential for perception and how they make use of the senses in daily activities do, of course, vary widely from one sociocultural group to another. Again, whereas for all human beings the visual sense is predominant, the way eyes are trained to see differs strikingly from people to people. To gatherers and hunters living in a dense forest, the eyes do not, obviously, function to full capacity as distance sensors. All that can be seen in a tropical forest—plants and animals—are already close by. Sight is trained to discern details in a cluttered setting rather than to comprehend open, expansive space. Indeed, open space can arouse dread. The Tasaday, a primitive people of Mindanao in the Philippines, when they were first taken out of their forest to view a patch of cleared land, described it nervously as the place "where the eye can look too far."[8]

Curiosity as to what lies beyond the protective all-encompassing forest is minimal for gatherers and hunters such as the Tasaday and the Mbuti Pygmies of the Congo basin. Sounds, on the other hand, can provide a comforting milieu. A tropical forest is full of sounds—rustling leaves, the impact of rain on vegetation, and the noises of a teeming, diversified fauna. To the Mbuti Pygmies, certain kinds of sound have a supernatural quality that gives intimations of a world beyond death. A favorite legend with the Pygmies tells the story of the Bird with the Beautiful Song. Killing the Bird results in instant and permanent death. Human songs also have power, a power that derives more from the sound than from the word content. The Mbuti sing to waken the benevolent spirit of the forest in times of stress. Human voices are answered by the "song" from a ceremonial trumpet, which is carried into the forest and blown at different points so that the sound may appear to emanate from the forest itself.[9] Odors, like sounds, are pervasive in a tropical forest: fragrances of growth and odors of decay are everywhere. The tactile sense of a near-naked people is frequently stimulated by tropical downpours and gusts of wind, by the leaves and branches they brush against, and, most important of all, by the exchanges of touch between human beings.

Outside of nurturing forests, people live exposed to the sky and to broad open spaces if only they make the effort to look. But most people choose not to look. The distant horizon seems threatening rather than beckoning. Eyes attend to what is at hand, to the humanized world of camp site or village, and to those parts of nature necessary to survival. Appreciation of scenery is much less common than we think. Almost everywhere, attachment is to homeplace, and the more intense feeling of awe is directed to a sacred locality. In the presence of a home or of a sacred place, all one's senses are actively engaged. Distancing—intrinsic to visual and aesthetic appreciation—is absent. The Tikopia are deeply attached to their tropical island but they do not share the anthropologist Raymond Firth's aesthetic delight in the beauties of the seascape.[10] The Aranda of central Australia reveal a profound love for their native soil. Mountains, creeks, and water holes are not, to them, merely scenic features in which the eyes may take passing delight; they are rather a living family tree, a record of their own past, and locales of intense personal as well as tribal experiences. In all the open space of the desert, much wandering and exploration is possible. But the Aranda, who have had a history of migration in search for water and food, do not care to wander. Their legends are full of the longing for home, of weary ancestors longing to return to the place whence they originated.[11]

Two peoples, the Chinese and the Europeans, have not only opened their eyes to the beauty of the world "out there," but have sought to capture it in nature-poetry and landscape painting. More than others, they have conceived the idea of scenery. If this emphasis on sight entails distancing and isolation—a movement toward a more differentiated and less encompassing world—then that has been the destiny of these two peoples. The story of the venture is long and intricate. We shall see, however, that the Chinese have moved far less in the direction of the visual than have the Europeans. Consider, for example, the evidence of the house. Both China and Europe had the courtyard house, but in China it remained popular for some two thousand years. Unlike the Europeans, the Chinese have not developed on their own the ideal of the picture window in their homes. Step inside the blank walls that enclose the traditional Chinese house and one is in a courtyard with perhaps a miniature garden at the corner. Move further into the private compound and one is wrapped in an ambience of calm beauty, an ordered world of buildings, pavement, decorative rocks, and vegetation. But nowhere is there a distant view. Only the sky offers open space. The pleasures of sight are mostly small-scale and intimate. Surrounded by walls, communication with the outside becomes possible only through the senses of hearing and smell. "Chinese literature," writes N. I. Wu, "abounds with examples describing city life through the sounds of peddlers on the streets and the scents of the flowering trees coming over the wall."[12]

To the Chinese, open space signifies separation. "Ten thousand *li*," as the expression goes, keep friends and lovers apart. A prominent theme in Chinese poetry is homesickness, a longing for the sights, sounds, and smells of the familiar and the circumscribed. Appreciation of outdoor nature and landscape came gradually. In the earliest literature, that of the early and middle Chou period (ca. 1000–500 B.C.), nature images fall into two extremes: at one extreme are the ordinary sights and sounds close to home; at the other, the esoteric and the transcendental—that is, the deities of mountains and clouds that are a feature of shamanistic beliefs. It was only in the fourth century A.D. that nature in the middle range—scenery and landscape—became manifest in poetry; and this range remained the most popular in the poems of the T'ang period (A.D. 618–907), during which landscape evocation in words attained a sensitivity that was never surpassed. Landscape painting matured later, during the Sung dynasty (960–1279).[13] In painting a landscape, the Chinese artist strives for atmosphere and a feeling of ubiquitous force rather than for scenery regarded as an arrangement of particulars "out there." Consider the picture entitled "Early Spring" (1072), which is the earliest signed and dated Chinese landscape. A modern critic claims that in "Early Spring" the artist Kuo Hsi tries to convey "the air of life." This "air" can be felt in the clouds, mists, and vapors, in the swift rivulets, and even in the soaring mountains, which are not dead matter but a dynamic force.[14]

China boasts different schools of art. Styles of landscape painting have changed over time. Nevertheless, throughout Chinese history the idea persists that nature, imbued with life, enfolds: a human being is a part of nature, wrapped by it. This fundamental attitude may be one reason why the Chinese have not been moved to develop the type of linear perspective that gained prominence in Western art during the Renaissance. Linear perspective, as we have noted, tends to isolate the viewer by giving him a position outside the scene. In contrast, the shifting and multilevel perspectives of the Chinese create the illusion of a world that envelops. It is significant, too, that unlike the European artist, the Chinese artist rarely paints with the landscape before him. His ideal is to experience nature in its manifold powers, to achieve a mystical identification with its essential spirit, and then try to recreate a vision of nature from within itself.[15]

Yet, in China as in Europe, the appreciation of nature grew and could only grow with a deepening sense of self. Recall the circumstances under which the depiction of landscape emerged. In the fourth century A.D., peoples of nomadic origin invaded north China, driving large numbers of native Chinese southward into the Yangtze basin, and beyond it, into a hilly and forested subtropical environment. What were the consequences of this movement to the South? On the one hand, the rules of society were relaxed to permit necessary adjustments to the new setting; on the other, the new setting offered mountains and streams of great beauty that were far more accessible to scholar-artists than had been the case in the long-settled valleys and plains of the North. In south China, court officials who fell out of favor or were disillusioned with transient human glories could find ready consolation among the mountains and the streams. This kind of escape into nature was possible in the fourth century and again during the Sung dynasty when the Mongols occupied north China and streams of Chinese once more migrated southward to establish their empire there.

As institutional bonds weaken, people of the scholar-official class seek consolation in union with nature. However, the quest for nature is unavoidably a lonely one. The seeker must, after all, abandon society. An artist who wanders into a place saturated with the sights, sounds, and fragrances of nature can easily believe himself to be steeped in milieu. But the effort of composition in the privacy of his study will remind him that the union is temporary, that to depict a thing is to stand outside of it. A poem recalls; and one recalls only what is absent. A landscape painting is indeed a perceptual presence—a presence perceived, however, only through the eyes; the feel of mist on the forehead and the scent of grass are lost.

Europeans, even more than the Chinese, have moved in the direction of the visual. In the Middle Ages, Europeans still lived for the most part in a traditional world that rewarded the senses—that was inchoate, colorful, and warmly human. From the sixteenth century onward, however, the world was shifting toward a cooler, larger, more deliberately conceived and precisely delimited order. The process may be characterized as one of sorting things out and spreading them over space, figuratively in the schemata of the mind and literally on the surface of the earth. We have already seen this process as it affects table manners, the house, and the theater. Here we shall focus on the sensory qualities of environment and their apperception.

The European medieval world was odoriferous to a high degree. Fragrances there were—those of herbs and roses, for example, and of blossoms from orchards that penetrated into the heart of even large medieval towns. But most odors, caused by the lack of personal and civic hygiene, were obnoxious. Body odors must have been strong even among members of the upper class, because people bathed infrequently and wore many layers of clothes that trapped sweat and dirt. Books of etiquette, composed in the thirteenth and fourteenth centuries, insist on the washing of hands, face, and teeth every morning but not on bathing. King John (1167–1216) took a bath once every three weeks, and his subjects presumably less often.[16] Medieval houses smelled strong for a variety of reasons, among them being the lack of ventilation. There were the musty odors from the damp walls, pungent cooking fumes, and noisome odors from the floor, incrusted with stale food and dog feces, and from the privies. Almost all medieval houses of any size had privies, connected by shafts in the wall either to water or to sewage pits. The problem lay with the shafts, which needed regular flushing if they were not to become offensive, but such flushing with stored rainwater was seldom available.

Great houses and palaces of the Renaissance period and later stank in unexpected places, because their residents and visitors were not yet fully trained to relieve nature discriminately. A Brunswick Court Regulation of 1569 warns: "Let no one, whoever he may be, before, at, or after meals, early or late, foul the staircases, corridors, or closets with urine or other filth, but go to suitable, prescribed places for such relief."[17] On August 8, 1606, the Dauphin of France "committed a nuisance" against the wall of his own bedchamber in the palace of St. Germain. During the reign of Louis XIV, visitors to the Louvre relieved themselves not only in the courtyards, but also on the balconies, on staircases, and behind doors.[18] Outside the domiciles and shops, the narrow streets were open sewers cluttered with foul-smelling garbage among which pigs rooted and fed. Butchers contributed greatly to the general foulness by slaughtering in the public thoroughfares. In fourteenth-century London, the Shambles presented a perennial problem to the city. Entrails and waste of the slaughtered animals, to be carted off to the Fleet, dripped from the carts and laid a swath of stink over the highway. Prominent citizens complained, but to little effect.[19] Bad odors detracted from the beauty of a city. Michel de Montaigne (1533–1592) wrote that his affection "for those beautiful cities Venice and Paris is lessened by their offensive smells."[20]

Odors diffuse and cannot be kept within bounds. An olfactory world offers pungency and variety, and it possesses a vaguely defined volume, but it lacks sharp lines of demarcation. Good and bad odors, where they occur close to each other, inevitably commingle. In a church, the smell of incense may remind one of the odor of sanctity and of heaven, but this fragrance necessarily mixes with the sour, evil odors of a crowded, unwashed congregation; and in practice incense was used less as a symbol than as a prophylactic, functional in the same way that the scented glove of a seventeenth-century Parisian was functional. Odors in their pungency and instability, their encompassing nature, and their ability to mix and arouse strong emotions, are of the essence of the premodern environment.

An awareness of place as enveloping is further strengthened by sounds that appear to emerge from all points of the compass. Noises permeated the streets of the medieval city from dawn to dusk. Street criers were everywhere and kept up their business at all hours of the day. In thirteenth-century Paris, criers proclaimed at dawn that the baths were open and the water hot; then followed bawling vendors advertising fish, meat, honey, onions, cheese, old clothes, flowers, pepper, charcoal, or other wares. Friars from different religious orders swarmed over the city, demanding alms. Public criers announced death and other news.[21] Street musicians provided entertainment but also could annoy those with well attuned ears. Some unmusical rogues played merely to have their silence bought off. During the reign of Elizabeth I, attempts by Parliament to suppress the caterwauling that passed for street music met with little success. Noises came out of industries and from a totally unregulated traffic of creaking carts and carriages, their wheels grinding on unpaved or cobblestoned roads. A sense of turmoil was contributed by neighing horses, grunting pigs, sheep bleating their way to market, and pedestrians on wooden clogs (to rise above the mud and filth) shouting and pushing their way through the crowd.

Not all sounds, however, were mere noise. The historian Johan Huizinga noted that one sound lifted city life onto a sphere of order and serenity: the sound of bells. "The bells were in daily life like good spirits, which by their familiar voices, now called upon the citizens to mourn and now to rejoice, now warned them of danger, now exhorted them to piety." The bell's authoritative and concerned voice unified a community, the outer edge of which was where its call could still be heard. Ringing bells, however, could also signify the rejoicing of a people. "What intoxication the pealing of the bells of all the churches, and of all the monastaries of Paris, must have produced, sounding from morning till evening, and even during the night, when a peace was concluded or a pope elected."[22]

The picture that we look at is always "out there," although we can enter it imaginatively. The music that we hear comes from a definite source, which we may be able to see, but the sound itself is less localized. The degree of localization depends on the sound waves' frequency. Bass sound of low frequency has the power to "touch" and surround the listener; it has a dark, directionless quality. The listener does not face the sound but rather feels immersed in it. High notes, by contrast, appear to be bright, sharp, and more precisely located in space. Attending a service in the Gothic cathedral, we have the sensation of being enclosed and steeped in an integral universe and of losing a prickly sense of self in the community of worshipers. The effect is caused, at an environmental level, by the pillars that soar and overarch to form a majestic vault, and by the subtle weaving of darkness and light, odors and fragrances that makes interior space seem almost a tangible substance. Sound contributes powerfully to this sense of oneness. As Kurt Blankopf put it,

The sound in Norman and Gothic churches, by surrounding the audience, strengthens the link between the individual and the community. The loss of high frequencies and the resulting impossibility of localizing the sound makes the believer part of a world of sound. He does not face the sound in "enjoyment"—he is wrapped by it.[23]

A landscape painting can produce a sensation of great open space, stretching above and beyond the viewer. Can music produce a similar effect? It can, though normally it does not. Music in most parts of the world has the power to generate a wide range of moods and feelings. Rare or absent among them, however, is the impression of a space that has distance and directionality, a space that stretches before rather than wraps around the listener. To produce an effect of perspective space, the sounds of music must display wide range in both frequency and intensity. The music must have high and low, loud as well as soft notes. Bass notes merge and diffuse; they swathe the listener. High notes, clear and focused, soar; they have sharp edges and give a clear sense of direction. Dynamic contrast further enhances an illusion of perspective space: loud sounds occupy the foreground, and as they grow softer the notes seem to fade into a distant acoustic horizon.

Great range in volume and pitch is a characteristic of Western music. This trait emerged toward the end of the sixteenth century, at a time when perspective painting was becoming popular. The musicologist Murray Schafer makes the comment that "just as objects are rank-ordered in perspective painting, depending on their distance from the viewer, so musical sounds are rank-ordered by means of their dynamic emphasis in the virtual space of the soundscape. . . . The classical Western composer places sounds in high definition before the eye of the ear."[24]

Classical music demands attention. Concentrated listening requires that the musicians be placed at one end of a hall and the audience, facing the musicians, at another. Attending a service in a Gothic church the individual is joined to his community and immersed in musical sounds that suffuse the building like incense. By contrast, in a concert hall where classical music is being played the listener remains an individual, isolated from the other members of the audience, and actively attending to the large, clearly defined musical space before him with "the eye of the ear."

Medieval people, of course, depended on their eyes and enjoyed what sight has to offer as much as anyone in modern times. However, they differed from us in two respects: their visual experiences were richly complemented by those derived from hearing and smell, and they lacked the notion of views and landscapes. The idea of a view is now so familiar that we tend to assume that it is how human beings normally see. Yet this cannot be correct. The view or scenery is a specialized way of structuring visual impressions; objects out there are arranged by the eye and the mind's eye so as to constitute a pleasing picture—and pleasing because of a perceived order in the objects that the picture arbitrarily frames. Medieval people focused more on the individual objects than on how they were arranged to form a larger unit called view or landscape. Perhaps they felt no compulsion to seek assurance in a large visual order because, at an intellectual level, the world's coherence was something that medieval people could take for granted; moreover, sounds, odors, and bright colors provided a sensuous and reassuring cocoon in which life could unselfconsciously proceed.

In actuality, the landscapes of the European Middle Ages lacked large-scaled visual order. At first, this assertion seems rash and groundless, for the words "medieval world" now tend to evoke images of picturesque villages or walled towns surrounded by neat fields. But such pictures are products of the modern mind. They are how we now choose to envisage the medieval environment. In those bygone days the people themselves might well have seen their world differently. We have reasons to believe so. Consider the material landscape, rural and urban. It was devoid of simple geometric order on a large scale. Roads were crooked rather than straight, and fields formed complex mosaics rather than rectangular patterns. The city had numerous houses, gardens, and courtyards of simple geometric design, but these small-scaled features did not, in small or large group, provide vistas—that is, expanses of ordered space that the eyes could readily apprehend as a unit. The church, though a prominent landmark, was not always successful in integrating its surrounding area to constitute a landscape. Located at the center of a town, the church could rarely be seen as a single architectural monument because houses crowded it on all sides and no avenue of any length approached it from which pilgrims might gain a comprehensive view. Moreover, although we can now appreciate the beauty of the flying buttresses that hold up a Gothic cathedral, their original purpose was not aesthetic. Medieval architects were not concerned with how their churches would look from the outside; their aesthetic verve was used to create internal spaces of sublime beauty—a beauty more felt than seen.[25]

Ambience and Sight

As a wayfarer approached a medieval town he would see in the distance an imposing wall, with towers and spires rising above it. The wall provided the town with a sharp boundary that is so unlike the fuzzy edges of a modern settlement. However, enter the gate and what one saw beyond the market and the lines of houses was a continuation of the countryside. Farms did not stop at the wall but continued beyond it even to the core of the town. Rural activities interdigitated in a complex fashion with urban life. Straight borders seldom extended for any length. Workshops and commercial establishments intermingled with residences. Mansions stood side by side with hovels. The profane activities of buying and selling and of lawyers consulting with their clients did not stop at the sacred portals of the church but continued well beyond them to the foot of the sanctuary. The border between the sacred and the profane was far more intricate and elusive in the medieval world than in the modern world where religious beliefs have weakened to become a small, separate compartment of life.[26] In a similar manner, the border between private and public space was indistinct, as we have noted earlier. The hall, for example, was the principal room in a private residence, but in what sense was the hall itself private space? On the commercial street of a medieval town, businesses of all kinds were allowed to appear without the benefit of spatial demarcation. Where did the stores end and the street begin? Storefronts encroached on the public thoroughfare, their merchandise spilling over it. There were no sidewalks, no separation of wheeled traffic from pedestrians, nor of pedestrians from the scavenging livestock. Splashes of color added to a sense of chaotic excitement in the medieval scene. Brightly painted statuary, for example, stood out vividly against the clean white facade of the church; large and richly colored signs protruded from the storefronts, and gaudily dressed crowds milled around the market square and in the streets on festival days. In a bustling medieval city the eyes would have to search hard to discern any large-scale visual order. On the other hand, they could feast on a tumult of contrasting and richly colored details, both architectural and human.

We can infer the nature of a perceptual world, in part, by what there is to perceive. Another line of evidence lies in language, in how people verbally express their awareness of the environment. The French historian Lucien Febvre, by studying the works of the poets of the sixteenth century, came up with the surprising discovery that the poets were far more men of sound than of sight. The sounds of running brooks and of singing birds constantly recur in the works of Clément Marot (1496–1544) and of Pierre de Ronsard (1524–1585). Marot's *chansons*, which abound in magpies, linnets, and goldfinches, refer carefully to their different warblings, but never to their plumages. Ronsard conjures up the sea and its creatures, but prefers to characterize them by the noises they make than by their shape. When this poet describes a kiss he chooses to evoke the experience in sound and fragrance rather than in visual images such as the shape and color of the lips. Jean Bouchet (1476–1559), in the title of a work, promises to describe a beautiful house. However, he manages to do this without once mentioning lines, colors, spatial harmony, and perspective—these pleasures of the eye. Instead he concentrates on sounds and voices—the pleasures of the ear. When Joachim du Bellay (1522–1560), working in Rome, feels homesick for France, he does not try to recall its physical form; rather he evokes a voice or a mood.[27]

It may be that, to poets, visual images are too direct, lacking in evocative power. But, according to Febvre, this preference for sound and the proximate senses of touch and smell to sight appears in the works of prose writers as well. Evidence of an indifference to views occurs even in the naming of inns, which in sixteenth-century France, were far more likely to be called "L'Homme Sauvage" or "Le Lion d'Or" than "Bellevue" or "Beau Site."

In contrast to our forebears, we take it for granted that the universe is there to be inspected, with that word's sense of deliberative action, rather than heard, which connotes a more passive mode of response. Yet, as Walter Ong reminds us, this emphasis on the testimony of the eye was not true of many early peoples, including the ancient Greeks who quite commonly thought of the world as an acoustic harmony.[28] Today we are still vaguely acquainted with the idea of the universe as the harmony of the spheres, a proportion and a movement that have auditory appeal. This idea was much more real and vivid in the sixteenth century. We have observed earlier that the Elizabethan theater was full of cosmic symbolism: the "heavens," for example, were painted on the canopy above the inner stage of Burbage's Theatre. However, the symbolism of the theater was also profoundly musical: human drama was music played within the harmony of the spheres or world music. Shakespeare, according to Frances Yates, thought in musical terms when he considered human destiny in its cosmic setting.[29]

Through much of the history of the stage, sound in fact mattered more than sight. Vitruvian theater in Renaissance times was still an actor's, not a scene-painter's, theater. Success depended on the eloquence of speech and on the music of the player's voice. Shakespeare's theater was also predominantly aural, suited to be the vehicle of great poetic dramas. People went to the Globe to hear even more than to see: they were an audience or, to use an older word, an "auditory." In France, tragic acting in the sixteenth century was primarily a vocal, even operatic, performance, which demanded great lung power and precise breath control, but little in the way of bodily gesture and movement. Montdory, the famous actor at the Théâtre de Marais, had so overtaxed his voice in one performance that he suffered a partial paralytic stroke, from which he never fully recovered. The tragedy ended his career. Montdory's contemporary at the rival Hôtel de Bourgogne, Montfleury, was struck by a similar, though less permanent, disability. Stories of this kind show to what degree actors were willing to stretch their vocal resources to maintain a reputation.[30]

Evidence from the history of the theater supports the view that in premodern times people were far more ready to perceive reality as aural, that is, as an encompassing world of sounds both human and nonhuman. Sight, where emphasized, tended to be particular and spectacular. Thus, in the Elizabethan theater the eyes, for lack of scenery, feasted on gaudy costumes and on special mechanical effects such as fire leaping from hell's mouth.

Vision and thought have several important traits in common. Both possess clarity. When we open our eyes, a diffuse ambience of sounds and smells yields to a sharply delineated world of objects in space. The effect of thought is similar. When we begin to think consciously, fuzziness gives way to clarity, and that which we try to understand seems arrayed before us, something that we can point to and say, "Now, do you see?" Sight gives us a world of discrete objects, as does touch, but unlike touch, sight can in addition easily discern a pattern, a relationship of these objects in space. And that act of visual intelligence resembles how the mind works, for thinking in its nature is relational and cannot rest content with merely entertaining the particular. Sight is the most active of the senses. We are free to open or close our eyes. We choose to see; indeed, from ancient Greek to late medieval times, thinkers have erroneously believed that we can direct the light of our eyes on the world like beams from a torch. Likewise, thinking is an activitiy: an individual must make an effort to think. In both seeing and thinking, a degree of psychological withdrawal or distancing occurs. A clearly seen object is "out there," detached from us, something that we cannot simultaneously merge with or possess. To think clearly and well we must carry our detachment a stage further, to the extent of shutting our eyes and excluding the world.

In an earlier age when people were less infatuated with sight and less rationalistic, environment probably seemed more fluid than it does now. Nothing then was strictly delimited. Material objects did not preserve their separateness and identity. Thus stones could come to life; leaves that fell into the river might turn into birds; animals could behave like human beings and human beings turn into animals; and it was possible for a person to be in two places at the same time. Before the sixteenth century, the idea of the impossible lacked both precision and currency. Even educated people showed little awareness of nature as under constraint, bounded by laws; rather they tended to see it as protean, all-powerful, and endlessly fertile. Distinctions commonly made in modern thought, such as those between real and imaginary, fact and fantasy, natural and supernatural, were blurred in the thought of the Middle Ages.[31] How could they be sharp and firm when everybody believed in ghosts, and the category of true happenings included ghosts as well as prophetic dreams and action at a distance? The fluidity of sensual experiences in a medieval setting thus finds a parallel in the flexible categories of thought.

To a modern thinker the tolerance of the premodern mind for incoherence is baffling. Lucien Febvre, for one, seemed baffled. Describing

Ambience and Sight

the French language of the twelfth century he was reduced to using a string of uncomplimentary epithets: concrete, impressionistic, naive, and anarchistic—anarchistic in the sense of displaying an almost total disregard for consistency in syntax and an almost total freedom to mix up time sequences in a narrative. Reading Old French produces an impression of skipping and arbitrary juxtaposition rather like that of viewing the scenes taken by an amateur camerman as he rushes from place to place. By the end of the fifteenth century the French language has shown notable progress in the direction of clarity and rigor: the subject of a sentence, for example, could clearly be distinguished from the object, and the sovereign verb around which other syntactic elements used to cluster like satellites ceded its preeminent position to the subject. Moreover, the new trend in composition required that superfluous details be excised and secondary details be subordinated to the central idea. Changes such as these made it easier for speakers and writers to organize their thought and maintain it as an accordant viewpoint or perspective.[32] As logic increasingly entered the narration of events, so it appeared also in the geometry of place: from the sixteenth century onward, writers paid greater attention to what is and is not visible from a certain standpoint, and to consistency in the relative size and scale of objects in a scene.[33]

Oral culture is social. Literate culture encourages individualism. When a group of people meet to talk they do not—nor do they have any compelling reason to —strive for coherence in what they say. Even when a storyteller or a politician addresses a group he is more concerned to persuade and establish a feeling of concordance with his listeners than he is with the logic and consistency of his story or message. Coherence as the sustained unfolding of a viewpoint is unnecessary; it is also difficult, perhaps impossible, to achieve for two reasons. One is the web of feelings inevitable in any congregation. Crosscurrents of approval and disapproval, pleasure and displeasure exist, hindering concentration on the part of both speaker and listener. The other reason, discussed at length by Walter Ong, lies in the nature of speech. Memory is short. A speaker cannot sustain an intricate storyline without the help of inscribed words. Drama could develop tight linear plot building up to a climax because drama in the Western world had been

controlled by writing since ancient Greek times and because drama was
not narrative but action. Narrative prose itself lacked a tightly organized structure until around the Romantic age. "Even *Tom Jones*,"
writes Ong, "always remains largely episodic by contrast with, say a
Thomas Hardy novel."[34] Of course, storytellers of the oral tradition
were and are well able to weave complicated epics of great length and
retell them with the essential content, though not the details, intact.
However, the complication lies in the number of separate incidents or
episodes, not in the links between them that, together with the details,
build up a plot. Moreover, the episodes in an epic are more or less
stereotyped expressions—clichés—such that given a key word or two
the details of a whole standard episode come effortlessly to the storyteller's mind, and given a key incident or two an entire epic can be constructed and told with eloquent fluency. Important to any speaker's
art is not coherence or originality but fluency and copiousness. *Copia*,
in Latin rhetoric, means "flow" or "abundance." Hesitancy in speech
is a defect. Concision, a virtue in writing, is a vice in speech because
words and ideas must be repeated if they are to be understood and
must come out in a torrent if they are to convince.[35] As Pliny the
Younger (61–113) put it, "It is the copious, the majestic, and the sublime orator, who thunders, who lightens, who, in short, bears all before him in a confused whirl."[36]

A happy group of human beings chatting away on the front porch
in a summer evening is, to a passerby, a pool of bright sounds that
ripple back and forth and of dark indistinct figures whose edges fuse.
Sounds envelop. Voices enjoin, even when raised in argument. De-
baters challenging each other are, like wrestlers, locked in combat.
Against these images of togetherness are those of solitude: a writer at
work and a reader reading silently in a corner of the library. Speech
is universal and natural to human beings. Writing, by contrast, is limited to certain cultures and unnatural in its loneliness, its silence, its
associations with death. Writing, Ong reminds us, cuts and dismembers.
"Stylus" means originally a stake, a spearlike instrument, and "scribe"
has its root meaning in the Proto-Indo-European word *skeri*, to cut
and separate. Writing calls for reflection. Rather than allowing ideas
to flow copiously, as in ideal speech and as life itself may be said to

Ambience and Sight

pour forth in unremitting abundance, a writer at work can and does pause frequently to prune and trim, to discriminate and discard, to constrain facts and ideas into a coherent pattern, a logical sequence, a consistent perspective.

Reading, unlike writing, can be an event in a public occasion. Cultivated Romans had books read to them while they feasted. Moreover, people in ancient times were accustomed to read aloud to themselves. Libraries, of which Rome had twenty-nine in the fourth century A.D., were not necessarily havens of silence.[37] We take unvocalized reading for granted; Augustine, however, was startled to see Ambrose reading soundlessly to himself.[38] A book contains the world of a single author, a world the reader enters and explores in the privacy of her room. In modern society, reading is widely accepted as a uniquely private act. The printed page, while it is silently read, belongs to one person and to no other. When the television is on, people feel free to congregate and watch the small screen, but in a crowded train, riders look furtively at the *Times* over the shoulder of its one rightful owner. We may reiterate our theme: sound, as in the voice of a storyteller, unites; sight, as in silent reading, isolates.

In the last four chapters we have explored wholes—the wholes of communal living, activities, and sensorial ambiences—and their segmentation, the process of segmentation being bound to a developing sense of self. This awareness of individuality and of self is a topic that appears repeatedly throughout the book. It is now time to gather the threads and discuss the nature of the self more systematically, before posing the last question, which is concerned with people's deliberate efforts to design and make wholes. To what extent can such conscious attempts at reintegration succeed?

SELF

7

Self

Western culture encourages an intense awareness of self and, compared with other cultures, an exaggerated belief in the power and value of the individual. The rewards of such awareness and belief are many, including the sense of independence, of an untrammeled freedom to ask questions and explore, of being clear-eyed, without illusion, rational, and personally responsible. The obverse is isolation, loneliness, a sense of disengagement, a loss of natural vitality and of innocent pleasure in the givenness of the world, and a feeling of burden because reality has no meaning other than what a person chooses to impart to it. This isolated, critical and self-conscious individual is a cultural artifact. We may well wonder at its history. Children, we know, do not feel and think thus, nor do nonliterate and tradition-bound peoples, nor did Europeans in earlier times.

Children take the world for granted. A precocious child may ask astute philosophical questions, such as what happens to the house when he is in bed and asleep, but the question cannot be pursued and does not lead to radical doubt. Children, in general, accept reality as given: what is has always been, or it was made at one time by God or some other powerful person for good reasons that need not be questioned. In the first few years of life, children's sense of self is still uncertain. They find it easier to describe themselves in the third person, objectively, than in the first person, subjectively. Until about the age of three, a child finds it easier to say, "Paul wants a ride," than "I want a ride." Emotions and feelings are projected outward. The world, richly endowed with the child's own moods, seems alive and there-fore capable of responding directly and personally to the child's needs and fantasies. In the excitement of a game, a stick becomes a horse and an overturned chair a fort to be defended. Yet, outside the con-text of play, children can be very matter-of-fact, more so than edu-cated adults. When children four to six years old are shown pictures of people—some crying, others laughing or looking angry—and asked to tell what they see, they are far more likely to provide factual an-swers of "man," "woman," "uncle," auntie," than "that man (or woman) is crying or laughing." Likewise, when young children are shown landscape paintings and asked whether the landscapes can be classified under the categories of "happy," "sad," or "neutral," they are baffled and may reply sensibly that landscapes cannot be either "happy" or "sad."[1] The evidence suggests that young children are not prepared to treat people as subjects with feelings and problems of their own; they also lack the ability to attribute mood to an inani-mate thing as an expressive or aesthetic quality that can exist inde-pendently of how the perceiver momentarily feels. In other words, the poetry of a small child's world lies more in action and the felt moment than in contemplative thought.

Young children are not acutely self-conscious. They lack the capac-ity to see self from the viewpoint of another. The distinction between self and other is not clearly drawn, and indeed a major feature of their world is that boundaries are flexible and infirm, including those between animate and inanimate, fact and fiction, reality and fantasy. Almost anything is possible; almost anything can happen. The world is fluid—not defined, segmented, and specialized as it is to an adult. At least one reason for this difference, we have already noted, is chil-dren's greater dependence on the emotion-laden proximate senses of touch and smell, and on the spatially unfocused sense of hearing, as distinct from sight. Moreover, compared with adults, children display greater synesthetic tendencies. Synesthesia is the blending of sensory experiences. The most common varieties are visual images aroused by sounds: when a child or an adult synesthete hears a sound he or she may also see a colored image. In extreme cases, a sound can call forth not only an image but a sense of touch and of taste as well. An obvious disadvantage of synesthesia is that it causes hallucination. The advantages are two. The world seems richer, more filled with rewarding stimuli; we remember our own childhood as irradiated with a brightness, a sensory splendor, that has dimmed with time. Another advantage of synesthesia is that it aids memory: an event is more likely to stay in the mind if it is not only an image but also a sound and an odor. To young children, whose vocabulary is limited, synesthesia helps to fixate experiences so that they can be grasped. As children come to depend more on language to perform this function their synesthetic power declines.[2]

The world begins to lose a little of its enveloping and diffuse wholeness once the child starts to use his expanding lexicon to differentiate and structure reality, and to interpose a system of symbols between self and direct experience. The process of distancing from the world and segmenting it is, of course, a gradual one. Words, not recognized in childhood as symbols, are the things they designate. It is natural for the child, and indeed for the adult most of the time, to regard words as properties of nature, not elements of a secondary nature created by human beings. Nonetheless, the child in picking up a more sophisticated and specialized vocabulary lives increasingly in a segmented and differentiated world; and that which the child isolates and differentiates includes people, classes of people, and ultimately the self. How far this process is allowed to continue varies with different human groups, but the trend is universal: it is what growing up means.[3]

In nonliterate cultures, the boundary between self and society is much less sharply drawn than it is in complex urban civilizations and particularly in Western civilization. The French anthropologist Dominique Zahan, characterizing African thought, writes: "To define the self, we separate it from the other, whereas in Africa the opposite is the rule." The African tends to define himself by that which he receives from others at any moment. His self is more social than individual. "This explains in part the real feeling of inadequacy often manifested by an ethnographer's informants since they deem themselves capable of furnishing testimony only when they feel supported by other members of their lineage." Single persons, unless they are celibate and live alone for ritual purposes, are treated with contempt and may even be ostracized by their own families. Celibacy constitutes an incomprehensible deviation from the accepted social and religious norm. A corollary of this emphasis on society and the social role is the weakly developed sense of the self as an integral entity. The individual psyche is not an undivided whole. Widespread in Africa, according to Zahan, is the belief that "the self possesses a point of fission, probably situated at the border of the conscious and the unconscious," and that this trait assures a person of a wide range of parahuman possibilities, including "the ability to be in two places at once, clairvoyance, and metamorphoses."[4]

To explore more deeply into the African idea of self, we may turn to two societies, the Dinka of the central Nile basin in the southern Sudan and the Tswana of Botswana and South Africa. In modern life the psychohistory of an individual, the drama of his or her mind, can seem very real and vivid to that individual, compared with which the external world is pallid and abstract. Almost the opposite would be true for the Dinka. All the drama and significance lie in external events; the self other than these events—these manifestations of power—is so bare of content as to be nonexistent. The objective dominates the subjective, as the whole dominates the parts, and what really matters are the objective and the whole, not the subjective and the individual. "The Dinka," writes the English anthropologist Godfrey Lienhardt, "have no conception which at all closely corresponds to our popular modern conception of the 'mind,' as mediating and, as it were, storing up experiences of the self." So what we should call the memories of experiences, "and regard as in some way intrinsic and interior to the remembering person . . . appear to the Dinka as exteriorly acting upon him. . . . Hence it would be impossible to suggest to Dinka that a powerful dream was 'only' a dream, and might for that reason be dismissed as relatively unimportant in the light of day." What, then, happen to the feelings—those of guilt and envy, for instance—that the Dinka, like all human beings, unavoidably have? The answer is that these feelings are expelled from the experiencing self to the external world. Because a sense of guilty indebtedness can come to the debtor suddenly (as memories often do), he finds it reasonable to interpret that unpleasant feeling as a Power directed at him by the creditor. Likewise, an envious man, not recognizing the envy in himself, easily transfers his experience of it to another person who thereby assumes the visage of a witch. The outside world, thus loaded with projected moods and passions, comes alive—a dense-textured, vivid, but often also frightening place.[5]

Compared with the Dinka, the Tswana have a stronger sense of self and of individual differences. The Tswana consider human nature to be unfathomable and unpredictable. They have proverbs of the following sort: "Unlike a field (which you can come to know every part of), you can never know a man"; and "smiling teeth kill," which means that a person can act one way and think in another. The Tswana also say that every person is made differently, that even people born of the same parents do not exhibit the same thoughts or feelings. Individuality is clearly recognized, but it is feared and suppressed. To be alone is unthinkable. "A person is a person by virtue of people." "We are human because of the way we are brought up and live with others." Society and fate severely limit what one can be and do. An individual has no control over the direction of his life. The Tswana say, for example, that "chieftainship cannot be bought (for oneself); you must be born into it." Choices exist, but their effect is either inconsequential or bad. People have the freedom to do as they please, but freedom is a temptation that leads almost invariably to the breaching of a custom rather than an opportunity that can be used to the advantage of both self and society. In child training, effort is directed toward producing a conforming and industrious person. Innovative behavior and the critical attitude are actively discouraged. Absent is the idea of developing a child's "whole personality." Without a positive, prideful sense of self, the Tswana lack any conception of unilateral moral obligations, wherein a person sets a standard and insists on abiding by it whatever other people think. Moral obligations are bilateral among the Tswana as legal obligations are in Western society. What a person must or must not do is always a social decision.[6]

The development of a sense of self, we have seen, is closely tied to the evolution of a world that is progressively more complex, specialized, and segmented. Space, time, and society are the principal categories that have been subjected to the processes of division and subdivision. But the differentiating mind has operated in the psychological realm as well. Consider aspiration, judgment, and value. In the Western world, the structure of aspiration is divided into means and ends, desires and goals; the structure of judgment is divided into success or failure, and that of value into practical and aesthetic.

Such distinctions are nonexistent or blurred in the thought of the Tswana. Their psychological world is far less sundered. In the West, desire belongs to the realm of dreams. What one wants may be a distant goal that can never be quite reached. In Setswana (the language of Tswana), the expression "to want" implies that some action is intended that either comprises what one wants, or will lead to what one wants. For the Tswana, "to want" is "to want to do," and "doing" denotes an activity that already contains the value of a desire. The Tswana are self-subsistent farmers and pastoralists. Their livelihood requires many kinds of work, nearly all of which are regarded as desirable. A similar union of means and ends occurs in the Tswana's notion of success, which implies qualities of coping as much as fruition. The route to success is itself a kind of success. Falling short of fruition is counted a disappointment rather than a failure, and almost surely it does not provoke a deeply personal sense of failure, because the achievement is a specific condition dictated by a group's beliefs, not by an individual's yearning. Moreover, the Tswana consider the family to be their paramount achievement. This means that what gives them the greatest pride and satisfaction is necessarily a closely meshed cooperative effort, one in which individual aspirations must be subordinated to the common good. Unlike people of urban culture, the Tswana do not see the practical and the aesthetic as distinct, often incompatible, values. Cultivating fields and husbanding cattle are works of such merit that, Hoyt Alverson reports, "the oral literature of the Tswana is filled with their apotheosis. Many of the oral accounts of husbandry and agriculture are purely aesthetic expressions making no reference to economic importance." When the people speak of the "beauty of Botswana," they mean the richness and fecundity of their habitat.[7] We have noted that the Tswana are keenly aware of differences among human individuals and of the unfathomable (hence also

unpredictable) nature of the self. We then see that their culture is ef-
ficiently designed to make the suppression of this knowledge possible.

Examples of how nonliterate peoples conceive of society and self
can easily be multiplied. A particularly revealing study is Dorothy Lee's
work on the Wintu Indians who live in northern California. Lee observes that their concept of self lacks boundedness. "With the Wintu,
the self has no strict bounds, is not named and is not, I believe, recognized as a separate entity." The self is at most a concentration, which
gradually fades and gives place to another. "For example, the Wintu
do not use *and* when referring to individuals who are, or live or act
together. Instead of analyzing the *we* into *John and I*, they say *John
we*, using the John as a specification." To the modern mind, society
is an aggregate of individuals and the self is analyzable into its component parts of head, body, and limbs. To the Wintu mind, society is
the basic unit; it is not a plurality of individuals. And the self is an
integral physical entity, not the sum of its constituent parts. The
Wintu's stress on society as an unpartitioned whole makes it reasonable to believe, for example, that "a man will lose his hunting luck
if he goes on a hunt while his wife is menstruating." A man is at one
with his wife in a way that is difficult for modern people to appreciate. And because the self is considered to be a whole the Wintu "does
not say *my head aches*; he says *I head ache*. He does not say *my hands
are hot*; he says *I hands am hot*." The physical self is an entity. What
about the interior or psychological self? The Wintu avoid references
to the interior. They regard, for example, action and feeling as phenomena with outward aspects that can be observed, rather than as
kinesthetic and emotional experiences of the self or as mental states
subject to introspection. Thus the word for "wade" is "to-make-a-
great-splashing." Feelings are seldom articulated directly. Expressions
such as "she is furious" and "he was happy" are extremely rare. Love
songs do not refer to the emotions of love but to their objective correl-
atives: love means "the sleeping place which you and I hollowed out
will remain forever." So thoroughly are the Wintu embedded in the
whole (the smaller whole of society and the larger whole of nature)
that they have great difficulty speaking about the individual self.
Dorothy Lee writes:

When I asked Sadie Marsh for her autobiography, she told me a story about her first husband, based on hearsay. When I insisted on her own life history, she told me a story which she called, "my story." The first three quarters of this, approximately, are occupied with the lives of her grandfather, her uncle and her mother before her birth; finally, she reaches the point where she was "that which was in my mother's womb," and from then on she speaks of herself, also.[8]

The West needs to be contrasted with a civilization of similar size and complexity. For this purpose, we may turn to China, a country with a long literary tradition in which biographies and autobiographies abound. Yet such works, compared with those in the West, are notably deficient in soul-searching, in that intense awareness of the ambiguities and ambivalences of the self that can be found in certain Western works, beginning with Augustine's *Confessions*.[9] A civilization, unlike simpler cultures, is constrained to acknowledge explicitly the problems of society and individual, and to review periodically the relationship of the whole to its parts. Chinese social thought, which arises out of the need to respond to actual and potential conflicts in life and institutions, lays stress on the individual's obligations to society. On the other hand, it recognizes that social well-being can result only from the cultivation of the individual. In a fundamental sense, self and society are mutually dependent. The self is to grow into the fullness of manhood, even sagehood, through public service and social participation. The sage does not stand apart from society; he is fully a member of it. And somehow this virtuous integration of the self with society entails also integration with the universe or nature.[10]

Confucians see no conflict between self, society, and nature. Within the Confucian tradition, certain kinds of individualism are possible and indeed encouraged. Excellence, for example, is encouraged in literature and the arts even when their practitioners depart from the canons. The Sung period (960–1279) saw an unprecedented blossoming of individual interests and tastes in art and culture among members of the gentry, the scholar-officials at the core of the establishment. A person can even espouse heterodox views and still remain in the bosom of orthodoxy. The philosopher Wang Yang-ming (1472–1529) illustrates this point. He is strongly persuaded that the universal moral law is innate and that truth is attainable by intuitive means without the aid of the classics. Nonetheless, as Theodore de Bary points out, "it does not even occur to Wang that there could be any essential conflict between subjective and objective morality, or that genuine introspection could lead to anything other than the affirmation of clear and common moral standards."[11] However much he stresses the intuitive path to truth, his outlook remains Confucian, with its underlying assumption of the integral harmony of self, society, and universe.

Individualism and self-consciousness gained importance in China from circumstances present also in other civilizations and from circumstances unique to the Chinese case. Generally speaking, civilizations are enormously complex hierarchies and networks of exchange in which conflicts between individuals and between groups are unavoidable. These conflicts promote awareness by highlighting the differences between self and other, "us" and "them." Moreover, civilizations are driven by ambitious people, whose ideology of achievement sets up competitive tensions in all spheres of life where these people have an influence. Achievement presupposes a cult of excellence; and excellence, unlike harmony, is inherently an aggressive and individualistic virtue.

A characteristic of civilization is that people must periodically make elaborate and explicit plans to run bureaucracies and build monuments. Plans call for systematic thought, and systematic thought can reveal flaws of reasoning, inconsistencies, and even irresolvable paradoxes that escape the looser cogitations of people in an oral culture. Being forced to confront inconsistencies and paradoxes in one's plans and projects can lead one to question more fundamental beliefs. At this stage awareness becomes painful.

The city is a striving after excellence, a monumental achievement of civilization. It is in the city that high pretensions to social harmony and intellectual coherence are likely to occur; yet it is also there that conflicts are most evident. To avoid the stress and strain of urban living, its confusion constantly mocking its claims to order, sensitive souls escape the city for self-cultivation, for communion with nature, or to search for immortality. Wherever dense urban life exists, we are likely to find yearnings for solitude in a natural setting. Taoism answers this need in China. Unlike Confucianism, it excludes society from its schema of harmonious relationship between man and nature. Social coherence is impossible when Taoism takes an extreme relativistic position with regard to morality. In the Taoist classic *Chuang Tzu* (ca. 300 B.C.), we already encounter the idea that "right" and "wrong" are just words that people apply to the same thing, depending on the partial viewpoint from which they see it. "For each individual there is a different 'true' and a different 'false.'"[12] Only nature or the Tao has integrity and a transcendent value; all else is either trivial or relative. The Taoist's faith (its naiveté, perhaps) lies in the belief that it is possible to know this Tao without human distortion.

Self-awareness is exacerbated by loneliness and the feeling of personal vulnerability. In China, people commonly associate loneliness with enforced separation and spatial barrier. For a variety of causes, the Chinese may find himself or herself separated from family, friend, or lover. One cause is war. Men are sent to guard distant frontier posts in barren steppes. Another is exile. When a high official falls out of imperial favor he is banished to a frontier province, which to the exile is an utter desolation compared with the cultivated life he has known in the capital. Even in good times, the Chinese seem acutely aware of geographical distance. Aspiring young scholars go to the capital to take examinations, on the successful outcome of which their futures depend. Magistrates are sent to serve in strange cities, far away from their home towns, to minimize the opportunities for favoritism. Young brides are removed from the seclusion and security of their homes to live among strangers in the husband's household. China is a densely settled country, yet to read its poems is to be aware, not of crowding, but of great open spaces—endless mountains and rivers—that keep kinsfolk and friends apart, forcing the isolated member to reflect on the loneliness of self.

Nostalgia, James Liu says, is a major theme in Chinese poetry. Another is time. Unlike the modern West, the Chinese idea of time is cyclical rather than linear. In common with agricultural peoples throughout the world, the Chinese derive their sense of temporal pattern from the periodicities of nature and especially from those of the seasons. However, a significant difference between civilized and nonliterate people is that the former have more reason to be aware of time as an irretrievable passing, as having a direction that cannot be reversed. Civilized life requires the making of plans that project beyond the proximate future. Monuments take years to build and are clear markers of time, both in the stages of their creation and in the stages of their decay. Moreover, in a large country like China, friends separated by official duties know that they may never see each other again. Experiences may not be repeatable. Though nature effortlessly replays its scenes, an individual's life is a single journey that ends in death. Hundreds of Chinese poems lament the fading of spring and the coming of autumn because they are reminders of human transcience. Old age, ending in death, inexorably isolates the self from society. When a philosophical Taoist withdraws from society, it is so that he can identify with the Tao of nature. To an educated Chinese not so philosophically inclined, nature offers no such consolation. On the contrary, its declining phases constantly suggest his own demise, with the difference that a human life, once ended, cannot be renewed. The human individual is ultimately alone, separate from both society and nature.[13]

Individualism in artistic expression, we have noted, was prominent in the Sung period. Individual assertiveness and preoccupation with self were even more visible and widespread during the later part of the Ming dynasty (1368–1644). The emergence of a vernacular literature is both a symptom and a cause. For the first time, educated readers of novels and short stories are confronted by colorful characters drawn from all layers of society. Human passions from the ridiculous to the sublime are depicted in explicit detail. Repressed desires and violence, sordidness and obscenity, inadmissible in classical literature, can be described in the novel, which has roots in the folk art of the professional storyteller.[14]

In the late Ming period, well-educated people themselves no longer felt bound to the more restrictive rules of proper social behavior. Intellectuals who scorned officialdom sought to lead a life that was totally free. For them this meant not only espousing unorthodox ideas but also indulging openly in the pleasures of wine and women. A supreme individualist of the time was Li Chih (1527–1602). His family background in commerce and Islamic religion might have prepared him to question the traditional values of the scholar-gentry class, but most Chinese of similar background, though their behavior could be judged somewhat unorthodox by strict Confucian standards, did not become iconoclasts, and certainly not of the extreme stripe that was Li Chih. Already a skeptic in his youth, he seems little influenced by the practices and beliefs of Islam. Though given a classical Confucian training, he did not take to it and was in fact repelled by anything and anyone identified with an organized creed. Attracted to Buddhism, he became a monk, but an unlicensed monk who did not submit to Buddhist discipline and indeed led a rather wild life and was accused of sexual misconduct. Mere eccentricity in behavior could be dismissed as that of a harmless madman. Li, however, was also a serious scholar who wrote books that argued in favor of individual freedom, of letting people satisfy their own desires and find their natural place in the world without harassment by busybodies—the humanitarians (*jen-che*). His most dangerous views were those on morality. "Yesterday's right is today's wrong. Today's wrong is right again tomorrow." Li's greatest threat to Confucianism was that he used historical scholarship to undermine morality's claim to unchanging values. Society as the Chinese knew it would obviously break down if Li's ideas enjoyed any currency. The authorities were sufficiently alarmed to proscribe Li's books and send Li to prison, where he committed suicide by cutting his own throat.[15]

A civilization, with its high concentration of people, its specialized activities and complex institutions, is bound to nurture a colorful range of human types. Although the recognition of this human diversity in literature is not inevitable, it did occur in China in the novels of the Ming and Ch'ing dynasties. In addition, colorful statesmen, warriors, philosophers, artists, and eccentrics adorn other genres of writing, including essays, memoirs, and histories. China has its share of assertive and introspective individuals. But individualism as it is known in the West, whether manifest in guaranteed freedoms and rights, or in extreme forms of alienation, failed to develop. Modern scholars have often noted that Chinese individualism lacked institutional support. China did not have a strong middle-class, a vigorous capitalism, a church that fought against the state for its prerogatives, and competing religions that argued for the primacy of conscience in confrontation with authority. We should also note that commitment to the social seems to be a deeply ingrained trait of the Chinese people. Confucianism did not create it, but rather built on it. The gentry actively sought public office. They became Taoists and withdrew to private life in their country estates only when they fell out of favor. Of course, true recluses of Taoist or Buddhist persuasion existed. They were committed, however, to lose the self in union with something else, whether this were the Tao of nature or Nirvana. What the Chinese do not seem to know, at least to judge from the literary evidence, is the condition of profound and sustained ennui or anomie—a total detachment from every object, person, and ideal. In the Chinese novel, characters of extreme heroism and villainy abound, but both kinds pursue their chosen courses with gusto. In the domestic novels, it is true, we often encounter women characters deprived of the challenges of work and satisfactions of sex. "The destructiveness of these frustrated creatures," writes C. T. Hsia, "can be truly frightening, but none arrives at the conclusion that life is meaningless and settles for an existence of amused boredom." The Chinese imagination finds it difficult to conceive of a self totally detached from society's values. With all its horrors and crudities, life is never simply absurd—one insipid thing after another, leading nowhere. Chinese fiction boasts a wide cast of characters, but it has not invented anyone like Dostoevsky's Underground Man or Camus's Stranger.[16]

Individualism, self, and self-consciousness—these and other related concepts are supremely the products of Western culture. In the West, the self has grown apart from others in prideful and nervous sufficiency. We are islands, each a world of its own; or, to use Goethe's metaphor, billiard balls, hard individuated objects that touch each other only at the surface. Islands and billiard balls suggest the qualities of boundedness and separation, though not of other key attributes of the individual, which include the idea that the self is the repository of experience, the source of feeling, knowledge, and action. So much emphasis can be put on the individual as maker and perceiver that the external world loses its objective standing: reality "out there" seems to be only a human construct.

These ideas evolved slowly and falteringly over the long span of the European past. In the Archaic age of Greece (750–500 B.C.) the self, like the self of many primitive peoples, lacks subjectivity. It responds to circumambient forces; it rarely initiates and its consciousness is unreflective. The self does not see itself performing an action, weighing and judging it. The self is one, not "one" as the result of reflection but "one" because experiences are unexamined. Without introspection, the self is undivided, and is certainly not felt as divided against itself. A commonly recognized split in the self is that between body and soul. Homeric man, however, has no unified concept of what we call "soul" or "personality." E. R. Dodds writes: "Homer appears to credit man with a *psyche* only after death, or when he is in the act of fainting or dying or is threatened with death: the only recorded function of the psyche in relation to the living man is to leave him."[17] Homeric man, it would appear, introspects only in extremis; near death he is aware of some separate essence abandoning the body. Although in Homer's thought psyche plays only a marginal role in a living person, the poet does recognize *thymos* as the generator of motion or agitation, and *noos* as the cause of ideas and images. However, thymos and noos are almost physical organs like the stomach. Postulating them does not imply the existence of spiritual entities different from the body. We still use expressions such as "I have no stomach for it," where the word "stomach" stands for something obviously physical, but also psychic.

An unmistakable individual voice, using the first person singular "I," first appeared in the works of lyric poets. Archilochus, who lived in the first half of the seventh century B.C., sang his own unhappy love rather than assume the role of a spectator describing the frustrations of love in others. When Archilochus characterized his thymos as "stirred up with suffering," or said of his general that "he is full of heart," he had in mind an immaterial sort of soul, with which Homer was not acquainted. Even better proof of an increasing awareness of self and its complex structure, according to Bruno Snell, is the suspicion that feelings may be contradictory, that feelings do not merely alternate in time between "passion and tranquility, between good fortune and misery, but that the present mood itself contains the seeds of discord." Ambivalent feelings, rarely found in Homeric epics, are explicitly stated in the lyric poetry of Sappho (ca. 600 B.C.) and Anacreon (died ca. 500 B.C.). The expression "bitter-sweet love," which has become a sentimental cliché, was invented by Sappho. From Anacreon comes the line: "Again I love and love not; I rave, nor do I rave."[18]

In the fifth century, says Dodds, the ordinary Athenian still regarded the psyche or soul as perfectly at home in the body. The soul is the life of the body. At this time the psyche still denotes the emotional rather than the rational self. In Attic writers, as in their Ionian predecessors, "the *psyche* is spoken of as the seat of courage, of passion, of pity, of anxiety, of animal appetites, but before Plato seldom if ever as the seat of reason." When psyche is represented as a higher state, the split in the self becomes more evident. For thinkers enamored of pristine ideas, it is easy to regard the body as an alien tunic, a prison, or even a tomb, from which the soul will one day be freed.[19] Another consequence of regarding the psyche as reason is a gain in the interiority and self-motivating power of the self. The self endowed with reason acts by virtue of an indwelling power, and does not merely react to forces that enter it from the outside. Strong emotions seem external because we often feel helpless before them. The expression "falling in love or into passion" suggests this feeling of helplessness. We do not "fall into reason." With reason we have a sense of control, both of the self and of external circumstance.

The idea of a self in control does not appear in Homer's world, which is permeated by forces that impinge on man and penetrate the core of his being. Simone Weil, in her translation of the *Iliad*, aptly subtitled it "a poem of force." Different words for "force" are used in the Homeric epics to describe sensations and states such as the vitality in the limbs of a man burning to tackle a great project, the muscular strength of the body, the sway of the ruler, the power that enables a defensive group to ward off its enemy, and the supremacy of an idea. Every unusual human performance is credited to an external power, a god or goddess. Human beings may act but cannot truly initiate. Whatever of importance happens in the human sphere is caused by the transactions of the gods with one another. Not only does human endeavor lack a beginning, it also has no proper end.[20] The human story is not written by the human beings themselves.

This notion of external control is characteristic of primitive peoples who have survived into the twentieth century. Common to their thought patterns is the preeminence given to objective reality, to events taking place "out there," and the neglect of the subjective realm in which individuals by their feelings and thoughts maintain the world. Greeks in the Archaic age share another trait with primitive peoples, and that is their fear of pollution. This trait again underlines the importance of the objective world to the ancients. Pollution is the automatic consequence of an action. As such it belongs to the world of external events, and operates with the same indifference to motive as does a typhoid germ. By contrast, sin is a perversion of the will, a disease of the inner consciousness. The idea of sin cannot appear without the idea of an inner responsible self. Whereas Achilles placed the responsibility of his decision on his goddess, fifth-century man, conscious of his freedom, proudly took upon himself the responsibility for his choice. Dodds observes: "Not until the closing years of the fifth century do we encounter explicit statements that clean hands are not enough—the heart must be clean also."[21]

The individual emerged as two major institutions underwent change during the Greek Archaic age. One was the family, the keystone of the archaic social structure. The head of a household was like a king in that he enjoyed unlimited and unquestioned authority over his children. By the sixth century, however, Solon had introduced certain safeguards circumscribing paternal power. The institution of the family remained repressively authoritarian throughout the archaic period, but toward the end, signs of discord began to appear. Voices other than the father's were heard. By the fifth century, with the rise of the Sophistic movement, generational differences and conflicts were openly expressed. Young men went so far as to claim that they had a "natural right" to disobey their fathers. The other major institutional change occurred in government. Kingship was eliminated, and in its place that characteristically Greek communal structure known as the *polis* (city-state) gradually emerged.[22] In its classical form, the polis required the action—the initiating act—of free citizens. Individuals, endowed with rights, asserted themselves. But they did so always for the common good. Despite gains in the idea of individual worth, what truly counted was the social whole. In classical thought from Plato to Cicero, "the whole is prior to the parts, is better than the parts, and is that for the sake of which the parts are, and wherein they find the meaning of their existence."[23] A strong support for the idea and reality of the whole was religion with its binding values and public rituals. Traditional Greek religion enforced social cohesion. Religion itself bore all the marks of an official institution. Temples were dedicated to the civic gods. Priests were civic magistrates. "On certain days," writes André-Jean Festugière, "all the citizens, in a body, men, women, and children, gather before the temple for a solemn sacrifice. . . . Athena is the goddess of Athens, of the Athenians considered as a social entity, before being the goddess of the Athenian as a private individual."[24]

Individualism in ancient Greece took various forms: in the assertion of rights, in the exercise of one's freedom to choose and initiate, in speaking with one's own voice, articulating one's personal and sometimes ambivalent feelings. The rules and customs of society were challenged by this growth in consciousness and self-consciousness, and modified to suit individual needs and dispositions. Some philosophers, however, carried their questioning to an extreme, sparing no institution or belief. Hecateus (fl. 500 B.C.) examined Greek mythology and found it "funny." He was apparently the first to do so. Xenophanes (ca. 570–480) discovered the relativity of religious ideas. "If the ox could paint a picture, his god would look like an ox." Heraclitus (ca. 535–475), with the words "dead is nastier than dung," deeply insulted Greek piety. He also attacked the popular cult of images, which he compared with talking to a man's house rather than to its owner. Enlightened skepticism was carried further by a later generation of speculative scientists like Anaxagoras (ca. 500–428) and Democritus (ca. 460–370), and by Sophists, particularly Protagoras (ca. 480–410), who thought a new art of living could be created if all the "barbarian silliness" were removed from the traditions. But the ultimate challenge to society — this whole that presumes to be greater than its parts — is to question its system of moral beliefs. And this the tragic poet Euripides (ca. 480–406) had done when he wrote in *Aeolus*: "There is nothing shameful but thinking makes it so"—a remark that was addressed to incest.[25]

Individualism flourished in the Hellenistic age. The sudden expansion of the spatial and cultural horizons that accompanied Alexander's conquests had the effect of broadening the mind. While science became more systematic, transcending its philosophical roots, philosophy itself fragmented into separate schools, which then contended vigorously with each other. "Despite the lack of political freedom," Dodds notes, "the society of the third century B.C. was in many ways the nearest approach to an 'open' society that the world had yet seen, and nearer than any that would be seen again until very modern times"[26] In the Hellenistic age, full but largely conventional participation in the life of the polis had ended. A bureaucratic State took over, making political tasks no longer the center of the citizen's concern. He could still choose to participate in politics, of course, as well as in the many other kinds of activity that a large and complex civilization offered. But, whereas in the past a citizen's many functions were given a unified meaning by the nature of the polis, in the third century B.C. and later, an educated man, to lead a full life, must himself select and integrate those activities that appealed to him. In other words, as communal cohesion weakened, the development of an integrated personality must proceed largely from within.[27]

In the polis or city-state, religion and public life were so tightly interlocked that injury to the one would have quick repercussions on the other. Both public religion and public life declined during the Hellenistic period. Uneducated people turned to the cult of minor gods, such as Asclepius who was thought to possess the magical power of healing, and to the cult of Tyche, "Luck" or "Fortune."[28] Educated people turned to a personal religion, one that supposed a direct compact between the cosmos and the self, by way of the mind, without the mediation of public rites. An individual's religion was thus freed from the bonds of community and place. A person had access to the stars wherever he was. His dignity and freedom lay in his mind and in the peace of his soul. A majority of philosophical pagans held this view from the third century B.C. to the fifth century A.D. Geography, the intermediate scale between the self and the cosmos, must be transcended. A common theme of Stoic thinkers was that place did not matter, that external circumstances counted for little. Seneca (3 B.C.-A.D. 65) wrote: "It is your soul you must change, not your environment." And, "Where one lives means little for one's peace of soul; it is the mind that must render all things agreeable to itself."[29] Marcus Aurelius (121–180) wrote: "Men seek retreats for themselves, houses in the country, seashores, and mountains; and you are wont to desire such things very much. But this is altogether a mark of the most common sort of men, for it is in your power to retire into yourself wherever you choose. . . . I affirm that tranquillity is nothing else than the good ordering of the mind." Compared with this tranquil and ordered mind, "the universe is transient, and life is opinion."[30]

Without doubt the foremost exemplar of a fully conscious and self-conscious individual in late antiquity was Augustine (354–430). On the one hand, Augustine as a neo-Platonist and student of Cicero embodied classical learning, including the philosopher's perennial bias in favor of the powers of the individual mind to apprehend and transcend reality; on the other, he combined a Christian's awareness of guilt and the taint of sin with a unique appreciation of the workings of sin in the cumulative experiences of a person's life. Augustine's explorations of self are modern in so many ways that we tend to forget that he was not afflicted by modern man's radical doubts and alienation. Throughout his adult life Augustine was steeped in faith, first as a Manichee, later as a Christian and a bishop fighting heresies with the utmost vigor. Augustine wanted seculsion, a life of study and prayer among a few friends and disciples; yet he accepted what he called "the burdens of the episcopate" and administered a large African diocese for thirty-five years. Augustine's total scholarly output, some two hundred and thirty-two titles, is a monument to the mind. Thinking calls for solitude. Yet, Peter Brown notes, "Seldom do we find him thinking alone: usually he is 'talking on such subjects to my friends.'"[31]

Augustine, though a good Platonist, found the exchange of ideas through correspondence unfulfilling. He yearned for the physical presence of his friends. His gregarious temperament, public office, and belief in objective truth all placed him in the midst of the world and its activities. Yet Augustine also turned inward. The world in the guises of society, nature, and even friends could not entirely satisfy. Society lacks truth. Its practices and customs are conventional. "Some are matters of superfluity and luxury, some of convenience and necessity." Institutions are what they are because people, from necessity or other reasons, have agreed to abide by certain rules. Culture therefore has no great claim on our allegiance.[32] As to nature, Augustine was indeed sensitive to its beauty. Still he marveled that people could be engrossed by the outer rather than the inner world. "Men go to gape at mountain peaks, at the boundless tides of the sea, the broad sweep of the rivers, the compass of the ocean, and the circuits of the stars; and yet they leave themselves unnoticed; they do not marvel at themselves."[33]

Lastly, there are the claims of friendship. Augustine enjoyed company but what he yearned for was the intimate call of one soul to another as in the City of God. That ideal could not be achieved on earth, certainly not in Hippo in the pastoral contacts between a very learned bishop and his illiterate flock. Peter Brown suggests that as "Augustine faced his congregation, perched up on his *cathedra*, he will realize how little he could ever penetrate to the inner world of the row of faces. . . . And his insistence on revealing his most intimate tensions in the *Confessions* is in part a reaction to his own isolation."[34] Even with kindred spirits, Augustine despaired that he could communicate all he felt, for a conversation to him meant dragging vivid thoughts "through the long, twisting lanes of speech." He was to conclude that people were perhaps too frail to bear the weight of revealing themselves to their fellows. Another difficulty lay in true self-knowledge. To reveal the self, there must be a self to reveal. Augustine became convinced that no man could ever sufficiently search his own heart, that "spreading, limitless room." What the conscious mind knows, accepts, and tries to govern might be only the surface of one's personality. "No one knows himself so well that he can be sure as to his conduct on the morrow."[35]

Yet no one in Augustine's time or earlier had explored human nature with the depth and subtlety of Augustine himself. We have noted that in the Hellenistic period individualism bloomed as old communal bonds began to break down. However, there was little knowledge of, or even interest in, the sources of human individuality. Insofar as people chose one line of conduct rather than another, it was to select and live by one system of philosophy among the several available at the time. The earlier Stoic philosophers did not appreciate human differences as such, because they were perceived as departures from the faculty of reason common to all men; and reason undergirded all morality. Later, the idea that people differed markedly in mental makeup, perhaps even more so than they did in bodily shape, was explicitly and favorably recognized. Cicero (106–43 B.C.), for example, opposed the view that differences in mental makeup were defects and blameworthy. On the contrary, "each must cling to that which is his own," and follow his own nature even if others were more admirable. Cicero, however, seems to have assumed personality or character as given.[36] Augustine's originality and modernity lie in seeing it as "a second nature" created by a person's past actions. To Augustine an individual's past is very much alive in his present. People are different from each other precisely because their wills are made different by the sum total of unique experiences and actions in the past.[37]

Augustine died in Hippo on August 28, 430, when the siege by the Vandal army was in its third month. This date suitably marks the beginning of the Dark Ages, which lasted some five hundred years.

The term "Dark Ages" arouses a certain malaise among modern historians for its blanket indictment of a long period in the past. But the term does accurately capture one general fact of that time, which is the dimming of self-consciousness—the nearly total absorption of the individual by the group. Historians have often commented on this phenomenon. They note, for example, the custom of collective punishments such as the interdict of a locality, or the amercements of villages and towns: communities were assumed to have a corporate character, and no one in authority bothered about how many innocent people suffered from these impositions. Historians also note the anonymity of writers, scholars, chancery personnel, architects, scribes, and so on. The medievalist Walter Ullmann writes in exasperation: "As often as not we are confronted with a *siglum* at the end of a gloss or of a *Summa*, but who was B? Who was M? . . . Who conceived Ely Cathedral? Who was the architect of Strasbourg Cathedral?" Hardly any personal correspondence has survived from the medieval period. Few anecdotal stories exist to give substance to major figures. We scarcely have any idea what the great kings and popes look like. To people in the Dark Ages, personalities were of little import; what mattered was the office, capable of being precisely measured by its own content. The office, allegedly of divine provenance, was objective, not of human making. It absorbed the individual.[38]

European society in A.D. 1000 was primitive and insecure. Insecurity called for unquestioning kinship bonds, acceptance of the idea of the objective norm, and the submergence of the self. But by the second half of the twelfth century, society had become more prosperous and open. People felt free to look around and feast their eyes on the enormous wealth of forms both natural and manmade in the world. At the same time, their eyes turned inward. The cultural milieu that favored knowledge of external nature also favored self-knowledge. Until the twelfth century, even the Church, curator of souls, showed far more concern with behavior than with intention; penances were attached to external acts rather than to internal states of mind. In 1135, however, Peter Abelard was able to write a book on ethics with the subtitle of "Know Thyself." For Abelard, sin lay solely in the intention. Monks of cenobitic or eremitic tradition developed the idea of self-knowledge as the path to God. Bernard of Clairvaux believed self-knowledge to be both the beginning and the end of the spiritual journey: "For you, you are the first; you are also the last." In the final analysis, religious experience is private and individual, known only to the Bridegroom and the soul. In the social sphere, medieval man in 1150 had career choices that were inconceivable during the earlier period called Dark. Self-regard and awarenesss rose to meet the demands of deliberative choice, which, for an ambitious young person, might occur in two stages. First, he had to decide whether he wanted to be a knight, a scholar, an administrator, or a monk. Then he had to face the fact that within each of these occupations there existed no simple, generally accepted ethic. Men debated at length over the nature of true knighthood and over the proper forms of monastic life.[39]

At the close of the thirteenth century, according to Jakob Burck-hardt, Italy began to swarm with people who were proud of being singular. Not only the tyrant asserted his individuality, but also the men he protected and used—the minister, secretary, poet, and com-panion, who were all determined to obtain the greatest satisfaction out of life in their brief period of power and influence. Fascination with the singular extended to locality. Patriots sang the praises of their own towns and cities. But this was not the deeply pious attach-ment to native soil known to the ancient Greeks and Romans. Renais-sance Italians were much more secular. Their poets wrote almost with tongue in cheek, mixing their laudations with barbed criticism and satire.

Cosmopolitanism and individualism are products of the same his-torical process. Allegiance to the cosmos means, in practice, no al-legiance—at least, no total commitment—to anything in particular on earth. Seneca and Marcus Aurelius, as Stoic philosophers, claimed cit-izenship in the whole world. This was also Dante's boast. When his recall to Florence was offered him on unworthy conditions, he wrote back: "Can I not everywhere meditate on the noblest truth, without appearing ingloriously and shamefully before the city and the people?" Artists exulted in their freedom from the constraints of residence. The sculptor Ghiberti (ca. 1378–1455) declared that "he who has learned everything is nowhere a stranger; robbed of his fortune and without friends, he is yet the citizen of every country." In the same strain an exiled humanist wrote: "Wherever a learned man fixes his seat, there is his home."

These statements reveal not only the pride of the individual but also the uncertainty of life and fortune in a period of great cultural efflorescence. Uncertainty created doubt in the operation of Divine justice. Self-assertion raised questions concerning the nature of that objective reality which placed reassuring limits on human endeavor. When freedom became a burden in the Hellenistic age, people turned to the cult of Luck or Fortune and to astrology. A similiar movement emerged during the Renaissance. As society underwent rapid change and fundamental Christian beliefs—including hope for immortality— wavered, men and women turned fatalistic or they sought certainty in the signs of the Zodiac. Astrology was not just the superstition of the common man: princes as well as free cities had their astrologers, and from the fourteenth to the sixteenth century, universities appointed professors of this pseudo-science to their faculties.[40]

Renaissance men took pride in their individuality and flaunted their differences on the public stage. At the same time, they sought privacy and pondered over the nature of the inner being. Those who could not stomach the stress and clamor of public life withdrew to their private estates in the country, and there occupied themselves with the family farm, quiet study, and leisurely conversation among friends. Even those bankers and merchants who lived in the heart of the city, who proclaimed their wealth and individuality in the size and design of their palaces, sought seclusion and private life in the private rooms and courtyards behind the monumental facades that lined the streets.[41]

Life in both the public and the private sphere confronted Reniassance man with the question of self and of the roles it could play. Many opportunities for advancement and applause were open to talented people. They might select one career rather than another. A choice must be made and yet it need not be confining. A person could be a scholar and an artist and still be the political emissary of a prince. One could play several roles in quick succession. If so, the question emerged as to whether an authentic self existed behind the various masks.

Stoic philosophers often linked morality with the human penchant for acting a part, which they disapproved of. Children, said Epictetus (ca. 50–138), are always switching roles. If you behave like children, "you will be at one time an athlete, at another a gladiator, then a rhetorician, then a philosopher, but with your whole soul you will be nothing at all." To Epictetus, a person's duty is to act well the part that is given, but to select the part belongs to another. "Do you wish to be a pentathlete or wrestler? Look at your arms, your thighs, examine your loins. For different men are formed by nature for different things."[42] There is comfort in the idea that what we are is beyond our willing. For the talented Renaissance man, however, the vocational choices are real. Society has made it possible for an individual to pick a part in which to play. Having decided to be one kind of person may only be the beginning of a problem, because Renaissance man can easily imagine himself in a different role. He has developed a habit of standing, as it were, outside or above his own personality, examining it critically. He is protean and schizophrenic.

Shakespeare's Hamlet is the great symbol of someone suffering from a crisis of identity. Hamlet's consciousness of playing a part that is in some sense alien to his real self appears as a theme in innumerable works of Renaissance and modern literature. Assuming that there is a real self, how does one find it? Montaigne's technique is, first of all, move to a place apart from the world. If the world is a theater of illusion, one's duty is to exit, to find a way of being elsewhere. For Montaigne personally, that elsewhere is his library. This solution may seem facile and unoriginal except that Montaigne knew well that solitude does not suffice. "It is not enough for a man to have sequestered himself from the concourse of people. . . . A man must also sever himself from the popular conditions that are in us. A man must sequester and recover himself from himself." The inner world, when we contemplate it, is not itself a unity but a phantasmagoric drama of conflicting parts. A sense of the true and unified self must be won, and it can be won, so Montaigne believed, by facing and noting the conflicts and changes; in other words, by writing an autobiography.[43]

Another reason for the growing concern in the Renaissance with the self and its roles is a sensitivity to the inevitable changes in an individual's life. Shakespeare put it well when he said that a "man in his time plays many parts, his acts being seven ages." Which age represents one's true self? Certainly not the "mewling and puking" infant, and just as surely not "the second childishness." But is it "the soldier full of strange oaths," or is it "the justice, in fair round belly with good capon lin'd"?[44] A writer explores the self in reflective essays and in autobiography, of which more and more began to appear in the course of the sixteenth century. A painter has another method of trying to fathom the self: painting self-portraits. To do so there must exist good mirrors; and indeed mirrors as their quality improved toward the end of the Middle Ages were themselves a cause of greater self-awareness.[45] Albrecht Dürer drew a picture of himself, with the help of a mirror, when he was thirteen years old. At least eight more self-portraits followed, in which Dürer cast himself in a large variety of roles, from the self-assured and handsome young man of 1493 to the nude "Man of Sorrows," with whip and scourge, of 1522. Which was the real Dürer?[46] In the seventeenth century, Rembrandt chased the elusive core of self even more obsessively, painting himself more than one hundred times, in different moods and roles, from youth to old age.[47]

Beginning in the sixteenth century, there appeared a decisive increase in the rate of social mobility, most especially in England but also in France. Lawrence Stone goes so far as to say that "between 1540 and 1643 English society experienced a seismic upheaval of unprecedented magnitude."[48] Horizontal mobility—the movement of individuals from one place to another and particularly to London—contributed to a sense of impending chaos. Whether this fluid social condition was viewed as threatening or as liberating depended on one's position in society and on one's ability to take advantage of the new opportunities to play new roles. Dissimulation, feigning, and pretense—execrable behavior in the eyes of medieval moralists—were viewed much more leniently in the sixteenth century. Machiavelli indeed recommended the play-actor's art to princes. For ordinary people, pretense and ingratiation were histrionic skills necessary to social and economic success. Until about a hundred and fifty years ago, society lacked respectable professions that would enable the ambitious to advance without having to descend to gross forms of flattery.[49] Even when such professions did become available, upward social mobility could still precipitate a lingering sense of guilt. Adaptability itself can seem an ambivalent virtue. As a person repeatedly changes places that is both geographical and social, the question arises again as to what is one's real self. A nostalgic answer, inconceivable to the ancient Stoic but characteristic of modern man, is that the authentic self is located in one's past—in unselfconscious childhood.

Social mobility gives an individual a sense of power to create his or her own position in the world. The world itself seems to lose a little of its givenness and objectivity, its essentially fixed character. It yields, after all, to one's ambitions, allowing one to rise and fall. The world may be viewed as society and as nature. Consider it first as society.

From the sixteenth century onward, the term society appears more and more often in literature and in speech. People see it as something of which they are a part but also as an external web of social agreements that they can critically examine. In this respect, the meaning of society differs radically from that of kingdom or nation.[50] A kingdom or nation seems to be more a growth of nature than a human contrivance. It possesses an organic coherence based on custom, that is, on the uncritically accepted beliefs and values of a people. Although countless individuals have contributed to a nation's tradition, yet the members of a nation can and do often feel that they are the recipients and mere beneficiaries of value rather than its curators and creators. By contrast, the use of the word *society* implies an acceptance of the idea that human groups are artificial entities, maintained by the wills and interests of individual actors. Human beings are members of a nation, subjects in a kingdom, citizens in a state, and players in society. We have here a spectrum. At one end is organic coherence, in which the whole is prior to and greater than its parts; at the other is an artificially constructed whole, sustained at every point by individual good will.

In a poem called "The Anatomy of the World," John Donne (1572–1631) noted:

> 'Tis all in pieces, all coherence gone;
> All just supply, and all relation:
> Prince, subject, father, son, are things forgot,
> For every man alone thinks he hath got
> To be a phoenix, and that then can be
> None of that kind, of which he is, but he.

Donne bemoaned the decay of social order and the vaunting pride of self. But it was of the firmament that he wrote the famous line, "'Tis all in pieces, all coherence gone." To the probing eye and mind of the sixteenth and seventeenth centuries, not only the social world but the greater world of nature showed signs of disorder and decay. It is worth noting that in this period Europeans made great gains in the use of sight. More and more ordinary houses sported large clear-glass windows, allowing light to flood in and dispel the age-old gloom. People could see better by wearing spectacles. Scientific optical instruments opened up nature at both ends of the scale. The gain in visual clarity and in the size of the visual world was exhilarating; on the other hand, it revealed hitherto unsuspected imperfections in nature. For example, until the seventeenth century, a common view held that whereas change and decay might be everywhere on earth and in the sublunary regions, beyond the orb of the moon the heavens remained as God made them. But in the supposedly immutable heavens, Galileo (Donne's contemporary) had discovered new stars and had found spots on the sun, arguing decay even on that majestic body. Kepler (1572–1630) dealt another blow to the old image of God's perfect design, by revealing that planets moved in ellipses rather than in perfect circles.[51]

Of course the human imagination both scientific and poetic could and did surmount the difficulties introduced by the new data. It was able to perceive order at a higher and more abstract level. However, the effort to do so suggests to thinking people that design is not simply a fact of reality that can be ascertained by merely opening the eyes; or that if it is, it may be illusory. To perceive true order in the midst of seeming disorder requires such persistence and ingenuity on the part of the human individual, including the invention of appropriate instruments and mathematical formulas if one were a scientist, that one begins to wonder whether one is not as much the creator as recorder of pattern in the universe.

Subjectivism is the hallmark of the modern age. Subjectivism grows with the conviction that reality is what we make of it. A source of this belief is the demonstrated human ability to transform nature for human ends. Terrestrial nature, instead of standing over people and dictating to them as a dominant power, yields to their initiative and rewards it abundantly. Nature as cosmos or as the totality of things still lies obviously beyond human control; yet we have just noted that it too can seem a human artifact because people with a reflective turn of mind are becoming more conscious of their own role in discerning its pattern. Does the pattern exist in external nature or does it exist only in the symbolic systems that humans use to describe nature? That this type of question can be raised by philosophers, artists as well as working scientists, suggests a blurring in their awareness of the boundary between what is really "out there" and what human beings construct materially and mentally.[52]

Nature and society, in the thinking of all human groups, are closely coupled. If even nature can seem artifactitious, then society is manifestly an artifact, created and maintained by people, subject to further change as its human constituents see fit. Society lacks an immutable nature because, in the final analysis, the individual is self-centered and protean. "Man makes himself and creates his own world" is a proud claim of modern times that continued to ring confidently in the first decade of the twentieth century. Since then we have become less sure of the rewards of such knowledge and power. The idea, long sensed but now clearly articulated, that what we take to be the world is largely the projection of our private compulsions, has robbed things and external events of their authority and solidity.[53] To the extent that the world loses its objective standing, much of its value and vitality also dissipate.

8

Self
and Reconstituted
Wholes

"Woe to him that is alone, for when he faileth he hath none to lift him up (Ecclesiastes 4:10)." That warning must be heeded by all, because human beings cannot be literally self-sufficient. We depend on others not only for survival but also for a sense of who we are. The illusion of self-sufficiency is, of course, possible. When the necessities of life are met without effort and when even certain luxuries appear daily, unasked, for our use, then it is easy to assume that we can be on our own and live in virtuous solitude apart from the contentious, hurly-burly world.

What does one do with solitude? Cato wrote: "Never is man more active than when he does nothing, never is he less alone than when he is by himself." This is true if one is a thinker. But few people are thinkers. Pascal wrote: "The king is surrounded by persons whose only thought is to divert the king, and to prevent his thinking of self. For he is unhappy, king though he be, if he thinks of himself."

In tracing the changes of the European house, we have noted its progressive segmentation. More and more rooms were added that enabled the householder and his family to withdraw for specialized activities and to be alone if they should so wish. The house itself stood apart from its neighbors. Aristocratic families wrapped themselves in palatial mansions on giant estates. As they lost political power they were also increasingly isolated from their own people—tenants, farmers, and laborers tied to them by tradition. Sumptuous social events in London and in great country houses filled their days, but these events too began to decline rapidly in number and liveliness in the course of the twentieth century. Roy Perrott, visiting an aristocrat of our time, noted from the palace window that lights began to twinkle from somewhere across the dark rolling sea of the park. "Yes: people without neighbors. That might be one definition of the landed lords." Like the novelist Anthony Powell, Perrott discerned a trait common among the aristocrats he visited—melancholy. "With few people close enough to distract them with pressure and demands, they had been cast in the role of contemplatives who seldom had the inner resources to find it satisfying."[1] This, Perrott thought, "was what the melancholia was all about."

Life that has grown too complex in the public sphere encourages people (not only aristocrats) to withdraw. The problem is how to withdraw without withdrawing from life; how to nurture a sense of self without losing touch with other people altogether; how to escape from the world and yet still be in the world—a world, however limited, of one's own design, or a world over which one has some control. A common type of solution to the problem is to seek or create a setting closer to nature. For a start, this setting may be found right in the city home. In the courtyard house—a type of house that once enjoyed worldwide popularity—are enclosed spaces, open to the sky, surrounded by walls or porticoes and decorated with ornamental and useful plants. Unlike large Baroque and Romantic parks, small open spaces of the courtyard house are intimately integrated with the living rooms. The gardens are part of a household's living space, not just areas embellished for show and prestige. Their association with the daily business of living is symbolized by the presence of fruit trees as well as decorative plants.[2]

English gardens of the late Tudor period are another example of the kind of cozy world for self and a few intimate others that human beings can successfully devise. In both town and country houses, gardens were places of retreat as well as sociability. Here is how L. E. Pearson envisages a scene in the time of Elizabeth I:

On a pleasant day, a visitor calling by appointment on the master of the household was almost sure to be told by the servant, "You will find him walking in the garden." Then he would be ushered to an orchard with paths of grass or gravel

Self and Reconstituted Wholes

and with flowers or vines growing about the trees. If a lady came to "gossip" with the mistress and the weather permitted receiving guests out of doors, she would expect to be shown into the garden.

The garden, in addition to being a secluded place for receiving favored guests, was used for strolling in before and after meals, for taking naps in the drowsy hours of the day, for reading and soft music, and for gentle sports. It also served as a place for assignations and the hatching of plots. "Elizabethans felt free to talk without being overheard in their gardens," Pearson observes. Conversations might be interrupted in private chambers, especially if doors opened to other rooms and, moreover, there was always the danger of eavesdroppers concealed behind hangings. "But in the garden they felt so much less restrained that Shakespeare could delight his audience with plots showing lovers and secret agents and businessmen betrayed while they made plans revealed to ears not intended to hear them"[3]

The garden was private space, but not cut off from the rest of the house, and not set apart from social life and the daily affairs of the household. Another type of retreat into nature called for the temporary abandonment of the townhouse in favor of the country estate. This move was also motivated by the desire for greater privacy and simplicity. Rather than merely stepping into the garden to spend a refreshing hour or so there, one left the city altogether for a season. The country house and its grounds were a working farm. One withdrew to a simpler life and to a slower-paced life, but not from life. Late in the fifth century B.C., three-quarters of the Athenian burghers had farms in Attica to which they repaired each summer when business permitted.[4] The farm was a source of wealth to the Athenian, but just as important it symbolized for him the forces—dark, chthonian, and mysterious—that renewed his natural vitality, enabling him to return to the city and resume life in the glare of the public arena.

The city stood for artifice, the uniquely human, and the call of excellence; whereas the farm stood for nature and the dark powers of creativity. In classical times the Athenian as well as the Roman strove for the kind of integrity that these two worlds in conjunction could provide. In later ages, too, people sought to attain a balance between city and country living, between their sense of themselves as public persons and as private individuals. Such a balanced and wholesome life was the happy lot of the well-to-do Florentine during the Renaissance. A merchant, for example, might own a *casa* in the city, which combined dwelling place with shop where he worked, and a villa or farm in the country. The farm produced cereals, vegetables, wine, oil, forage, and wood. It supplied all a Florentine household's needs: the surplus could be sold. "Blessed villa," cried Alberti the humanist, "sure home of good cheer, which rewards one with countless benefits: verdure in spring, fruit in autumn, a meeting-place for good men, an exquisite dwelling."[5]

We have seen two kinds of withdrawal, both not from life but from one kind of life to another that was closer to biological needs and to nature. We now turn to a third type of withdrawal, more self-conscious, individualistic, and sentimental. A person of delicate feelings, disillusioned with the bustle and meretricious life of the city, recognizes that one does not have to tolerate human venality, that one can always retain peace of mind and ideals in the solitude of the farm or in the midst of nature. This theme of high-minded living in retirement is a commonplace of both Chinese and Western nature poetry. In Chinese literature, we may take as illustrative the works of T'ao Yuan-ming (A.D. 372?–427), a reluctant magistrate who served in his post for only eighty-three days. He wrote fondly of his country cottage where "in early summer the woods and the herbs are thriving and numerous birds delight in their sanctuaries." On his farm, T'ao claimed (with no doubt a touch of poetic license) that after he had done the work of plowing and sowing, he would retire to the cottage and there read his books. From a later period, the T'ang dynasty, the great poet Li Po said: "If you were to ask me why I dwell among green mountains, I should laugh silently. My soul is serene. The peach blossom follows the moving water. There is another heaven and earth beyond the world of men."[6]

In Western literature, the retirement theme rises to prominence periodically, ever since its first blossoming, partly in reaction to the expansive growth of cities, during the third century B.C. Rome under Augustus witnessed another efflorescence of bucolic poetry: Vergil's poems describe an ideally happy life in a beautiful land of ancient

Self and Reconstituted Wholes

beeches and dark oaks. Yet, as the classicist Gilbert Highet notes, every one of Vergil's bucolic poems has sadness mixed with its charm. "As in a late Italian afternoon, his idyllic landscapes are sunny, but they have long, sloping shadows and areas of black coldness."[7] Horace, Vergil's contemporary, was given a farm outside of Rome by his patron Maecenas. On his farm Horace celebrated his seclusion, contrasting the peaceful life there with the smoke, the ostentatious wealth, the bustling business and violent pleasures of Rome. Yet he also seemed ambivalent about this life of withdrawal made possible by other people's labor and his possessions. In one perplexing poem, he put the praises of simple country living into the mouth of a notorious city usurer, a real person whose whole soul was absorbed in laying out his money at interest on the calends of each month.[8]

The retirement theme in literature reached a peak of popularity in eighteenth-century England. As Samuel Johnson (1751) put it, "There is, indeed, scarce any writer who has not celebrated the happiness of rural privacy."[9] The literati of the age were citified because culture, political opportunities, and pecuniary inducements had brought them to London and kept them there. Lack of success in London easily led some writers to adopt the fashionable classical pose of retiring to their country homes for a life of dignified leisure apart from the distractions and corruption of the city and the court. Moreover, as Myra Reynolds has pointed out, many of the more prominent of the century's nature-poets wrote their best poems in their youth while they still resided in the country. Not being able to conquer the city, they consoled themselves with the idea that the country was, after all, the better place to live in.[10]

Poetic descriptions of the countryside are full of unspecific rural sounds and scenes: the "lowing herd" and the beetle's "droning flight," "brawling springs," the "dim-discovered spires," "drooping winds [that] among the branches sigh," "cheerless shades," and numerous symbols of mortality such as "ruin'd seats," "twilight cells and bow'rs." In such a setting the appropriate mood is one of gentle melancholy and solemn meditation. "And, in the summer, you wou'd probably find me sitting under a Tree with a Book in my Hand, or walking thoughtfully in some pleasant Solitude" (Henry Needler,

1710). Most modern readers are familiar with this sentiment from a few exemplary poems that have made their way into anthologies, and foremost among them is Thomas Gray's "Elegy in a Country Churchyard" (1751). But hundreds of gloomy nature poems were published in the eighteenth century, all much alike in theme and tone, and many are egregiously self-centered.[11] A pervasive theme is the supposition of refinement in the author who, unlike the common herd, is capable of reflection, of discerning in country scenes evidences of the vanity of all human striving. "Far from the busy world's detested noise. . . . There, in a melting, solemn, dying strain, let me, all day, upon my lyre complain" (Elizabeth Rowe, 1739). Self-indulgence stands out in this poem as in so many others, and with self-indulgence goes theatrical posing, as in the example of a Henry Needler "walking thoughtfully in some pleasant Solitude."[12]

The retirement theme in eighteenth-century literature draws its inspiration from classical authors such as Vergil and Horace, and from classical values, prominent among which are order and moderation. The city represented excess and chaos, whereas the countryside represented order and tranquility. But in the eighteenth century, writers also revealed a deeply romantic and individualistic strain, which moved to the fore as the century progressed. Romantic individualism suspected established society for its order rather than disorder, for its monolithic presence before which individuals must conform, and for its inability to accommodate personal needs and emotions. Nature, on the other hand, appealed to the romantic imagination because it was wild and because it lent itself to subjective readings. Nature, unlike the city, lacked a precise semiotic; therefore, an individual could readily project his or her own mood and meaning on it. Nature did not, as it were, answer back. A person who felt constrained and unfree to express feelings in the midst of other people might have no such inhibition among the mountains and the trees. T. S. Eliot's comment on Thomas Hardy is to the point: Hardy's work, wrote Eliot, "represents an interesting example of a powerful personality uncurbed by any institutional attachment or by submission to any objective beliefs. . . . He seems to me to have written as nearly for the sake of 'self-expression' as a man well can. . . . In consequence of his self-

Self and Reconstituted Wholes

absorption, he makes a great deal of landscape, for landscape is a passive creature which lends itself to an author's mood. Landscape is fitted too for the purposes of an author who is interested not at all in man's minds, but only in their emotions."[13]

This comment on Hardy's work may not be entirely fair, but Eliot is surely correct in associating nature or landscape with a tendency toward moody subjectivism among educated Europeans. A thinker seeks solitude in order to think, but that kind of isolation is as accessible in a city library as in the country. Moreover, the fact is that few people care to think deeply or for long. Much easier is "leisurely learning" or "meditation" by the bubbling brook, a state so lacking in energy and discipline that the consequence, inevitably, is a sort of somnolence and melancholy celebrated by the Augustan poets. The romantic individualist is a much wilder and more passionate creature, but even with him melancholy threatens as subjectivism turns into solipsism. "We receive but what we give," wrote Coleridge, "And in our life alone does Nature live."

The dream of a serene life in the midst of nature, however, is far from being confined to disaffected individuals possessed with the means to withdraw from society when it proves too burdensome and frustrating. Older, more widespread, and politically more potent is the dream of Eden; that is, of the existence of a composed life, not alone but with others, in an unspoiled natural setting. We may pause to consider briefly these Edenic fantasies because they are a primary source of inspiration for the design of idyllic coherent wholes—the utopian communities that humankind has yearned for and has periodically tried to establish.

From civilized societies are numerous legends that hint at a beautiful world, variously named Arcadia, Eden, Isles of the Blest, Garden of Immortals, Paradise. These places differ from each other in detail but share certain basic characteristics such as egalitarianism, geographical isolation, and the richness of the natural environment. The people in them also tend to be depicted as free of disease, long-lived, and showing a fondness for music.[14] Let the Taoist paradise from *Lieh Tzu* (ca. 300 B.C.) stand as a representative dream. The place, called Northendland, is far removed from any known nation. Its climate is

Self and Reconstituted Wholes

mild. Its people follow nature without wrangling and strife. Arrogance and envy, princes and lords, marriage and private property are all unknown to them. Men and women, young and old, live together in harmony and happiness. They love music; taking each other by the hand, they dance and sing in chorus, and their singing may continue into the night. When they feel hungry or tired they drink the water in the rivers and find their vitality restored. King Mu of Chou, on his journey to the north, discovered this country and stayed there for three years, completely forgetting his own kingdom. When he finally returned home, he lost all interest in wine and meat, and would have nothing to do with his concubines and servitors. It took him months to recover.[15]

This type of fantasy appears in nonliterate communities too, but there it is more likely to be depicted as a "happy hunting ground" in the afterlife than as a geographical locality in this one. Motivation also differs. With primitive people, hardships in life encourage the belief in a more generously endowed environment in the hereafter. With materially advanced people, it is not necessarily hardship that drives them to dream of Eden; rather, it is disillusionment with civilized society. King Mu of Chou obviously lacked nothing in services and goods, and yet was discontent. If we look at history we shall find that legends of terrestrial Eden are the inventions of the elite and well-educated members of society rather than the dreams of the downtrodden. Society makes demands on the privileged that can make life with all its glitter and material comfort seem futile—a strenuous theater in which each person must be adept at various roles played before a constantly alert and critical public. Although complaints about city life are often couched in terms of its vainglory, crassness, and ceaseless demands, implicit in them is the burden of consciousness, of the constant need to be "on one's toes," of living in an artificial world, that is, a world that does not, like nature, run on its own but must be consciously maintained.

Eden, by contrast, is simple, natural, whole, and wholesome. In it there is no strife, not only in the sense of the struggle to make a living or against one's rivals, but also in the sense of an agitated mind that is always taking stock, assembling and disassembling ideas, materials, and people in the attempt to achieve coherence. Since the early Middle

Ages, European explorers and travelers have kept an eye out for Paradise. Columbus himself thought he had discovered it in the interior of the Orinoco basin during his third trip to the New World. In the eighteenth century, although scientific explorers like Louis de Bougainville and James Cook no longer believed in the existence of a Biblical paradise on earth, they nevertheless attributed paradisiacal qualities to the tropical islands they found in the Pacific. That Age that we call Enlightenment was also a time when the light of reason, or rather the obligation to sustain it, seemed almost too heavy a burden for the *philosophes*, who yearned for the supposed freedom and wholesome simplicity of native lives in distant places. Egalitarian communities of the kind we sketched in chapter 2 were perceived in a romantic haze that made the discernment of their human and social defects all but impossible. This tendency, admirable in its generosity despite its fruition in error, is a recurrent trait of educated people living in the metropolitan centers of the Western world.[16]

Paradise was not only a ready-made place at the source of the four rivers, in Ethiopia, or somewhere west across the Atlantic, it was also an ideal community that could be deliberately created in the midst of nature, far away from the temptations and foulness of city life. Basil the Great (ca. 330–379) wrote: "I am living in the wilderness wherein the Lord dwelt. Here is the ladder which leads to heaven and to the encampments of the angels which Jacob saw. Here is the wilderness where the people, purified, received the law, and then going into the land of promise beheld God."[17] This vision takes us to the long story of monasticism in Western Christendom, which emerged in recoil against the excessive worldliness of the institutional Church, and which periodically had to renew itself as it found this worldliness seeping into and corrupting its own fabric. One source of monasticism was individualism. Individuals were dissatisfied with Rome and with ecclesiastical politics. Individuals were concerned with the salvation of their own souls. Some individuals sought the isolation of the Egyptian and Syrian deserts and became hermits; some lived alone in cells but the cells were close enough to each other so that some form of communal life could develop among these athletes of the spirit. Communal life finally triumphed in the highly regulated and disciplined monasteries. When individuals joined a monastery they yielded their autonomy to the abbot. They took this path deliberately, by graduated steps, in a succession of vows that called for deepening self-examination; and they did this with the ultimate purpose of a mystical union with God.[18]

On earth monastic life strove for the perfection of paradise, a life in which people did not own property, were essentially equal, practiced brotherly love, worked, prayed, and sang together in a setting that is often beautiful, surrounded by nature. The monastic community is one of mankind's more successful experiments in utopian living. By giving thought, people have demonstrated their ability to create a "cohesive whole." But the price of success was discipline and simplification. That image of Eden or Taoist paradise in which people somehow managed to live in innocence and harmony without the tolling bell—symbol of constraint—must remain in the phantasmagorial realm. The monastic community may exemplify pure living but it is unnatural and without innocence. It is an artifact, with the simplification of all artifacts. It is a one-sex community that cannot reproduce itself by natural means. It is intensely self-aware. Its discipline curbs spontaneity and natural affection. Ease in the sense of being able to take one's world for granted, of being able to go through the duties and pleasures of the daily round unreflectively, may well occur and may even be the norm of monastic life, but it is alien to its fundamental ethos, which is one of wakefulness.

Utopias are conscious attempts at reconstituting social wholes. The monastic experiment reaches an extreme of discipline and simplification. Other experiments, also driven by religious impulses but with a firmer commitment to this world, are less extreme in their disciplinary demands, and the social wholes they have created are more complex and less stable. Among such endeavors the most important, in terms of historical impact, are the covenanted communities of New England. The Puritans who landed on American shores supposed that they were inaugurating a new age of the Church, a new Reformation, a new community that was to take shape like a garden in the protective wilderness. John Winthrop and his band crossed the Atlantic to settle in Massachusetts Bay under commission from God. There was unity of purpose, but Winthrop anticipated friction in his future settlement because of the heterogeneous background of his people, who were Puritans from different English communities and from different levels of English society; indeed some were orthodox Anglicans unaffected by Puritan ideals. To be successful in God's commission, Winthrop warned his charge, "we must be knit together in this work as one man." But how, if not by constant vigilance? In the Old World, through generations of living, towns had assumed a pattern that seemed as stable as nature itself. The economic and social facts of life in them were no doubt often harsh and unfair, like nature's own demands, but there was also an innocence in habitude, in the drowsy acceptance of what always had been. In New England, by contrast, everything around the settlers reminded them, as Page Smith puts it, "of the precarious, man-made, consciously fashioned character of their communities." Settlers lived nervously, not only because of external pressures from storms, fire, and pestilence, but also because they were aware of the fragility of the internal bonds. The terms of the covenant might not be met. Each person had to be concerned with his or her own behavior and that of the whole community. "One's own sins imperiled the group; one could, by failing to observe the stern demands of the covenant, bring down God's wrath upon one's neighbors as well as oneself." Although John Cotton of Boston might describe the colony as Paradise and the garden of Eden, it and other Puritan settlements lacked one major ingredient of Eden, namely, ease.[19]

In the course of the nineteenth century, more than one hundred ideal communities with a total membership exceeding one hundred thousand men, women, and children, were tried out in the United States. "The history of these experiments," Mark Holloway observes, "is one of few successes, many failures, and constantly renewed endeavour. Only three or four communities have lasted longer than a hundred years. Many vanished within a few months of their foundation."[20] In general, the long-lived ones were those of religious inspiration. Religion provided the idealists with objective or transcendental values and rules to which all must give assent because they came ultimately from God. The problem with secular utopian communities was that they lacked authority derived from a transcendental source. Their stability depended much more on subjective good will and on shared ideals, the validity of which did not go beyond the dreams and desires of individuals. Friction and stress emerged as people disagreed on particular practices, and complete breakdown threatened when these disagreements extended to principles. Moreover, groups inspired by religious faith enjoyed a greater degree of homogeneity because to be a member one must assent to a specific set of doctrines and practices, and submit to rituals of a sacred-mysterious nature. In comparison, the conditions for membership in a secular utopian community were lax. People from different social and economic backgrounds could join. Almost always they included intellectuals who tended to be individualistic, personally ambitious, restless, and unused to the hardships and monotony of work in the shops and on the farms.

New Harmony in Ohio (1825–1827) illustrates the kinds of difficulty that could arise when people attempted to build a new whole — a "heaven on earth"—without the discipline of doctrinaire religion. This social experiment seemed favored to succeed for a variety of reasons. In the first place, its founder, Robert Owen, was a wealthy philanthropist who, from his reforms at New Lanark, acquired a European reputation. Second, the Owenites entered ready-made homes, and took over thousands of acres of farmsteads, orchards, and cultivated fields from their previous owners the Rappites. And third, there can be no doubt that the membership included some very talented and dedicated individuals. But in its two years of existence New Harmony never came close to being a harmonious community. Owen's unsteady leadership contributed to the failure, but it is doubtful that even the wisest leader could create a social whole out of such diverse elements. The hundreds of people who came within a few weeks of the clarion call to found a new civilization were men and women of all classes and vocations, embracing dozens of different nationalities, creeds, professions, and trades. It is one thing to organize tasks and activities so that people find themselves in the same place, but quite another to make them heed each other's presence beyond the merest social acknowledgment. As one contemporary observer put it, the New Harmonists, for all their communitarian ideals, "continued strangers

Self and Reconstituted Wholes

to each other." They failed to connect despite "all their meetings, their balls, their frequent occasions of congregating in the hall, and all their pretence of co-operation." In the hall the better-educated members kept to themselves, and when a ball was held the lower classes did not join the dance but read the newspapers scattered over the side-tables. Such differences in social practice and educational background hindered personal exchange even when the willingness to do so was there. Still more divisive were differences in principles and ideals. Soon after the foundation of the community, one group broke off and settled on another part of the estate because its members objected to Owen's deistic beliefs. A second schism, initiated by hard-working English farmers, followed: they objected to Owen's advocacy of teetotalism. Educational policy lay close to the heart of the intellectuals; not surprisingly, it became a source of bitter contention. Differences large and small might all be overcome in the course of time if there had existed an overarching principle of indisputable authority to which all naturally deferred. But there was no such principle. In June 1827, Robert Owen left for England, and New Harmony, as an experiment in communitarianism, was finished.[21]

Dreams of Eden and assays in utopia emerged out of disillusionment with the city, not necessarily with a particular place, but with the city as the symbol of civilization—large, complex, and corrupt. Edens and utopias were, by comparison, small, simple, and pure. Because they were envisaged at this modest scale, they seemed well within human capability to achieve. In fact, as we have just noted, although a harmonious physical environment could be built easily enough, a harmonious society—even one with less than a thousand members—proved resistant to human design. The successful ones were almost invariably homogeneous in composition, bound by dogmatic faith, experienced in the basic skills of livelihood but intellectually unadventuresome.

In this period of bold experimentation in communal living, roughly from the sixteenth to the nineteenth century, the city itself was shedding its chaotic complexity by segmenting space into areas of specialized and homogeneous use. We have already described some of these steps toward disentanglement. Thus carriage ways were separated from pedestrian walks, industries and residential quarters moved apart, as did also the rich and the poor. The changes came about in a haphazard fashion. Indiscriminate mixing of functions and social classes persisted into the eighteenth century. Note, for example, that Henry and Hester Thrale, wealthy patrons and friends of Samuel Johnson, lived next to the brewery in Southwark. Hester Thrale, it is true, had come to detest her Southwark home but her guest Johnson seemed unfazed: he wrote some of the *Lives of the Poets* in a room that looked out into the brewery's courtyard filled with the bustle and noise of workmen, horses, and wagons.[22] In Paris, it was only at the beginning of the nineteenth century that first individual buildings and then entire quarters became homogeneous in population.[23]

The ultimate in residential homogeneity is the suburb. Without the help of prophets, or religious or idealistic fanfare, though certainly with careful planning, suburban Edens have sprouted vigorously over the Western European and North American landscapes through the nineteenth and twentieth centuries. These middle class and upper-middle class quarters seem the fulfillment of an age-old human longing, which is to live among people who share one's beliefs and values in the midst of greenswards and trees. Suburbs, like religious utopian communities, are small, simple, and pure. Unlike them, suburbs are almost exclusively dormitories, not also places of sweat and toil. In other words, simplification of life has proceeded much further in the suburb. Dissociated from work and from the religious fervor of utopian communities, suburban living lacks seriousness. It does not have the seriousness of shared labor. Its cooperative efforts are voluntary, and serve useful rather than essential ends. Participation in social activities depends on an individual's mood and on peer pressure, rather than on a compelling sense of duty. In religious utopian communities, social acts such as dancing, group singing, and play-acting are also acts of worship. This is evidently not the case with suburban coffee klatches and with groups that meet periodically to read *Moby Dick*.

Communal living in the suburb is vitiated by the countervailing desire for property. Houses stand on their own lawns, and within the house individuals can readily find solitude by withdrawing into their own rooms. In fact, the superiority of suburban living lies in this

Self and Reconstituted Wholes

segmentation of space, which allows individuals to be alone, to explore and deepen their own sense of being. In the isolation of one's house and in the privacy of one's room, it is possible to think seriously and at length. Unfortunately, few people have that desire or capacity for serious reflection. Educated men and women are more tolerant of solitude than are those without education, but the difference seems minor. Augustan poets, by the testimony of their own works, are far from happy in their country villas. And modern aristocrats, shorn of residual lord-of-the manor obligations, become melancholic figures in their ancestral seats. To this gallery we add the vaguely discontented suburbanities, forced to draw on their meager inner resources to impart meaning to a world that outwardly is already so satisfactory. The burden of leisure, once carried only by the privileged few, is now much more widely shared.

Countering these forces of withdrawal are those of reintegration. Experiments in utopian living are an example of reintegration, preceded by the act of withdrawal. Geographical withdrawal is not, however, necessary. A new society can be erected within an existing one, differing from it not so much in values and ideals as in the fact of their translation into reality. This creative effort has traditionally been the prerogative of ambitious princes. Federigo de Montefeltro (1444–1482), a brilliant representative of the princely order in the period of the Italian renaissance, sought to make his court and state into a work of art. This impulse to build a world was aesthetic rather than religious. But whether the driving force came from art or religion, the aim was the same—to create a harmonious whole—and likewise the route, which was by way of will and discipline. In the arrangements of the court, Montefeltro saw to it that nothing was wasted, that all had their object. Everything was carefully watched and controlled. The court, far from entertaining vice and dissipation, served as a sort of military school for the sons of other great houses. The palace that Montefeltro built contained luxurious living quarters but also a celebrated library. In his city-state, the duke encouraged the construction of houses and the extension of cultivable land, and in general worked hard to ensure that farmers, artisans, and merchants prospered. Confident of his people's love, the duke habitually went about unarmed.[24]

Self and Reconstituted Wholes

The opposing forces of segmentation and integration could be seen to operate simultaneously in European societies in the modern period. They were, for example, clearly at work in eighteenth-century aristocratic Germany, as W. H. Bruford's study shows. Segmentation operated at the large scale of social reality, integration at the smaller scale of art. In eighteenth-century Germany the medieval estates of nobility, burghers, and peasants had hardened almost into castes. The nobility considered themselves a different race. Some thought that even in a future life they would receive preferential treatment. Boys of good family were educated privately by tutors so as to avoid mixing with boys of lower social standing in the schools. On public occasions the nobility made every effort to keep social inferiors at a distance. "In the theatre they sat apart from the common man, either in the front seats or in boxes. . . . At public concerts too a space was left between the chairs of the quality and the rest. . . . At ceremonious court concerts, on the analogy of the solar system, the very great were left surrounded by a number of empty chairs in direct proportion to their rank."[25]

Communal life was being diluted by keeping the social categories rigidly separate. As if to compensate, art of mixed genres flourished. The nobility, for example, greatly favored operas and patronized them with munificence. Singing, acting, dancing, naval battles in little gilded vessels, and extravagant landscapes manipulated by machines were all included in a show. Banqueting was another mixed art for which no expense was spared. Medieval banqueting, we have seen, combined ceremony with rowdiness, but the mixture came about naturally. In the eighteenth century, the serving of meals became an art form that joined the pleasures of the table with those of the concert room, the theater, and even the sculpture gallery. The court confectioner was a sculptor and an architect. He might produce, for the delectation of banquet guests, a whole formal garden "the length of the table, with a little fountain of perfumed waters in the centre edged with statues, avenues of trimmed trees, beds of flowers in natural colors and little sugar ladies and gentlemen promenading."[26]

But without doubt the most ambitious art form was the idealized city of a prince. Capitals like Mannheim (1606), Karlsruhe (1715), and

Self and Reconstituted Wholes

Ludwigsburg (1704–1733) had been built at the whim of a prince. They were grandiose stages of symmetrical design, either a chessboard or a cartwheel. Who would occupy such a stage, and what sort of show would be put on? In fact, the scenarios were pretty much standardized and evolved around the needs and rituals of the court. Every major decision of the prince—for example, the size of the palace and the duration of his stay in it—had more or less predictable effects on the number of people, the sort of people, and the kinds of activities that would appear in the city. A ruler might be deliberate with his decisions and design his capital with the care and control of an artist; or he might make them, as it were, on the spur of the moment and call a town into being almost absentmindedly. Bruford describes how, within ten years (1777–1786), a farm could be transformed into a bustling and civilized town through the favors and decisions of a duke.

A relative of the mistress of the duke of Pfalz-Zweibrücken owned a farm near Homburg (Pfalz) that she wished to sell. The duke was persuaded to visit. The farmer, his family, and servants were made to look very attractive, the finest cattle were brought there for the visit (in short a stage). The court doctor assured the prince that it would be impossible to be ill in such surroundings. The duke easily fell a victim. He summoned an architect. The stables and byres had to be enlarged, a cottage for the farmer and his family had to be built. . . . In a few weeks the farm had grown into a village with the workmen and their families. . . . At first the duke just drove over every afternoon, but presently he wanted to dine there. This necessitated further alterations—a new kitchen wing, a large dining room. And so the farm grew and grew until the duke was living there permanently. Soon a regular Schloss had been built, with stables for 1,000 horses, an "orangerie" with rooms for the gentlemen-in-waiting, pages, officers, doctors, chaplains, gardeners; a picture gallery and library, a theatre, a zoological garden, and barracks for 1,400 men. Finally a whole town had to be called into being.[27]

Deliberate attempts to reconstitute wholes occur, of course, also at smaller scales. We have noted in chapters 4 and 5 the progressive segmentation of space, catering to privacy and intensified awareness, in the development of the house and the theater since medieval times. Segmentation reached a peak in the later part of the nineteenth century. Thereafter architects, playwrights, and producers have been moving deliberately toward a greater integration of space and of

Fig. 20. Excessive enclosure: walls and doors. This drawing shows a degree of enclosure that Americans found—and still find—repugnant. From E. C. Gardner, "Where Shall the Pictures Be?" (1878).

people using that space. What structural feature clearly differentiates a Victorian house from a modern one of comparable size? Even a casual impression provides the correct answer: a Victorian mansion has numerous rooms of modest size sharply separated from each other by doors (Fig. 20), whereas a modern house has "spaces" rather than rooms, spaces (a few quite large) that flow into each other. In a Mies van der Rohe house, one is struck by the austerity of form and of interior furnishing, but also by the promiscuous merging of space. Perhaps only the bathroom is truly enclosed and has a door. Elsewhere, separation is only suggested by panels, a column, or a change of orientation.[28] In 1905, when Henry James returned from his long exile in Europe to the United States, he noticed a "diffused vagueness of separation between apartments, between hall and room, between one room and another, between the one you are in and the one you are not in, between the place of passage and place of privacy." He objected to the substitution of "gaping arches" and "resounding voids" for "enclosing walls and practical doors." He disliked all the gimmicks that contributed to the loss of "the essence of the room-character, that room-suggestion which is so indispensable not only to occupation and concentration, but to conversation itself, to the play of the social relation at any other pitch than the pitch of a shriek or a shout."[29]

Henry James's criticism was misplaced. He failed to recognize ambiguity in the American house. The American house retained the open

Self and Reconstituted Wholes

plan for a much longer period of time than did the European house. What James considered faddism was in fact tradition, but a tradition that an innovator like Frank Lloyd Wright was later able to transform into something that, superficially, seemed radically new. In organizing his plans Wright turned back to the seventeenth century, when builders used the large chimney at the center of the house as the point of departure for structuring the whole layout. Sigfried Giedion observed that Wright worked fundamentally and as far as possible with the house as one room; the single interior space was then differentiated to meet special needs (Fig. 21).[30]

Contradictory forces were at work shaping the American house during the last quarter of the nineteenth century. On the one hand, following the European example, the American house moved toward specialization: rooms multiplied and were each designed for a special purpose. On the other hand, an architect such as Eugene C. Gardner also sought for the ideal of multiple use and integration. The living room, ostensibly a formal area for the reception of guests, might also be used for family activities. A bedroom could also serve as a study, a playroom for the children, or a sewing room for the housewife. This equivocation over the correct use of space had the effect, according to David Handlin, of making the rooms larger than they needed to be, at least, to European eyes: one part of a room was carefully designed and furnished for an exclusive function but there had to be some vaguely defined space outside it for other possible uses. A second level of ambiguity exists. "On the one hand spaces were parceled out more than ever before into designated rooms. . . . On the other hand the same houses were usually planned to achieve the opposite result. By opening sliding doors, removing screens, or pushing back portieres, most of the rooms, especially those on the first floor, could be thrown together to become one inter-connecting space."[31]

This ambiguity and equivocation of the modern American house neatly mirrors the conflict between polarized American ideals: individualism and community, selfhood developed in the privacy of one's own space and democratic togetherness. But, let it be said again, the communal ideal is one evoked deliberately by individuals. Community

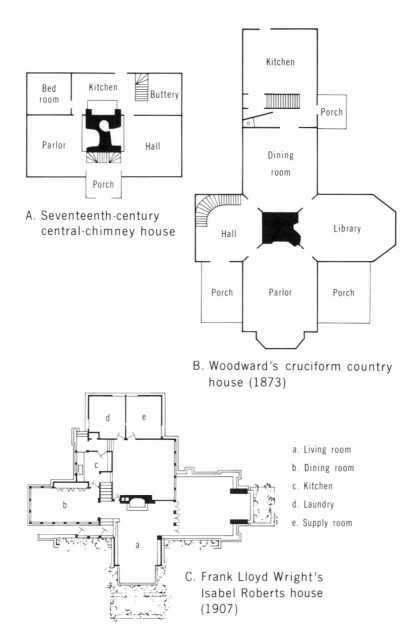

A. Seventeenth-century central-chimney house

B. Woodward's cruciform country house (1873)

a. Living room
b. Dining room
c. Kitchen
d. Laundry
e. Supply room

C. Frank Lloyd Wright's Isabel Roberts house (1907)

Fig. 21. American central-chimney houses. (A) Central-chimney house in seventeenth-century New England. After Abbott L. Cummings. (B) Woodward's plan of a cruciform country house, 1873. Diagonally sliding doors can be used to convert the house almost into a single room. Modified from G. E. Woodward, *Suburban and Country Houses* (New York, 1873). (C) Frank Lloyd Wright's Isabel Roberts house, River Forest, Illinois, 1907. Modified from Sigfried Giedion, *Space, Time and Architecture* (Cambridge: Harvard University Press, 1965), p. 401.

of the kind that modern men and women can personally experience is an artifact of individualism.

Theater has its roots in religious celebrations and festivals. It was very much a communal affair. However, by modern times (and especially in the nineteenth century), drama other than music-hall comedy had become a specialized art form designed for the entertainment of a small social class in Europe's capital cities. Segregation, social and spatial, was extreme. Players and spectators dwelt in different worlds, kept apart by the frame of the picture stage and, in some theaters, by the orchestra pit. In the popular Italianate auditorium, social divisions were manifest in the architectural arrangement of horseshoe-shaped galleries and boxes piled one on top of the other, each layer of which catered to a different clientele. The audience was further divided between those who could see the whole stage and those who could see only a segment. At the Comédie Française, for example, only half of the audience had an unobstructed view of the stage. The view of the other half was partially blocked, with the result that audience involvement with players was further reduced.

Against this constriction of theater's role in society were forces both within and outside the world of theater that pushed, from the late nineteenth century onward, for expansion and involvement. Social barriers as well as barriers between audience and players were to be lowered, if not removed. To encourage maximum attendance by people of different social backgrounds, theatrical troupes were established in the provinces. This step served to reduce the capital city's overwhelming dominance on drama and to combat the idea that playgoing was only for the social elite. Plays with social and political themes were introduced so that ordinary people could appreciate the relevance of the theater and be affected by the performances long after they had come to an end. Governments dreamed of introducing patriotic plays that could strengthen the unity of a nation. The Soviet government, for example, commissioned a "Mystery of Liberated Labour" for May 1, 1920. It is ironic that an atheistic government should use the form of medieval mystery play to celebrate its revolution. In France at the turn of the century, several pioneers of people's theater, "notably Maurice Pottedner (1867–1960) and Firmin Gémier

Self and Reconstituted Wholes

(1869–1933), declared that they wanted the theater to develop as a 'social religion', preaching the civic virtues and supplying its adepts with a sense of union and communion. Gémier spelt this out by pointing to the original meaning of the word religion: that which binds together."[32]

This movement toward involvement and integration naturally required radical change in the concept of physical space in the theater. Space must be arranged so as to minimize the separation between players and audience. As early as the 1880s, subscription made possible the building of a people's theater (*Volkstheater*) at Worms, which was distinguished by its semicircular auditorium with a stage that thrusted outward into the audience. Other steps to enhance integration, taking place mostly between the two world wars, called for the staging of performances in buildings not intended for use as theater; constructing flights of steps and bridges from the stage into the audience area; and moving the stage to the center so that it is surrounded by tiers of spectator seats. In an old-fashioned proscenium theater the stage is designed to show off flat painted perspective decor to its best advantage. Spectators contemplate scenes "out there" on the illuminated stage. In the new theater the settings consist of sculptural and architectural masses such as steps, blocks, and columns that can be viewed from any direction. In fact the word "view" is no longer wholly appropriate. What confronts the spectator is not a picture, with its suggestion of illusion and distance, but an objective presence. The things on stage are three-dimensional objects that can be used—that is, touched, leaned against or stood upon. They are, in this sense, real presences. So, of course, are the players brought physically close to the audience; but so also are the spectators who are drawn into the performance and who become collaborators. This trend at bridging the gap between players and audience continues after the second world war. Following an ancient custom, players may again direct their gestures and speech to the audience, or even seem to address their remarks to a particular individual, as though to initiate an impromptu exchange. Even when such direct solicitation does not occur, the audience is drawn into the play and becomes willy-nilly a part of the act by virtue of the interdigitation of performance and audience

Self and Reconstituted Wholes

areas. Where the stage ends and the space for spectators begins is deliberately fudged. This fudging is carried to an extreme in what is called "environmental theater," (Fig. 22). Richard Schechner, an exponent of environmental theater, describes it as a

globally organized space in which the areas occupied by the audience are a kind of sea through which the performers swim; and the performance areas are kinds of islands or continents in the midst of the audience. The audience does not sit in regularly arranged rows; there is one whole space rather than two opposing spaces. The environmental use of space is fundamentally collaborative; the action flows in many directions sustained only by the cooperation of performers and spectators.[33]

In this century we see certain trends in the theater toward community and participation, toward the type of communal involvement characteristic of the Middle Ages, and even beyond it to the idea of the festival in which everyone is a celebrant. The extreme form of this movement is a deliberate attempt to return to what the Greeks called *dromenon* (or action) as distinct from drama, which is action seen from the outside, contemplated. Every dramatist of any importance, says Nicola Chiaromonte, from Aeschylus to Molière, from Molière to Strindberg, Chekhov, and Pirandello understood the theater as the place where the world could be seen and appraised.[34] The response to a dramatic presentation is always more intellectual than visceral. But an intellectual response, far from being necessarily cold and distant, can be passionate and sustained. Indeed the level of involvement between a spectator sitting in the darkness of the auditorium and the drama on the illuminated stage can be so intense that the slightest distraction, such as a neighbor's cough, could seem a sacrilege.

By contrast, in the dromenon, the festival, or modern forms of participatory play, noise and movement are everywhere. Opportunity to focus on some event or display over a period of time seldom occurs. Few things are sustained. One's own moods and behavior shift rapidly from participatory frenzy (losing one's self-consciousness in gesticulation), to amusement, embarrassment, bafflement, and boredom — and perhaps back again to a high state of arousal. Environmental theater is

A. Orthodox

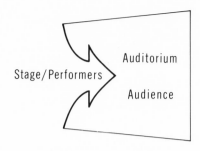

Stage/Performers

Auditorium

Audience

B. Confrontation

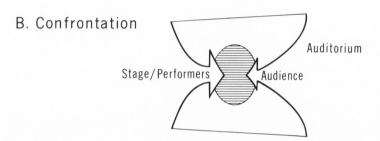

Stage/Performers

Auditorium

Audience

C. Environmental

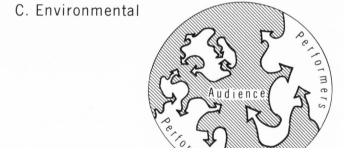

Performers

Performers

Audience

Fig. 22. Different kinds of relationship between performers and audience in the theater. In orthodox theater, the stage is the illuminated magic space, the auditorium is the dark secular space (A). Performers are active, the members of the audience are passive—at least with regard to bodily position. In confrontation theater (B), the audience is provoked into some sort of participation. In environmental theater (C), the distinction between stage and auditorium, performers and audience, is minimal. After Richard Schechner, *Environmental Theater* (New York: Hawthorn Books, 1973), pp. 38–39.

Self and Reconstituted Wholes

not dromenon or festival, but it does aspire to bring the audience into the play, and it has some of the fluidity and informality of a festival. Many members of the audience, Schechner admits, are embarrassed by the uncertain ways they respond to a performance. They think the play "doesn't work" because they cannot focus on it; their involvement, which can be emotional, is too episodic. People come up to Schechner and tell him, "I was moved by some parts of the play, but I kept thinking my own thoughts." Or "Sometimes I felt good, but at other times I felt threatened." Or "I watched the audience so much that I lost part of the play." Or even, "I fell asleep." To all these responses Schechner nods in approval: "they are splendid."[35] If so, are we to conclude that ordinary life is also splendid? How does the theatrical experience differ from ordinary life, in which we go through much the same moods and suffer similar sorts of muddle? Environmental theater seems to say that we should never stand aside from life and be merely spectators, and that the yearning for clear images is vain pride and can lead only to illusion.

After the second world war, two of the more conspicuous manifestations of the desire to generate communal life in the city are the shopping plaza and the central-city neighborhood. Europeans needed such places to replace those destroyed during the war. Americans needed them to combat the diffuseness of the sprawling suburbs and either the glass-and-steel sterility or the decay of the urban cores. What steps must be taken to ensure that the new shopping centers combine bustling activity with intimacy, as in Old World markets, but without the noise, confusion, and dirt? And how does one create complex, lively, and humane neighborhoods? Clearly the physical setting has an important role in the quality and extent of human intercourse. What this role is can be stated fairly easily where the activity is specialized, as, for example, football games, or the servicing of passengers and airplanes in an airport. Where the activities are many and complex and where their measure of success is not simply one of efficiency or productivity, the relationship between environment and behavior becomes far more problematic. Our ability to construct an intricate physical setting far outstrips our ability to put together a vibrant human world, even one of modest size. The successes we have had seem as much happy accidents as the fruits of forethought.

Consider the limited world of the shopping center. How does one build a center that is successful? The physical components are the easiest to specify. Crowds alone generate a sense of activity, but this feeling can be enhanced by architectural devices. For example, it helps to vary the shopping frontage and shop-front design and keep the concentration of such visual patterns at eye level; it helps to provide two or three layers of stores, thus amassing goods and displays within a narrow compass; and it is desirable to control carefully the heights of the buildings in the mall and the widths between the facades.[36] Since the early 1950s, regional shopping forums began to multiply in American suburbs. They were an ambitious attempt to re-create, as Victor Gruen their foremost proponent puts it, the beauty and bustle of "the long-lost town squares of our urban past." They were intended to be not only a commercial place but also a "social, cultural and recreational crystallization point" for a sprawling suburban region.[37] To this end, planners and developers have added year by year new facilities such as restaurants, cinemas, children's play areas; and at the larger centers, exhibit halls, general office buildings, and hotels.

A new gleaming "town" comes into being, without the hazards of motorized traffic. In a brief decade, the commercial success of the suburban shopping center is thoroughly established. It has proven its popularity with retailers, middle-class housewives, and their young children. But "a town square of our urban past" it is not. Like all human efforts at social planning, the shopping center, with all its virtues, is a greatly truncated world: it remains overwhelmingly a place for consumption. It does not produce goods, it excludes all serious political activity, and it is a social recreational center only for a special class of people and in a limited sense. White-collar working males are a small minority, likewise the old and the poor, and in general people who do not have private transport. Social exchange is largely confined to business chatter between buyers and sellers, and to gossip among friends in breaks between bouts of shopping. Unlike the routines of an old town square, people do not simply stroll over to a shopping mall to sit under the tree, soak in the sun, and enjoy a leisurely game of chess; nor do young people go there at night for purposes of self-

Self and Reconstituted Wholes

display and courtship. Recreation as just sitting and looking is not done. The message to buy is compelling, so that even the times in the coffee shop or restaurant seem "breaks" from the serious business of acquiring material goods.

How to restore the decaying neighborhoods of the central city is a task of a different order. Again, master planners could at first think only of architectural solutions. Run-down neighborhoods and business districts were razed, and in their place rose gleaming office or residential towers. Urban renewal, as this procedure came to be widely known in the fifties, was a term of hope. Where successful it meant vigorous business transacted in new buildings during office hours, and abandonment at night; or it could mean a convenient though rather sterile living environment for middle-class people who held white-collar jobs downtown. At night these office workers returned to their highrise apartments, which sparkled like bejeweled bracelets, but the streets outside showed little sign of life even if safe. In other words, the cost of success was simplification. Often urban renewal utterly failed. Neat-looking buildings put up with unbounded optimism as the answer to housing for the underprivileged became, within a few years, warrens of crime and of despair.

One of the earliest and most eloquent critics of urban renewal was Jane Jacobs. She denounced the naïveté of planners who saw the salvation of urban neighborhoods in simple-minded architectural terms. What demonstrated the planners' naïveté was their faith in segmentation and cleanliness. Influential architects believed that functions should be kept apart, and that above all residences should be protected from the traffic and bustle of the streets. They acted as though they thought that people would be happy if they could live in a clean, simplified, and neatly compartmentalized environment. Jacobs thought the opposite. In her view, to revitalize an urban neighborhood one must plan for complexity, even if the cost of complexity were a certain amount of confusion and dirt, for these are evidences of life. The problem is how to generate exuberant life in a city's streets and districts. Four conditions, according to Jacobs, are indispensable. (1) The district should have multiple functions to insure the presence of people who go outdoors at different schedules, for different reasons, but who are able to use many facilities in common. (2) Most blocks must be short; that is, opportunities to turn corners must be frequent. (3) The district must mingle buildings that differ in age and condition so that they vary in the economic yield they have to produce. (4) There must be a sufficiently dense concentration of people who are there for different purposes, including that of residence.[38]

To live in a neighborhood of exuberant diversity may not be to everyone's taste. Even if it were generally considered desirable, we quickly see how hard it is to achieve. Of the four conditions stated by Jacobs, only one can be established with relative ease, and that is the physical design of short blocks. All the others are much more difficult to realize. And this includes the close-grained mingling of buildings of greatly different age and style. As an exercise in physical design this type of juxtaposition may be attainable, but there is no guarantee that the attractive stage would then be taken over by people of different social class, working at different jobs, and living in harmony. Of course vibrant urban neighborhoods have existed in the past and still exist today. But a complex urban fabric is the product of political, social, and economic forces that extend far beyond a particular place or time. No individual or group has the power to call these large diffuse forces into being and direct their paths toward the re-creation of a richly textured society. Moreover, if we reflect a little, it is doubtful that we would even want to restore the kinds of constraint—economic inequality, assumptions of hierarchical order, tolerance and bonhomie imbued with condescension, to name a few— that made a certain sort of communal life possible in our past.

Nevertheless, we want community and we want freedom. Community is a web of socioeconomic exchanges, personal contacts, and affectional bonds that, in the final analysis, emerge from the needs of group survival. Cooperative tasks can be difficult and unpleasant; some forms of social exchange may even go against personal inclination and be felt as a burden. But such moods are normally overcome without great stress, because the customs and values of the group are accepted unquestioningly. Customs and traditional values have a timeless quality. Duties, even those that call for sweat and pain, are easy enough to perform if they are perceived as inexorable—a part of the

Self and Reconstituted Wholes

necessary order of things. Certainly all is not work and toil in a robust community. There must be sufficient leisure for informal visiting, for staying around to talk, for people to immerse themselves in a warm ambience of sounds and smells. Communal bonds are forged out of the performance of common tasks and rites, but as important to the forging are those numerous unstructured occasions when people are simply in each other's presence.

Freedom, the state wherein constraints are removed, is inimical to community. Freedom from material want and the threat of enemies enabled members of the upper class, then the middle class, to isolate themselves by space from people not of their kind; and among their own kind to withdraw further in search of solitude. These steps were taken as external constraints were removed. They were taken voluntarily to fulfill desires. What could the desires be? First, there was the desire to be freed of certain bonds and obligations. We have seen that even in our gregarious past—the late Middle Ages—a bishop was obliged to counsel a lord and his lady against following their inclination to dine apart from their people in the common hall. Second, there was the desire to engage in one's own projects without interference, and one such project might be the exploration of self.

Self and world are inseparable. Questioning in depth of the one leads to the questioning of the other. As self-knowledge increases, so does a critical knowledge of nature and society, or the world. The world, subjected to critical evaluation, loses its objectivity and cohesiveness. An individual finds it more difficult to accept society's values and to partake in its affairs as a matter of course. On the other hand, friendship in the sense of a profound sharing of selves and a sustained exchange of views becomes possible. Deep personal relationships presuppose the existence of persons, that is, complex and self-aware individuals; but such individuals can emerge only as the cohesive and unreflective nature of community begins to break down.

Given the freedom and the opportunity to explore self and world, few individuals in fact do so. Removed from necessity and the hurly-burly of life, most men and women find that they lack the inner fire to sustain vigorously projects of their own making. Life is in danger of losing its pungency as the world relaxes its unyielding demands.

Self and Reconstituted Wholes

Melancholy or boredom threatens. To keep such eventuality at bay, people resort to a variety of measures. One is conspicuous consumption. In the eighteenth century, aristocrats built palatial country houses for which they must then find reasons to visit at different times of the year. The reasons must carry an air of inevitability. Where necessity is absent it has to be invented. On a particular day the emperor of the Austro-Hungarian empire went into residence at Schönbrun; on another fixed day he left for Laxenburg; on another he returned to Hofburg. Lesser nobles moved likewise, as though under constraint, through the circuits. At each residence, lavish entertainments helped to dispel ennui. Having gradually abandoned the tumultuous political world, the great lords sought to substitute for it the complex artificial cosmos of the opera.

The upper bourgeoisie, in distinction to aristocrats, found salvation in home life and in the cultivation of intimate personal relationships. A moral seriousness pervaded these endeavors. But the seriousness was hard to maintain in the home as institutional religion began to decline, and hard to maintain between individuals because it called for the kind of self-awareness and commitment that few people possess. The intensity of Bloomsbury friendships may be widely admired but it cannot be widely shared or imitated. There remains for the middle class the social round and conspicuous consumption. As balm for what David Riesman once called the "ṣuburban sadness," such activities are not greatly effective; and the reason for their lack of power is that they seem arbitrary. To feel, for example, that one *has* to attend a neighbor's party is already evidence of the arbitrariness of the occasion. What color of dress should one put on, red or blue? The answer, obviously, is that if it really matters the question would not arise. In a traditional community, objective values are intact. Meaning is manifest in things, people, and activities; it is not a point of view or the result of a personal investment of energy. One attends a function because it is there, a statement that would not seem whimsical but merely self-evident. Paradoxically, necessity gives ease to life. Necessity, not only as a fact recognized by the mind but as a weight fully felt by body and soul, sustains the objective character of the world.

NOTES

Notes

1. Segmentation, Consciousness, and Self

1. Walter J. Ong, "World as view and world as event," *American Anthropologist* 71 (1969): 634–47.
2. See Robert Sack, *Conceptions of Space in Social Thought: A Geographic Perspective* (Minneapolis: University of Minnesota Press, 1981).
3. Christopher Alexander, *Notes on the Synthesis of Form* (Cambridge: Harvard University Press, 1964), pp. 46–70.
4. Alan F. Westin, *Privacy and Freedom* (New York: Atheneum, 1967), pp. 14–15.

2. Cohesive Wholes

1. Jules Henry, *Jungle People: A Kaingáng Tribe of the Highlands of Brazil* (J. J. Augustin, 1941), p. 18.
2. Ibid., p. 33.
3. Ibid., p. 17.
4. Ibid., p. 69.
5. Lorna Marshall, *The !Kung of Nyae Nyae* (Cambridge: Harvard University Press, 1976), p. 249.
6. Patricia Draper, "Crowding among hunter-gatherers: the !Kung Bushmen," *Science* 182 (19 October 1973): 301–3.
7. Marshall, *The !Kung*, pp. 244–45, 249–50.
8. Eric R. Wolf, *Peasants* (Englewood Cliffs, NJ: Prentice-Hall, 1960); Teodor Shanin, *Peasants and Peasant Societies* (Harmondsworth, Middlesex: Penguin, 1971).
9. Hsiao-T'ung Fei, *Peasant Life in China* (London: Routledge & Kegan Paul, 1939), p. 98.
10. Hsiao-T'ung Fei, *Earthbound China: A Study of Rural Economy in Yunnan* (Chicago: University of Chicago Press, 1945), p. 82.
11. Kenneth A. Lockridge, *A New England Town: The First Hundred Years, Dedham, Massachusetts, 1636–1736* (New York: W. W. Norton, 1970), pp. 93–118; Stephanie G. Wolf, *Urban Village: Population, Community, and Family Structure in Germantown, Pennsylvania 1683–1800* (Princeton: Princeton University Press, 1976), p. 157.

12. John Mogey in his Foreword to Elmora Messer Matthews, *Neighbor and Kin: Life in a Tennessee Ridge Community* (Nashville, Vanderbilt University Press, 1965), p. xiii.
13. Elmora Matthews, *Neighbor and Kin*, pp. 89, 125, 144.
14. Lyn H. Lofland, *A World of Strangers: Order and Action in Urban Public Space* (New York: Basic Books, 1973).
15. Gerald D. Suttles, *The Social Order of the Slum: Ethnicity and Territory in the Inner City* (Chicago: University of Chicago Press, 1968), pp. 74–75.
16. Herbert J. Gans, *The Urban Villagers: Group and Class in the Life of Italian-Americans* (New York: The Free Press, 1962), pp. 21–22.
17. Gans, *Urban Villagers*, pp. 80–103.
18. Jacques Gernet, *Daily Life in China on the Eve of the Mongol Invasion 1250–1276* (London: George Allen & Unwin, 1962), pp. 92–93.
19. Gernet, *Daily Life in China*, p. 93.
20. Cao Xueqin, *The Story of the Stone*, translated by David Hawkes, (Harmondsworth, Middlesex: Penguin Books, 1973), vol. 1, "The Golden Days."
21. *The Hsiao Ching*, translated by M. L. Makra (New York: St. John's University Press, 1961), p. 15, 35.
22. Y. P. Mei, "The status of the individual in Chinese social thought and practice," in Charles A. Moore, ed., *The Status of the Individual in East and West* (Honolulu: University of Hawaii Press, 1968), p. 340.
23. *Analects*, book 17, chapter 19; also book 15, chapter 4.
24. H. G. Creel, *What is Taoism?* (Chicago: University of Chicago Press, 1970), p. 3.
25. J. Huizinga, *The Waning of the Middle Ages* (Garden City, NY: Anchor Doubleday, 1954), pp. 9–10.
26. Lauro Martines, ed., *Violence and Civil Disorder in Italian Cities 1200–1500* (Berkeley and Los Angeles: University of California Press, 1972).
27. Diane Hughes, "Domestic ideals and social behavior," in Charles E. Rosenberg, ed., *The Family in History* (Philadelphia: University of Pennsylvania Press, 1975), p. 121; on the large and heterogeneous retinue of the cardinal-princes of Italy, see Lauro Martines, *Power and Imagination: City-States in Renaissance Italy* (New York: Vintage Edition, 1980), pp. 220–21.
28. Mark Girouard, *Life in the English Country House: A Social and Architectural History* (New Haven: Yale University Press, 1978), p. 10, 27.
29. Peter Laslett, *The World We Have Lost: England Before the Industrial Age* (New York: Charles Scribner's & Sons, 1971), p. 80.
30. Peter Brown, "Society and the supernatural: a medieval change," *Daedalus* 104, no. 2 (Spring 1975): 143.
31. Douglas Hay, "Property, authority and the criminal law," in Douglas Hay, Peter Linebaugh, John G. Rule, E. P. Thompson, Cal Winslow, *Albion's Fatal Tree: Crime and Society in Eighteenth-Century England* (New York: Pantheon Books, 1975), p. 29.
32. Hay, "Property," p. 47.
33. Otto Gierke, "The idea of organization" in *Political Theories of the Middle Age* (Cambridge at the University Press, 1968), pp. 22–30; see also Walter Ullmann, *The Individual and Society in the Middle Ages* (Baltimore: The Johns Hopkins Press, 1966), pp. 24–25.
34. Quoted in E. M. W. Tillyard, *The Elizabethan World Picture* (London: Chatto & Windus, 1960), p. 88.

35. Tillyard, *Elizabethan World Picture*, p. 90.
36. A. J. Lovejoy, *The Great Chain of Being* (Cambridge: Harvard University Press, 1933).
37. Tillyard, *Elizabethan World Picture*, p. 26, 28.

3. Food and Manners

1. There are exceptions, of course. With some people, eating is a personal and private affair. See Havelock Ellis, "The evolution of modesty," in *Studies in the Psychology of Sex*, 3rd ed., vol. 1, part I (New York: Random House, 1963); Theodore Besterman, ed., *The Mystic Rose* (London: Methuen, 1927); Carl D. Schneider, *Shame, Exposure and Privacy* (Boston: Beacon Press, 1978); and Clifford Geertz, "Deep play: notes on a Balinese cockfight," *Daedalus* 101, no. 1 (Winter, 1972): 7.
2. Quoted in H. D. F. Kitto, *The Greeks* (Harmondsworth: Penguin Books, 1957), p. 33.
3. Reay Tannahill, *Food in History* (New York: Stein and Day, 1974), p. 80.
4. Chapter "Wei Ling Kung," in *Lun Yü*. See James Legge, *The Four Books* (New York: Paragon Reprint Corp., 1966), p. 219.
5. James Legge, *The Li Ki* transl. of the *Li Chi* (Oxford: Clarendon Press, 1885), "Shao I" in *Li Chi*, pp. 78-79. Quoted in K. C. Chang, "Ancient China," in K. C. Chang, ed., *Food in Chinese Culture: Anthropological and Historical Perspective* (New Haven: Yale University Press, 1977), pp. 37-38.
6. Chapter "Hsiang T'ang," in *Lun Yü*, Legge, *The Four Books*, p. 130.
7. Chang, *Food in Chinese Culture*, pp. 34-35.
8. Ying-shi Yü, "Han China," in Chang, p. 79.
9. Michael Sullivan, *The Birth of Landscape Painting in China* (Berkeley and Los Angeles: University of California Press, 1962), pp. 29-30.
10. Chang, *Food in Chinese Culture*, pp. 7-8, 31.
11. Yü, "Han China," p. 68.
12. Chang, *Food in Chinese Culture*, p. 10.
13. Petronius, "Dinner with Trimalchio," in *The Satyricon*, transl. William Arrowsmith (New York: Mentor Books, 1960), pp. 38-83; for other descriptions of the dinner in literary works influencing Petronius, see L. R. Shero, "The *Cena* in Roman satire," *Classical Philology* 18 (1923): 126-43.
14. Tannahill, *Food in History*, p. 94.
15. J. P. V. D. Balsdon, *Life and Leisure in Ancient Rome* (New York: McGraw-Hill, 1969), p. 53.
16. Described by the young Pliny in a letter to Baebius Macer. See Frank Dawson Adams, *The Birth and Development of the Geological Sciences* (New York: Dover Publications, 1954), pp. 36-37.
17. Balsdon, *Life and Leisure in Ancient Rome*, p. 49.
18. Marjorie and C. H. B. Quennell, *A History of Everyday Things in England 1066-1799* (New York: Charles Scribner's Sons, n.d.), pp. 124-25.
19. Quoted by Frederick J. Furnivall in *Early English Meals and Manners* (London: N. Trübner & Co., 1868; reissued by Singing Tree Press, Detroit, 1969), p. lxvi.
20. Tannahill, *Food in History*, p. 227.
21. Bridget Ann Henisch, *Fast and Feast: Food in Medieval Society* (University Park: The Pennsylvania State University Press, 1976), pp. 110-11.

22. Elizabeth Burton, *The Early Tudors at Home 1485–1558* (London: Allen Lane, 1976), p. 129.
23. W. H. Lewis, *The Splendid Century: Life in the France of Louis XIV* (New York: Morrow Quill Paperbacks, 1978), pp. 208–9.
24. Gerard Brett, *Dinner Is Served: A History of Dining in England 1400–1900* (London: Rupert Hart-Davis, 1968), p. 116.
25. On methods of cooking, see Louis Stouff, *Ravitaillement et alimentation aux XIVe et XVe siècles* (Paris-La Haye: Mouton, 1970), pp. 258–62. The menu for the Archbishop of Besançon is from Robert Mandrou, *Introduction to Modern France 1500–1640* (New York: Harper Torchbooks, 1977), p. 25.
26. Mildred Campbell, *The English Yeoman* (New York, Barnes & Noble, 1960), pp. 246–47.
27. From *The Habits of Good Society* (1859). Quoted in Norbert Elias, *The Civilizing Process: The History of Manners* (New York: Urizen Books, 1978), p. 121.
28. Quoted in Thomas Wright, *The Homes of Other Days* (London: Trübner & Co., 1871), p. 430.
29. Charles Cooper, *The English Table in History and Literature* (London: Sampson Low, Marston & Co., n.d.), pp. 17, 19.
30. Michel de Montaigne, *Essays*, transl. J. M. Cohen (Harmondsworth, Middlesex: Penguin, 1958), chapter 13 "On Experience," p. 367.
31. Elias, *The Civilizing Process*, p. 107; Alfred Franklin, *La Civilité, l'étiquette, la mode, le bon ton du XIIIe au XIXe siècle* (Paris: Emile-Paul, 1908), vol. 1, p. 278. Even in the sixteenth century it was the custom among German princes to provide individual spoons to guests.
32. Brett, *Dinner Is Served*, p. 129.
33. Mrs. C. S. Peel, "Homes and habits," in G. M. Young, ed., *Early Victorian England 1830–1865* (London: Oxford University Press, 1934), pp. 111–19.
34. Elias, *The Civilizing Process*, p. 64.
35. Wright, *Homes*, p. 377.
36. Harold Nicolson, *Good Behavior* (Garden City, NY: Doubleday, 1956), pp. 129–45.
37. Elias, *The Civilizing Process*, pp. 77–79.

4. House and Household

1. Gaston Bachelard, *The Poetics of Space* (Boston: Beacon Press, 1969).
2. For the courtyard house in Mesopotamia see C. L. Woolley, "The excavation at Ur 1926–1927," *The Antiquaries Journal* (London) 7 (1927): 387–95. For a summary of changes in the style of the house in the ancient Near East see S. Giedion, *The Eternal Present* (New York: Pantheon Books, 1964), pp. 182–89. For the evolution of house shape from oval to rectangular in ancient Egypt see Alexander Badawy, *Architecture in Ancient Egypt and the Near East* (Cambridge: MIT Press, 1966), pp. 10–14. For changes in house type from the semi-subterranean dwelling to the courtyard pattern in Boeotia see Bertha Carr Rider, *Ancient Greek Houses* (Chicago: Argonaut, 1964), pp. 42–68. For the development of the Chinese house since Neolithic times see K. C. Chang, *The Archaeology of Ancient China*, 3rd ed., (New Haven: Yale University Press, 1977). For prehistoric Mexico see Marcus C. Winter, "Residential patterns of Monte Alban, Oaxaca, Mexico," *Science* 186, no. 4168 (1974): 981–86.

3. Nelson I. Wu, *Chinese and Indian Architecture* (New York: George Braziller, 1963), pp. 33–35; and Andrew Boyd, *Chinese Architecture and Town Planning 1500 B.C.-A.D. 1911* (Chicago: University of Chicago Press, 1962), p. 33.

4. G. Glotz, *The Greek City and Its Institutions* (London: Routledge & Kegan Paul, 1965), pp. 302–3; T. G. Tucker, *Life in Ancient Athens* (London: Macmillan Co., 1906), pp. 90–92, 194.

5. Jérôme Carcopino, *Daily Life in Ancient Rome* (New Haven: Yale University Press, 1940), p. 25.

6. J. P. V. D. Balsdon, *Life and Leisure in Ancient Rome* (New York: McGraw-Hill, 1969), pp. 21–22.

7. *The Letters of Caius Plinius Caecilius Secundus* (London: George Bell and Sons, 1905), p. 14 and 334.

8. U. T. Holmes, Jr., *Daily Living in the Twelfth Century: Based on the Observations of Alexander Neckham in London and Paris* (Madison: University of Wisconsin Press, 1952), p. 231.

9. Thomas Wright, *The History of Fulke Fitz-Warine: An Outlawed Baron in the Reign of King John* (London: Warton Club, 1855), p. 178.

10. Thomas Wright, *The Homes of Other Days: A History of Domestic Manners and Sentiments in England from the Earliest Known Period to Modern Times* (London: Trübner & Co., 1871), p. 148.

11. William Langland, *Piers Plowman*, Text B, Passus X, 97–101. See B. A. Henisch, *Fast and Feast: Food in Medieval Society* (University Park: The Pennsylvania State University Press, 1976), p. 204.

12. *Statutes of Eltham*, Harleian MS. 642. Quoted in Joan Wildeblood, *The Polite World: A Guide to English Manners and Deportment from the Thirteenth to the Nineteenth Century* (London: Oxford University Press, 1965), pp. 100–101.

13. Olwen H. Hufton, *The Poor of Eighteenth-Century France* (Oxford at the Clarendon Press, 1974), pp. 49–50.

14. Edward Shorter, *The Making of the Modern Family* (New York: Basic Books, 1977), p. 42.

15. Eugen Weber, *Peasants into Frenchmen: The Modernization of Rural France 1870–1914* (Stanford: Stanford University Press, 1976), p. 159.

16. Alan Everitt, "Farm labourers," in Joan Thirsk, ed., *The Agrarian History of England and Wales* (New York: Cambridge University Press, 1967), vol. 4: 1500-1640, pp. 442–43.

17. M. W. Barley, *The House and Home: A Review of 900 Years of House Planning and Furnishing in Britain* (Greenwich, Conn.: New York Graphic Society, 1971), pp. 40–41.

18. W. G. Hoskins, *Provincial England: Essays in Social and Economic History* (London: Macmillan, 1963), pp. 133, 144–45.

19. Mildred Campbell, *The English Yeoman Under Elizabeth and the Early Stuarts* (New York: Barnes & Noble, 1960), p. 214.

20. Hoskins, *Provincial England*, pp. 104–5.

21. W. G. Hoskins, "The Elizabethan merchants of Exeter," in S. T. Bindoff et al., eds., *Elizabethan Government and Society* (London: The Athlone Press, 1961), pp. 163–87.

22. Paul Zumthor, *Daily Life in Rembrandt's Holland* (New York: Macmillan Co., 1963), pp. 4–5.

23. Madeleine Jurgens and Pierre Couperie, "Le Logement à Paris aux XVIe et XVIIe siècles," *Annales ESC* 17, no. 3 (1972): 499.

24. Jean-Pierre Babelon, *Demeures Parisiennes sous Henri IV et Louis XIII* (Paris: Le Temps, 1965), pp. 69–114.

25. Richard A. Goldthwaite, "The Florentine palace as domestic architecture," *American Historical Review* 77, no. 4 (1972): 977–1012.

26. Goldthwaite, "Florentine Palace," p. 983.

27. Ibid., 998.

28. L. E. Pearson, *Elizabethans at Home* (Stanford: Stanford University Press, 1957), pp. 55, 56.

29. Philippe Ariès, *Centuries of Childhood: A Social History of Family Life* (New York: Vintage edition, 1965), pp. 392–93; W. H. Lewis, *The Splendid Century: Life in the France of Louis XIV* (New York: Morrow Quill Paperbacks, 1978), p. 197.

30. H. M. Baillie, "Etiquette and the planning of the state apartments in baroque palaces," *Archaeologia* 101 (1967): 183; W. H. Lewis, *The Splendid Century*, p. 60.

31. Baillie, "Etiquette," pp. 182–93; Mark Girouard, *Life in the English Country House: A Social and Architectural History* (New Haven: Yale University Press, 1978), pp. 126–28.

32. Barley, *The House and Home*, pp. 23–25; Margaret Wood, *The English Medieval House* (London: Phoenix House, 1965), p. 55; Jean-Louis Flandrin, *Families in Former Times* (Cambridge: Cambridge University Press, 1979), pp. 98–99.

33. Wright, *Homes of Other Days*, p. 263.

34. Quoted in David H. Flaherty, *Privacy in Colonial New England* (Charlotte: University Press of Virginia, 1972), p. 77.

35. Lewis, *The Splendid Century*, pp. 8, 48.

36. Ariès, *Centuries of Childhood*, p. 395.

37. Flaherty, *Privacy*, p. 73.

38. Ibid., p. 40.

39. Wright, *Homes of Other Days*, p. 124.

40. Ariès, *Centuries of Childhood*, p. 395.

41. Wright, *Homes of Other Days*, p. 107.

42. Elizabeth Burton, *The Early Tudors at Home 1486–1558* (London: Allen Lane, 1976), p. 86.

43. M. St. Clare Byrne, *Elizabethan Life in Town and Country* (London: Methuen, 1961), p. 50.

44. Elizabeth Burton, *The Pageant of Stuart England* (New York: Charles Scribner's Sons, 1962), p. 100.

45. Barley, *The House and Home*, p. 35.

46. Girouard, *Life in the English Country House*, p. 219.

47. Lewis, *The Splendid Century*, p. 202; for the treatment of servants by Victorians, see Frank E. Huggett, *Life Below Stairs: Domestic Servants in England from Victorian Times* (London: John Murray, 1977), and Merlin Waterson, *The Servants' Hall: A "Downstairs" History of a British Country House* (New York: Pantheon Books, 1980).

48. Christina Hole, *English Home Life: 1500 to 1800* (London: Batsford, 1947), pp. 8–9.

49. Pearson, *Elizabethans at Home*, pp. 47–48.

50. Barley, *The House and Home*, p. 40.

51. Ariès, *Centuries of Childhood*, pp. 359, 398.

52. Girouard, *Life in the English Country House*, p. 286.

53. The private museums of great houses might be crowded with a superfluity of knickknacks. Here is how Teresa of Avila (1515–1582) described an apartment of her friend, the Duchess

of Alba. "Imagine that you are in an apartment — I fancy it is termed a private museum — belonging to a king or great nobleman, in which are placed numberless kinds of articles of glass, porcelain, and other things, so arranged that most of them are seen at once on entering the room. While on a visit to the Duchess of Alba I was taken into such a room. I stood amazed on entering it and wondered what could be the use of such a jumble of knick-knacks." See Victoria Sackville-West, *The Eagle and the Dove* (London: Michael Joseph, 1943), p. 89.

54. Quoted by Ettore Camesasca, "Anatomy of the house," in *History of the House* (New York: G. P. Putnam's, 1971), pp. 367–68.

55. John Lukacs, "The bourgeois interior," *The American Scholar* 39, no. 4 (1970): 623.

56. Artemidorus Dalianus, *The Interpretation of Dreams*, transl. Robert J. White (Park Ridge, NJ: Noyes Press, 1975); George Steiner, "The language animal," *Encounter* (August, 1969), p. 17; Bachelard, *The Poetics of Space*, pp. 17, 25–26; Carl Jung, *Memories, Dreams, and Reflections* (London: Collins, The Fontana Library, 1969), p. 184; Clare C. Cooper, "The house as symbol of self," *Institute of Urban and Regional Development* (Berkeley: University of California), reprint no. 122, 1974, pp. 130–46.

57. James S. Allen, "Bergasse 19, Sigmund Freud's Houses and Offices, Vienna, 1938," *The New Republic*, November 13, 1976, p. 34.

58. See Daniel Mornet, *Les Sciences de la nature en France au XVIIIe siècle* (Paris, A. Colin, 1911).

59. Jerome H. Buckley, "Victorian England: the self-conscious society," in Josef L. Altholz, ed., *The Mind and Art of Victorian England* (Minneapolis: University of Minnesota Press, 1976), pp. 3–15.

5. Theater and Society

1. Gilbert Murray, "Excursus in the ritual forms preserved in Greek tragedy," in Jane Harrison, *Themis* (Cambridge at the University Press, 1927), p. 341.

2. Francis M. Cornford, *The Origin of Attic Comedy* (London: Edward Arnold, 1914).

3. Margarete Bieber, *The History of Greek and Roman Theater* (Princeton: Princeton University Press, 1961).

4. A. E. Haigh, *The Attic Theatre*, 3rd ed. (Oxford at the Clarendon Press, 1907), pp. 323–48.

5. Oscar G. Brockett, *History of the Theatre* (Boston: Allyn and Bacon, 1977), p. 61.

6. Benjamin Hunningher, *The Origin of the Theater* (New York: Hill and Wang, 1961), pp. 48–49.

7. Grace Frank, *The Medieval French Drama* (Oxford at the Clarendon Press, 1960), pp. 24–26.

8. Glynne Wickham, *The Medieval Theatre* (London: Weidenfeld and Nicolson, 1974), p. 60.

9. V. A. Kolve, *The Play Called Corpus Christi* (Stanford: Stanford University Press, 1966), p. 24.

10. William Tydeman, *The Theatre in the Middle Ages: Western European Stage Conditions, c. 800–1576* (Cambridge: Cambridge University Press, 1978), pp. 149–50.

11. Frank, *Medieval French Drama*, pp. 163–64.

12. Wickham, *Medieval Theater*, p. 113.

13. Richard Southern, *The Medieval Theatre in the Round*, 2nd ed. (London: Faber & Faber, 1975), pp. 73, 80.

14. Southern, *Medieval Theatre in the Round*, p. 91; Tydeman, *Theatre in the Middle Ages*, p. 165.

15. John F. Danby, *Shakespeare's Doctrine of Nature* (London: Faber paperback edition, 1948), pp. 18–19.

16. Patrick Murray, "The idea of character in Shakespeare," in *The Shakespearian Scene* (London: Longmans, 1969), pp. 1–53.

17. Frances A. Yates, *Theatre of the World* (London: Routledge & Kegan Paul, 1969), p. 124.

18. Irwin Smith, *Shakespeare's Globe Playhouse* (New York: Charles Scribner's Sons, 1956), pp. 61, 83.

19. Alfred Harbage, *Shakespeare's Audience* (New York: Columbia University Press, 1941), pp. 92–116; Brockett, *History of the Theatre*, p. 183.

20. W. L. Wiley, *The Early Public Theater in France* (Cambridge: Harvard University Press, 1960).

21. Ibid, pp. 191–92.

22. Eugène Despois, *Le Théâtre français sous Louis XIV* (Paris: Hachette, 1874), pp. 154–61.

23. Wiley, *Early Public Theater*, p. 226.

24. T. E. Lawrenson, *The French Stage in the Sixteenth Century* (Manchester: Manchester University Press, 1957), pp. 161–67.

25. Wiley, *Early Public Theater*, p. 192. "Contemporary illustrations show that for special performances or overflow crowds tiers of benches could be set up round the acting area, so crowding the action that the audience was sometimes uncertain whether a new arrival was a late member of the public or a character making an entrance in the play." Quotation from Peter D. Arnott, *An Introduction to the French Theatre* (London: The Macmillan Press, 1977), p. 41.

26. M. C. Bradbrook, *Themes and Conventions in Elizabethan Tragedy* (Cambridge: Cambridge University Press, 1950), p. 8.

27. *Ten Books of Architecture of Vitruvius*, transl. by M. H. Morgan, Book 5, chapter 6, section 9.

28. Leonardo da Vinci, *A Treatise on Painting*, transl. by J. F. Rigaud (1892); Lily B. Campbell, *Scenes and Machines on the English Stage: A Classical Revival* (New York: Barnes & Noble, 1960), pp. 28–30.

29. Lawrenson, *The French Stage*, pp. 176–77.

30. Stephen Orgel, *The Illusion of Power: Political Theater in the English Renaissance* (Berkeley: University of California Press, 1975), p. 9.

31. Yates, *Theatre of the World*, p. 85.

32. Orgel, *Illusion of Power*, pp. 35–36.

33. Kenneth Clark, *Landscape into Art* (New York: Harper & Row, new edition, 1976); and *The Romantic Rebellion: Romantic versus Classical Art* (New York: Harper & Row, 1973).

34. Cecil Price, *Theatre in the Age of Garrick* (Totowa, NJ: Rowman and Littlefield, 1973), pp. 80–81; Brockett, *History of the Theatre*, pp. 289, 381.

35. Philippe Ariès, *Centuries of Childhood: A Social History of Family Life* (New York: Vintage edition, 1965).

36. Roy C. Flickinger, *The Greek Theater and Its Drama* (Chicago: University of Chicago Press, 1926), pp. 237–41; Campbell, *Scenes and Machines*, p. 138.

37. Arthur Tilley, *Molière* (Cambridge at the University Press, 1921), pp. 205, 337.

38. J. W. Krutch, *Comedy and Conscience After the Restoration* (New York: Russell & Russell, 1949).

39. George Rowell, *The Victorian Theatre 1792–1914* (Cambridge: Cambridge University Press, 1978), pp. 38–39, 43, 83.

40. Price, *Theater in the Age of Garrick*, pp. 84–101.

41. Edith Melcher, *Stage Realism in France between Diderot and Antoine* (Bryn Mawr, Pennsylvania: Lancaster Press, 1928), p. 18; Brockett, *History of the Theatre*, p. 378.

42. Elizabeth Burns, *Theatricality: A Study of Convention in the Theatre and in Social Life* (New York: Harper Torchbook, 1973), p. 75.

43. Raymond Williams, *Drama from Ibsen to Eliot* (London: Chatto and Windus, 1965), pp. 130–31; also "Social environment and theatrical environment: the case of English naturalism," in Marie Axton and Raymond Williams, eds., *English Drama: Forms and Development* (Cambridge: Cambridge University Press, 1977), pp. 203–23.

44. Frederick Penzel, *Theatre Lighting Before Electricity* (Middleton: Wesleyan University Press, 1978).

45. Raymond Williams, *Drama in a Dramatised Society* (Cambridge: Cambridge University Press, 1975).

6. Ambience and Sight

1. Desmond Morris, *The Naked Ape* (London: Corgi Books, 1968), pp. 94–96; Michael Southworth, "The sonic environment of cities," *Environment and Behavior* 1 (1969): 49–70.

2. J. S. Wilentz, *The Senses of Man* (New York: Thomas Y. Crowell Co., 1968), p. 114.

3. J. J. Gibson, "The smelling system," in *The Senses Considered as Perceptual Systems* (Boston: Houghton Mifflin Co., 1966), p. 145; Ralph Bienfang, *The Subtle Sense* (Norman: University of Oklahoma Press, 1946), p. 109. Trygg Engen, "Why the aroma lingers on," *Psychology Today*, May 1980, p. 138; R. W. Moncrieff, *Odour Preferences* (London: Leonard Hills, 1966).

4. Ashley Montagu, *Touching: The Human Significance of the Skin*, 2nd ed. (New York: Harper & Row, 1978); John Napier, *Hands* (New York: Pantheon Books, 1980).

5. Aristotle, Metaphysics, 980a (transl. by W. D. Ross; Oxford: Clarendon Press, 1908).

6. P. H. Knapp, "Emotional aspects of hearing loss," *Psychomatic Medicine* 10 (1948): 203–22.

7. T. G. R. Bower, *The Perceptual World of the Child* (Cambridge: Harvard University Press, 1977); D. M. Maurer and C. E. Maurer, "Newborn babies see better than you think," *Psychology Today*, October 1976, pp. 85–88; William Goldfarb and Irving Mintz, "Schizophrenic child's reaction to time and space," *Archives of General Psychiatry* 5 (1961): 535–53.

8. John Nance, *The Gentle Tasaday* (New York: Harcourt Brace Jovanovich, 1975), p. 22.

9. Colin M. Turnbull, "Legends of the BaMbuti," *Journal of the Royal Anthropological Institute* 89 (1959): 55–60; Turnbull, *The Forest People* (London: Chatto & Windus, 1961), p. 223.

10. Raymond Firth, *We, The Tikopia* (London: George Allen & Unwin, 1957), p. 29.

11. T. G. H. Strehlow, *Aranda Traditions* (Melbourne: Melbourne Univeristy Press, 1947), pp. 30–33.

12. Nelson I. Wu, *Chinese and Indian Architecture* (New York: George Braziller, 1963), p. 32.

13. James J. Y. Liu, *The Art of Chinese Poetry* (Chicago: University of Chicago Press, 1962), pp. 55-57; Burton Watson, *Chinese Lyricism: Shih Poetry from the Second to the Twelfth Century* (New York: Columbia University Press, 1971), pp. 79, 124.

14. Tseng Yu, "Kuo Hsi's Early Spring," *Orientations*, September 1977, pp. 37-43.

15. Hugo Munsterberg, *The Landscape Painting of China and Japan* (Rutland, VT: C. E. Tuttle Co., 1955); Michael Sullivan, *The Birth of Landscape Painting in China* (Berkeley and Los Angeles: University of California Press, 1962).

16. Lawrence Wright, *Clean and Decent* (London: Routledge & Kegan Paul, 1960), p. 39.

17. Norbert Elias, *The Civilizing Process: The History of Manners* (New York: Urizen Books, 1978), p. 131.

18. W. H. Lewis, *The Splendid Century: Life in the France of Louis XIV* (New York: Morrow Quill Paperback, 1978), p. 174.

19. D. W. Robertson, Jr., *Chaucer's London* (New York: Wiley, 1968), pp. 23-24.

20. Michel de Montaigne, *Essays* (Harmondsworth, Middlesex: Penguin Books, 1958), p. 136.

21. D. C. Munro and R. J. Sontag, *The Middle Ages* (New York: The Century Co., 1928), p. 345.

22. Johan Huizinga, *The Waning of the Middle Ages* (Garden City, NJ: Doubleday Anchor Books, 1954), pp. 10-11.

23. Kurt Blaukopf, "Problems of architectural acoustics in musical sociology," *Gravesner Blätter* 5, nos. 19/20 (1960): 180; quoted in R. Murray Schafer, *The Tuning of the World* (New York: Knopf, 1977), p. 118.

24. Schafer, *Tuning*, p. 156.

25. Reyner Banham, *Age of the Masters: A Personal View of Modern Architecture* (New York: Harper & Row, 1975), p. 50.

26. J. R. Green, *Town Life in the Fifteenth Century* (London: Macmillan and Co., 1894), vol. 1, pp. 155-56; Carolly Erickson, *The Medieval Vision: Essays in History and Perception* (New York: Oxford University Press, 1976), pp. 75-76.

27. Lucien Febvre, *Le Problème de l'incroyance au XVIe siècle: La Religion de Rabelais* (Paris: Albin Michel, 1942), pp. 393-403; Robert Mandrou, *Introduction to Modern France 1500-1640* (New York: Harper Torchbook, 1977), pp. 50-55.

28. Walter J. Ong, "World as view and world as event," *American Anthropologist* 71 (1969): 636-37.

29. Frances A. Yates, *Theatre of the World* (London: Routledge & Kegan Paul, 1969), pp. 118, 124-28.

30. Peter D. Arnott, *An Introduction to the French Theatre* (London: The Macmillan Press, 1977), pp. 21, 41.

31. Febvre, *Le Problème*, pp. 406-7.

32. Ibid., pp. 331-33.

33. C. S. Lewis, *The Discarded Image* (Cambridge at the University Press, 1964), pp. 101-2.

34. Walter J. Ong, *Interfaces of the Word: Studies in the Evolution of Consciousness and Culture* (Ithaca: Cornell University Press, 1977), p. 89.

35. Ong, *Interfaces*, pp. 103-4, 144; see also Shelly Errington, "Some comments on style in the meanings of the past," *Journal of Asian Studies* 33 (1979): 231-44.

36. *The Letters of Caius Plinius Caecilius Secundus*, William Melmoth transl., (London: George Bell & Sons, 1905), p. 31.

37. J. P. V. D. Balsdon, *Life and Leisure in Ancient Rome* (New York: McGraw Hill, 1969), p. 149.
38. Peter Brown, *Augustine of Hippo* (Berkeley and Los Angeles: University of California Press, 1969), p. 82; Augustine, *Confessions*, Book VI, iii, 3.

7. Self

1. S. Honkavaara, "The psychology of expression," *British Journal of Psychology Monograph Supplement* 32 (1961): 41–42.
2. Lawrence E. Marks, "Synesthesia," *Psychology Today*, June 1975, pp. 48–52; A. R. Luria, *The Mind of a Mnemonist* (New York: Basic Books, 1968), p. 27.
3. Roger Brown, *Words and Things: An Introduction to Language* (New York: The Free Press, 1968).
4. Dominique Zahan, *The Religion, Spirituality, and Thought of Traditional Africa* (Chicago: University of Chicago Press, 1979), pp. 8–10.
5. Godfrey Lienhardt, *Divinity and Experience: The Religion of the Dinka* (Oxford: The Clarendon Press, 1961), pp. 149–51.
6. Hoyt Alverson, *Mind in the Heart of Darkness: Value and Self-Identity among the Tswana of Southern Africa* (New Haven: Yale University Press, 1978), pp. 68–69, 112, 189.
7. Alverson, *Mind in the Heart of Darkness*, pp. 117–24.
8. Dorothy Lee, "Linguistic reflection of Wintu thought" and "The conception of the self among the Wintu Indians," in *Freedom and Culture* (Englewood Cliffs, NJ: Prentice-Hall, 1959), pp. 121–30, 130–40. Quotation from p. 140.
9. Wang Gungwu, "The rebel-reformer and modern Chinese biography," in Wang Gungwu, ed., *Self and Biography: Essays on the Individual and Society in Asia* (Sydney: Sydney University Press, 1975), pp. 194–206.
10. Y. P. Mei, "The individual in Chinese social thought," in Charles A. Moore, ed., *The Status of the Individual in East and West* (Honolulu: University of Hawaii Press, 1968), pp. 333–48.
11. William Theodore de Bary, "Individualism and humanism in late Ming thought," in Theodore de Bary, ed., *Self and Society in Ming Thought* (New York: Columbia University Press, 1970), p. 156.
12. H. G. Creel, *What is Taoism?* (Chicago: University of Chicago Press, 1970), p. 3.
13. James J. Y. Liu, *The Art of Chinese Poetry* (Chicago: University of Chicago Press, 1962), pp. 50–57.
14. C. T. Hsia, *The Classic Chinese Novel: A Critical Introduction* (New York: Columbia University Press, 1968).
15. Theodore de Bary, *Self and Society*, pp. 188–89, 192–93.
16. Hsia, *The Classic Chinese Novel*, p. 22.
17. E. R. Dodds, *The Greeks and the Irrational* (Berkeley and Los Angeles: University of California Press, 1951), p. 15.
18. Bruno Snell, *The Discovery of the Mind: The Greek Origins of European Thought* (Cambridge: Harvard University Press, 1953), p. 60.
19. Dodds, *The Greeks and the Irrational*, pp. 139, 152.
20. Snell, *Discovery of the Mind*, pp. 29–30.
21. Dodds, *The Greeks and the Irrational*, pp. 36–37.

22. M. I. Finley, *Early Greece: The Bronze and Archaic Ages* (New York: W. W. Norton & Co., 1970), pp. 90-108.
23. Hans Jonas, *The Gnostic Religion* (Boston: Beacon Press, 1963), pp. 330-31.
24. André-Jean Festugière, *Personal Religion Among the Greeks* (Berkeley and Los Angeles: University of California Press, 1960), p. 6.
25. Dodds, *The Greeks and the Irrational*, pp. 180-82.
26. Dodds, *The Greeks and the Irrational*, p. 237.
27. Georg Misch, *A History of Autobiography in Antiquity* (London: Routledge & Kegan Paul, 1950), vol. 1, p. 181.
28. M. P. Nilsson, *Greek Piety* (New York: W. W. Norton, 1969), p. 86.
29. Seneca, *Letters from a Stoic (Epistulae Morales ad Lucilium)*, transl. Robin Campbell (Harmondsworth, Middlesex: Penguin Books, 1969), letters 28 and 55, pp. 76, 108.
30. Marcus Aurelius, *Meditations* (Chicago: Henry Regnery, Gateway edition, 1956), pp. 30, 80.
31. Peter Brown, *Augustine of Hippo: A Biography* (Berkeley and Los Angeles: University of California Press, 1969), p. 180.
32. *On Christian Doctrine*, book 2, chapter 25:38.
33. *Confessions*, book 10, chapter 8:15.
34. Brown, *Augustine*, p. 210.
35. *Epistola*, 130, ii, 4; quoted in Brown, *Augustine*, p. 405.
36. Misch, *A History of Autobiography*, pp. 191, 196.
37. Brown, *Augustine*, p. 174.
38. Walter Ullmann, *The Individual and Society in the Middle Ages* (Baltimore: Johns Hopkins Press, 1966), pp. 32-33, 43-44.
39. Colin Morris, *The Discovery of the Individual 1050-1200* (New York: Harper Torchbooks, 1973), pp. 75, 121-22, 157.
40. Jakob Burckhardt, *The Civilization of the Renaissance in Italy* (London: Phaidon Press, 1951), pp. 82-84, 207, 314.
41. Richard A. Goldthwaite, "The Florentine palace as domestic architecture," *American Historical Review* 77, no. 4 (1972): 977-1012.
42. Epictetus, *Enchiridion* (Chicago: Henry Regnery, Gateway edition, 1956), pp. 178-79.
43. Jean Starobinski, "Montaigne on illusion: the denunciation of untruth," *Daedalus* 108 (Summer 1979): 87, 93-94.
44. Shakespeare, *As You Like It*, act 2, scene 7.
45. Georges Gusdorf, "Conditions et limites de l'autobiographie," in G. Reichenkron and E. Haase, eds., *Formen des Selbsdarstellung: Analekten zu einer Geschichte des literarischen Selbstportraits* (Berlin: Duncker & Humblot, 1956).
46. E. Panofsky, *Albrecht Dürer* (Princeton, NJ: Princeton University Press, 1943), vol. 1, p. 15.
47. Paul Delany, *British Autobiography in the Seventeenth Century* (London: Routledge & Kegan Paul, 1969), p. 13.
48. Lawrence Stone, "Social mobility in England, 1500-1700," *Past and Present*, no. 33 (April 1966): 16.
49. Jacques Barzun, *Classic, Romantic and Modern* (Garden City, NY: Doubleday Anchor Books, 1961), p. 46.
50. Lionel Trilling, *Sincerity and Authenticity* (Cambridge: Harvard University Press, 1972), p. 19.

51. M. H. Nicolson, *Mountain Gloom and Mountain Glory* (New York: W. W. Norton, 1963), pp. 132–33, 161; and *The Breaking of the Circle* (New York: Columbia University Press, 1962).
52. Werner Heisenberg, *Physics and Beyond* (New York: Harper Torchbooks, 1972); Nelson Goodman, *Ways of Worldmaking* (Indianapolis: Hackett, 1978).
53. Gabriel Josipovici, *The World and the Book* (London: Macmillan, 1971), p. 299.

8. Self and Reconstituted Wholes

1. Roy Perrott, *The Aristocrats* (London: Weidenfeld and Nicolson, 1968), p. 33.
2. Richard Wright, *The Story of Gardening* (New York: Dover Publications, 1963), pp. 81, 105.
3. Lu Emily Pearson, *Elizabethans at Home* (Stanford: Stanford University Press, 1957), pp. 4, 66–67.
4. Lewis Mumford, *The City in History* (New York: Harcourt, Brace, and World, 1961), p. 128.
5. J. Lucas-Dubreton, *Daily Life in Florence in the Time of the Medici* (London: George Allen & Unwin, 1960), p. 95.
6. Robert Payne, *The White Pony* (New York: Mentor Books, 1960), pp. 130–31, 163.
7. Gilbert Highet, *Poets in a Landscape* (New York: Knopf, 1957), p. 51.
8. W. Y. Sellar, *Horace and the Elegiac Poets* (Oxford at the Clarendon Press, 1891), pp. 127, 180.
9. Samuel Johnson, *The Rambler* (London: W. Suttaby, 1809), vol. 3, no. 135, p. 131.
10. Myra Reynolds, *The Treatment of Nature in English Poetry between Pope and Wordsworth* (Chicago: University of Chicago Press, 1909), pp. 329–31.
11. Eleanor M. Sickels, *The Gloomy Egoist: Moods and Themes of Melancholy from Gray to Keats* (New York: Columbia University Press, 1932).
12. George G. Williams, "The beginning of nature poetry in the eighteenth century," *Studies in Philology* 27 (1930): 583–608.
13. T. S. Eliot, *After Strange Gods: A Primer of Modern Heresy* (London: Faber & Faber, 1934), pp. 54–55.
14. Arthur O. Lovejoy et al., *A Documentary History of Primitivism* (Baltimore: Johns Hopkins Press, 1935).
15. *The Book of Lieh-tzu*, A. C. Graham, transl. (London: John Murray, 1960), pp. 102–3.
16. Henri Baudet, *Paradise on Earth: Some Thoughts on European Images of Non-European Man* (New Haven: Yale University Press, 1965); Bernard Smith, *European Vision and the South Pacific 1768–1850* (London: Oxford University Press, 1960).
17. Quoted in George H. Williams, *Wilderness and Paradise in Christian Thought* (New York: Harpers & Brothers, 1962), p. 39.
18. Peter F. Anson, *The Quest for Solitude* (London: J. M. Dent, 1932), pp. 16–31; see also, Herbert B. Workman, *The Evolution of the Monastic Ideal* (Boston: Beacon Press, 1962).
19. Page Smith, *As a City Upon a Hill* (Cambridge: MIT Press, 1973), pp. 7–8.
20. Mark Holloway, *Heavens on Earth: Utopian Communities in America 1680–1880* (New York: Dover Publications, 1966), p. 19.
21. Holloway, *Heavens on Earth*, pp. 101–16; see also Philip W. Porter and Fred E. Lukermann, "The geography of Utopia," in David Lowenthal and Martyn J. Bowden, eds. *Geographies of the Mind* (New York: Oxford University Press, 1976), pp. 197–223.

Notes to Chapter 8

22. W. Jackson Bate, *Samuel Johnson* (New York: A Harvest/HBJ Book, 1979), pp. 432, 478, 529.
23. Adeline Daumard, *Maisons de Paris et propriétaires parisiens au XIXe siècle* (Paris: Éditions Cujas, 1965), p. 90.
24. Jakob Burckhardt, *The Civilization of the Renaissance in Italy* (London: Phaidon Press, 1951), p. 29.
25. W. H. Bruford, *Germany in the Eighteenth Century: The Social Background of the Literary Revival* (Cambridge at the University Press, 1939), p. 57.
26. Bruford, *Germany*, p. 94.
27. Bruford, *Germany*, pp. 95–96.
28. A. James Speyer, *Mies van der Rohe* (Chicago: The Art Institute of Chicago, 1968), p. 48.
29. Henry James, *The American Scene* (Bloomington: Indiana University Press, 1968), p. 167.
30. Sigfried Giedion, *Space, Time and Architecture* (Cambridge: Harvard University Press, 1965), p. 398.
31. David P. Handlin, *The American Home: Architecture and Society 1815-1915* (Boston: Little, Brown and Co., 1974), pp. 344–45.
32. David Bradby and John McCormick, *People's Theatre* (London: Croom Helm, 1978), pp. 17–18.
33. Richard Schechner, *Environmental Theater* (New York: Hawthorn Books, 1973), p. 39.
34. Nicola Chiaromonte, "The political theater," in *The Worm of Consciousness and Other Essays* (New York: Harcourt Brace Jovanovich, 1977), pp. 140–42.
35. Schechner, *Environmental Theater*, p. 31.
36. Wilfred Burns, *British Shopping Centres: New Trends in Layout and Distribution* (London: Leonard Hill, 1959).
37. Victor Gruen, *The Heart of Our Cities: The Urban Crisis: Diagnosis and Cure* (New York: Simon & Schuster, 1964), pp. 190–91.
38. Jane Jacobs, *The Death and Life of Great American Cities* (New York: Random House, 1961), pp. 150–51.

INDEX

Index

Yi-Fu Tuan, born in China in 1930, was educated at Oxford University and the University of California, Berkeley. He is a professor of geography at the University of Minnesota and has been a visiting professor at Oxford, the University of Hawaii, and the University of California, Davis. In his most recent books—*Topophilia, Space and Place,* and *Landscapes of Fear*—he uses the methods and resources of both the social sciences and the humanities to deal with human-environmental relations.